Rude Citizenship

Rude Citizenship

Jamaican Popular Music, Copyright, and the Reverberations of Colonial Power

· ·

LARISA KINGSTON MANN

The University of North Carolina Press Chapel Hill

Set in Charis by Westchester Publishing Services

The University of North Carolina Press has been a member
of the Green Press Initiative since 2003.

Library of Congress Cataloging-in-Publication Data
Names: Mann, Larisa Kingston, author.
Title: Rude citizenship : Jamaican popular music, copyright, and the
    reverberations of colonial power / Larisa Kingston Mann.
Description: Chapel Hill : University of North Carolina Press, [2022] |
    Includes bibliographical references and index.
Identifiers: LCCN 2021041590 | ISBN 9781469667232 (cloth) |
    ISBN 9781469667249 (paperback) | ISBN 9781469667256 (ebook)
Subjects: LCSH: Popular music—Jamaica—History and criticism. | Popular
    music—Social aspects—Jamaica—History. | Music trade—Jamaica. |
    Copyright—Music—Jamaica. | Music and race—Jamaica.
Classification: LCC ML3486.J3 M36 2022 | DDC 781.63097292—dc23
LC record available at https://lccn.loc.gov/2021041590

Cover photographs: *Front*, Debbie Bragg, *Passa Passa Street Party in Kingston,
Jamaica* (detail) (Everynight Images / Alamy Stock Photo); *back*, sound
system (crazy82 / Shutterstock.com).

To my mother, Dr. Esther Kingston-Mann, a historian of peasants resisting enclosure of land, and my father, James Newton Mann Jr., an ethnomusicologist, poet, and composer, I dedicate this work on people resisting the enclosure of music. And to Andrea Lewis, mentor and friend in Jamaica.

Contents

Table

Acknowledgments

I am grateful for family, friends, and colleagues in academia and the musical/DJ communities for support and for holding me to a higher standard of accountability than any institution. I am sure I can always do better, but as well as I have done, it is with your help. My mother, Dr. Esther Kingston-Mann, has read everything of mine, and I of hers, which has made an indelible impression on my scholarship. My father, James Newton Mann, was a model for deep listening, ethnographic methods, and a musical inspiration. Kendra Salois is a thoughtful and inspiring writing collaborator and friend, Ali Colleen Neff's intellectual and emotional generosity is only matched by her insight, and Erin Macleod's great ideas and comradeship kept me going. Aram Sinnreich has been a stalwart friend and mentor. I am lucky to have friends and colleagues who make me smarter when I talk to them. In Jamaica, Andrea Lewis was invaluable for her wisdom, her street smarts, and her guidance in all things Jamaica-related; Dr. Sonjah Stanley-Niaah for inspiring scholarship and just as invaluable practical help; Afifa Aza for heart soul and mind connections; and Tarik Jabari Perkins especially for generosity and insight. There are too many artists, studios, and DJ crews to list but special shout-outs to Earl "Chinna" Smith, Small World Studios, Payday Music, Tandra Lytes Jhagoo, Warrior Queen, Andre France, Sam Diggy, Elijah & Skilliam, Footsie, and the Heatwave Crew. I could never have survived graduate school and the adjunct life (mentally and financially) without my comrades in Surya Dub, Dutty Artz, and Heavy NYC, as well as my esteemed DJ/academic colleagues infiltrating academia every year more and more. My dear Ravish Momin has been a great sounding board and support. I am thankful for Elaine Maisner's encouragement and guidance at the University of North Carolina Press. My research was supported by Temple University, Fordham University, and the University of California, Berkeley, as well as by DJing with and for communities in New York City and across the world.

Rude Citizenship

Introduction

Community Originality and Colonial Copyright

· ·

In 2009 in Kingston, Jamaica, a new vocalist stepped onstage during a singing competition called Magnum Kings and Queens of Dancehall, in which singers perform before a panel of judges including notable producers, musicians, and television personalities.[1] The vocalist, Tanto Blacks, handed the DJ a CD, who cued it up and hit play. As the music started, Blacks leaped into action—striding across the stage, gesturing to the audience, singing, and swaying to the music. As with all the previous singers, after only two verses, the DJ cut the music, and it was time for feedback. First, Miss Kitty, a local TV and radio personality, praised the vocalist's energy and attitude. But then another judge, a respected Jamaican producer named Skatta,[2] offered his commentary. Referring to the backing track, Skatta said: "That riddim,[3] it *lame*." Shaking his head, he continued, speaking to the other judges: "I wish he use a more original riddim, not one that they make themselves. . . . Use one more established riddim that been tested! Not this amateurish thing! One that has passed the test already, been played out [in public]."

Consider the way Skatta uses the word "original." He uses it in a way that diverges from commonly accepted definitions, including the definition relied on by law as the basis of copyright ownership. A copyright lawyer would find his use a rude shock, something to be corrected—and quickly! By law, and in mainstream U.S. and European musical traditions, if the artist made the music himself or herself, a song could be called "original."[4] In contrast, Skatta uses the word "original" as a value judgment, one that decenters an individualistic and linear approach to music making. Skatta places the onus of judgment on the public: the musical element of a riddim—a.k.a. the instrumental track—is original when it has been "played out" in front of an audience and "established." The way Skatta uses "original" directs our attention to the aspects of culture that originate not in individuals but in a community. Another aspect of his use reflects a concern with standards: for a work to be original it must not be amateurish but meet (here undefined) standards that could include professionalism or rigor. Skatta is not simply suggesting artists cater to public tastes but asserting that public tastes are part of the creative process. Even if he is using "original" as a value judgment (akin to the term "creative"), that judgment differs from the legal definition (which is not concerned with quality but with an act of origination) and situates the recognition, if not creation, of that value in the public. In recording studios, you can also hear the word in a different but related way. Some people use "original" as a kind of praise. I usually observed older male speakers, often Rastafarians, who gave the beginning of the word heavy emphasis, heightening the sound of the word "origin" contained within the longer word. "Original" signals a collective recognition, a collective relationship to a shared worldview, and—given the root word, "origin"—a shared history and cultural origin among the listening and performing community. In this context, the word "original" directly contradicts the legal definition, or more accurately, it translates the concept into local parlance.

The interchange at the Magnum Kings and Queens of Dancehall competition illustrates how Jamaican popular musical practices rudely challenge basic assumptions about communities, creativity, and the role of law, even though Jamaicans are in no way isolated from the commercial, capitalist twenty-first-century music industry. In a single word, we see authority and value shifted away from the places where mainstream society assumes it to reside—places that are defined by a system that was not created to serve the interests of the poor and Black. The public Skatta refers to is primarily the public for Jamaican popular music: an audience dominated by members of the Jamaican underclass, who often subversively reject moral judgment of their social position (the competition winner was not Tanto Blacks but an artist called Poor and Boasy [*boasy* means "proud"]). If you want to understand the conditions that enable cultural expression to move communities toward autonomy and liberation, Jamaican popular music provides an illuminating example of a living tradition that often challenges colonial ways of looking at the world. This living tradition is not invisible to those in power but is often seen by them as rude, which in a way it is: it does not respect or abide by the terms of engagement the state defines as proper.

How do Jamaican popular music practices enable Jamaicans to resist colonial power? This book pursues this question in an idiosyncratic way: I use copyright law as a refractory lens to split Jamaican popular music practices into a rainbow of different social functions and dynamics. As a branch of *intellectual property law*, copyright law relies on a set of rules to differentiate between what can be property and what cannot. This ability—to define people, things, land, culture, and knowledge as either property or not—forms the base of colonial power. Setting the story of Jamaican popular music against the framework of copyright law, I show how Jamaicans responded to the historical conditions around them with their own particular disrespect for coloniality, a diasporic and decolonizing logic.

What Does It Mean to Study Popular Music?

Any study of music requires that we take the object of our studies as "the creative act, not just the created object."[5] Rather than starting with a written or recorded piece of music, or even focusing on the technologies people use to make recordings, getting at music's meaning requires that we consider musical practices in their social context. We cannot presume music's meaning derives from specific processes that produce recordings or from technologies already identified as musical instruments. Because music and its meaning vary so widely across culture, we would miss a lot if we relied only on definitions and practices within our own experience and scholarship. In the Jamaican context, live, interactive moments of musical engagement are at the heart of music's social function and the engine of meaning making.

On "the Popular" in Jamaica

In the Jamaican context, the term "popular" requires some unpacking. While popular culture is often discussed as synonymous with "mass culture," the demographics of popularity in Jamaica require a more careful definition. The majority of Jamaica's population are descended from African people that the British enslaved, African people who escaped from slavery, and—although this is contested—a small number of Indigenous Taino people. The rest of the population is composed primarily of a small minority of white people, many of whom still own the majority of property on the island (as they did when it was a colony, prior to 1834, when they also owned other human beings); a small minority of Chinese people; and even fewer Indian and Lebanese people, who are also concentrated in the middle and upper classes (hereafter called "the upper classes" except when their interests or actions diverge). After slavery ended, and even after independence in 1962, elites were not required to relinquish or share control of the island's land and institutions. Thus the gap between the few elites and the large numbers of poor has remained wide, with not many people in the middle. The divide between the masses and the upper classes is racial, color based, and ethnic as well as wealth and income based. In colonial Jamaica, to the extent that advancement was possible for anyone, that advancement was tied to the ability to distance oneself, visually and culturally, from the poor and Black. After independence, although the direct colonial relationship with Great Britain no longer existed, the value of maintaining that cultural distance remained, or even increased.[6]

The masses are both the majority and a denigrated social group: the poor. At the same time, the poor, particularly the urban poor, have been the primary creators and audience for Jamaican popular music.[7] In general, upper-class Jamaicans have aspired to emulate "a global bourgeois class, [which] meant adopting the consumption patterns of the West and acquiring its cultural capital."[8] Against the cultural works associated with Britain (and more recently, a U.S.-dominated popular music landscape), Jamaican popular music and its practitioners have been characterized as having moral failings consistent with colonial hierarchies of power and taste.[9] This has meant that music associated with the poor and Black has continually been excluded and denigrated by upper-class Jamaicans. Those in charge of centralized media channels like radio and television and those controlling formal education and cultural events maintain this hostility.[10]

Some results of this exclusion have not been entirely negative. We will see how the urban poor majority have become arbiters of their own kind of cultural authority, not wholly dependent on the upper classes for approval. A foundational Jamaican scholar of popular music, Carolyn Cooper, has suggested that one such culture associated with the urban poor, dancehall music, is a "radical underground confrontation with the patriarchal gender ideology and the pious morality of fundamentalist Jamaican society." This book tracks how that confrontation also extends to ideologies of property as well.[11] Property rights are underpinned by a system of knowledge, one that is challenged by Jamaican popular music, which has its own systems of knowledge. Katherine McKittrick describes how Black music "affirms, through cognitive schemas, modes of being human that refuse antiblackness just as they restructure our existing system of knowledge."[12] Anti-Blackness is not identical to coloniality, but for the purpose of this study, it is not too much of a stretch to say that coloniality acts like a particular structuring form of anti-Blackness—it is a dynamic that includes not only attitudes to skin color but also attitudes and institutions that classify people and practices, using Blackness as a defining limit of what is acceptable or desirable. While not always explicitly identified as Black, Jamaican popular music practices embody the interests of people most marginalized along race and class lines in Jamaica—a condition that tracks Blackness. This book investigates how poor Jamaicans have claimed, negotiated, rejected, or redefined ownership and identifies sites and moments in which poor communities have gained a measure of cultural autonomy. This is what allows musical practices to function as a site of community healing and resistance to the depredations of the colonial class system.[13] That autonomy is based partly in the lack of attention, and even in the negative attention, paid to those sites by the state and elite institutions.

The Jamaican state has had a more complex relationship with poor people than simple exclusion. The majority of Jamaicans are Black, and the foundational experience of Jamaica was as a British colony depending on the enslaved labor of Africans. This means that Black Jamaicans are able to claim a kind of authenticity that elite Jamaicans' association with white British culture and institutions does not allow. While Black people are also present in elite institutions in Jamaica, their presence is one that requires negotiation with and often assimilation (even if strategically) into anti-Black ways of being and relating. Over and over again, Jamaican elites, especially at election time, have uneasily reached with one hand for symbolic and material allegiances with the poor while using the other to block their access to power. Popular music provides an unusually clear view of this seemingly contradictory symbiotic relationship between those at the top of the Jamaican social system and people who in some ways position themselves outside it and against it. Much of this book will be concerned with how that positioning happens in everyday practices, especially those prevalent in popular music.

Central Concepts and Ongoing Practices in Jamaican Popular Music

In the chapters that follow, I develop my analysis using three main concepts. I borrow the concept of phonographic orality from Jason Toynbee's work on Jamaican music, blues, and hip-hop. From the Jamaican sociologist Obika Gray, I borrow the concept of exilic space.[14] Both identify features of Jamaican popular music that help poor Jamaicans position themselves outside and against Jamaican, and to some extent global, systems of power. The third concept—coloniality—describes the system that organizes dominant assumptions in such a way that markers of race, color, and class sort out who has most access to the centers of power. Theories of coloniality also highlight how the concept of modernity itself is embedded in these racialized dynamics so that being associated with white colonizers is not identified as being "white" but as being "modern." This dynamic is apparent at the state level in discussions of "modernizing copyright," which is usually used to mean enforcing copyright in a way consistent with colonial notions of property and creativity. In using this concept, I draw especially on the work of Anibal Quijano and Walter Mignolo, refracted through such Caribbean scholars as Aaron Kamugisha and Obika Gray.[15]

Phonographic Orality: Syncretism for Survival in the Era of Recordings

Phonographic orality describes a particularly Jamaican way of making culture. Since Jamaica was created as a colony in the seventeenth century, the music of the majority has been syncretic, as one would expect of an island where the majority were torn away from their own cultures (and discouraged from practicing them) while thrown together with people from other parts of the world and forced, as well, to participate in the dominant version of British culture. Syncretism generally describes the practice of weaving together selections or scraps of various cultural influences; in Jamaica, these cultures were not brought together on equal terms in which all were able to participate and benefit equally in cultural practices and the making of cultural works. A shallow definition of syncretism, focusing on the mixing and combining of culture but not the terms that allowed various cultures and practitioners to flourish, would obscure the realities of racialized inequality that deeply shape Jamaican life and worldwide dynamics of cultural engagement.[16] Stuart Hall has described Caribbean identity as "positioned in relation to cultured narratives which have been profoundly expropriated, [and, therefore,] the colonized subject is always 'somewhere else': doubly marginalized, displaced always *other* than where he or she is, or is able to speak from."[17] This displacement is reflected in diasporic people's continual reliance on syncretic practices, whereby displaced peoples and their descendants weave together multiplicitous identities from the cultural resources that surround them, including fragments of the past and elements of the new societies in which they have found themselves.[18] Works of the dominant culture as well as roots and references to past homelands and memories become fodder for the project of survival in a colonial context. In Jamaican music, musicians have combined African musical practices from the enslaved people brought to the island with the European,

Chinese, Lebanese, Latin, and Indian influences of free or indentured migrants, as well as with influences from other Caribbean islands. The method of combination, in Jamaica, has developed in a way that continually enacts a clash with colonial order: this is the practice of phonographic orality. Toynbee uses this term to describe the practice of live, interactive performance that includes audio recordings (phonograms) as an element. Its quintessential expression may be the Jamaican tradition of using riddims: the DJ plays a recording of the instrumental parts of a song separated from the vocals so that a live performer can sing their own vocal line over it, or a producer records a succession of new vocal lines over a preexisting instrumental recording, which may have been in continual circulation for the past twenty years in popular culture.[19] This practice (and phonographic orality more generally) dates back to the beginning of replay and broadcast technology but came into its own with the rise of radios, jukeboxes, and record players. Both in the recording and performance process, phonographic orality centers memory, community, and live, virtuosic improvisation with and by means of recordings. The term describes how the practices of oral culture that reinforce memory-based creative practices—especially repetition and reuse—can encompass the use of phonograms. As Skatta emphasized in his critique of Tanto Blacks's performance, using prerecorded music for creative acts is not secondary but is instead a central aspect of the creative process. The use of recordings as raw material rather than finished product and the musical practitioners' ongoing interest in interacting with those recordings have continually set Jamaican popular music against copyright law.

Exilic Spaces: Fostering the Play of Freedom

Scholars of Jamaican music have described how Jamaican popular music has continually challenged social norms and legal regulations that attempt to define the island's majority in colonial terms. To do this in the face of sustained hostility by the cultural and economic upper classes has required a kind of sheltering space where poor Jamaicans can produce this relatively autonomous cultural life. What the Jamaican scholar Obika Gray has termed "exilic social space"[20] provides protection from those entities who hold the poor in a permanent state of "social dishonour." Gray develops his argument from his observations of how people live in poor urban neighborhoods, especially in Kingston, places that lack resources and infrastructure on a fundamental level. Often identified as "downtown" (many of them are on the lowlands nearest Kingston Harbor), such neighborhoods are visually identifiable as places of official neglect and poverty: they have unpaved streets, unfinished buildings with roofs open to the sky or streets lined with leaning corrugated zinc walls, and they are cut through with the occasional open sewer line ("gully"). Residents experience inconsistent access to running water and electricity, and they find very few avenues to participate in social mobility. In many ways, people appear to have been exiled from institutions of power. But Gray identifies how the Jamaican state's shaky foundations have allowed these communities to play a powerful role in public life; this is especially the case for so-called gangsters or dons, who act as authoritative figures in these neighborhoods and sometimes are treated with respect by state actors as well. Instead of the state providing services to the poor, it is sometimes the dons who offer access to resources (including water and education, as well as money and guns). Because these poor neighborhoods are not wholly open to or dependent on the state, they allow people living there to craft lives and worldviews with relative independence from the social order defined by the state. Gray focuses on political power, but this independence is reflected also in cultural practices, including the music that is generated in poor urban communities. People in exilic spaces can appropriate and reinterpret cultural resources to engage both in dissent and in "the repair of cultural injuries."[21] Cultural injuries include the injuries to dignity and selfhood inflicted when elites represent poor Black Jamaicans as worthless, dangerous, and disreputable. Jamaican popular music, nurtured in these exilic spaces, has been a way for poor Jamaicans to redefine their relationship to central concepts of citizenship and personhood. Before we investigate them further, however, it is important to identify the hostile forces against which exilic spaces provide some respite.

Coloniality: The Organization of Dominant Power

The term "coloniality" highlights aspects of Jamaican history and social order that help explain how power flows within and among its peoples and institutions and who has access to it. A central dynamic is its creation of a hierarchical system of social classification, often nominally by skin color, which structures people's relationship to labor, resources, power, and respect. Anibal Quijano has observed that the idea of race, while designed to suit the labor needs of colonialism's ruling classes, has "proven to be more durable and stable than the colonialism in whose matrix it was established."[22] Coloniality identifies structures and dynamics that continue beyond the end of formal colonialism. In Jamaica, this pretty well describes a political and economic system with a very small predominantly white minority concentrated at the top, middle and upper classes that include Black as well as brown people of varying ethnicities, and the vast majority of the Black and poor population. Coloniality, after the removal of explicit rule by colonizers, functions by erasing or hiding a color-based classification system through an ideology in which seemingly objective and desirable values like modernity, respectability, and good taste are modeled on anti-Black social and cultural conditions.[23] Gray has described how in Jamaica coloniality functions especially through social norms. This works powerfully in social realms outside of what is often recognized as "the political," including personal deportment and manners. This is especially illuminating for Jamaican experiences of coloniality, which differ from most of the countries (primarily in South America) where theories of coloniality were derived. In Jamaica, Black people have never been the minority, but even among the Black majority, comportment and civility are allocated along racialized lines that divide the population. After independence, and when the state and its elite intellectuals (even many of its politically radical ones) were at odds over the appropriate forms and distributions of power, they tended to remain more in agreement about cultural norms of conduct, reading the poor as "rude" rather than as challenging coloniality. These norms remained white supremacist, despite postindependence Jamaica's celebration of a mixed society. (Jamaica's national slogan is "out of many, one people.") In fact, this assertion of mixed heritage tended to erase and minimize Blackness and Black people who made up the majority of society, including the poor.[24] In that context, anything that celebrated and centered Blackness (including the manners or mannerisms of the poor) could only be conditionally and precariously welcomed into the representation of Jamaica or its structures of formal power.

Coloniality also explains the generally authoritarian and predatory functions of a state whose institutional structure was never intended to grant full participation to the majority of people. This is the coloniality of citizenship in the Caribbean. Aaron Kamugisha describes this as a "complex amalgam of elite domination, neoliberalism and the legacy of colonial authoritarianism, which continue to frustrate and deny the aspirations of many Caribbean people."[25] Many scholars have highlighted the state's role in excluding, through law, people who do not fit colonial requirements. These requirements have shaped norms and institutions that structure labor, family life, sexuality, and, most crucially for this book, citizenship, sovereignty, and autonomy.[26] Citizenship in Jamaica (and in other Caribbean nations) has entailed what the anthropologist Deborah Thomas has called "dominant paradigms of belonging that were rooted in colonial hierarchies and inequalities."[27] The terms by which one can claim citizenship tend to reinforce inequality, privilege, and deference to whiteness or colonial authority; paradoxically such inclusion is predicated on exclusion, conformity to colonial social norms, and violence, including the violence of precarity and structural poverty.[28]

While Jamaican society, like all colonial societies, structurally denies the benefits of full citizenship to poor Black people, who are systematically less able to claim protection or support from the law, we still must ask: What does or should citizenship mean, and why should people want it? We may better understand citizenship as a negotiation with the state in which some demands go beyond the legal definition to include tropes of belonging and identity. I agree with Thomas that it would be fruitful to reformulate our understanding of citizenship away from a fixed set of rights and obligations between actors and the state and toward seeing citizenship as "a set of performances and practices that is grounded in specific historical circulations and that is directed at various state and nonstate institutions and extraterritorial or extra-legal networks."[29]

The following pages pursue this reformulation through identifying key Jamaican performances and practices that have allowed varying levels of redefinition from the ground up. The term "citizen" can be used both to affirm and to transcend the colonial basis of current national boundaries and institutions. Remembering Gray's points about comportment, we can see how those in power use the language of manners to frame reformulated claims to citizenship as improper. It is notable that "rudeness" and the character of the "rudeboy" are terms claimed early in Jamaican popular music as a simultaneously somewhat heroic but threatening identity. This reclaiming of the terminology of bad manners in a double-edged way is a theme in Jamaican popular music that illustrates how poor Jamaicans claim social power.

I also use the term "sovereignty" to evoke a dynamic that accounts for the ability not only to make claims on a ruling institution (like a state) but also to assert one's rights over one's own experience and body independent of or even against the demands of the state, because inclusion in citizenship does not guarantee one's ability to make claims on the law. Instead, it brings one into a new struggle over what it means to be visible to the state.[30]

Many activists in Jamaica and beyond struggle, rightfully and importantly, for legal recognition and protection, so the specific terms of definition and protection become crucial to whether those communities are further oppressed by their inclusion. Meanwhile, other activists and marginalized communities either avoid the scrutiny of the state or, as in the case of Jamaican popular music, assert their rights even when those rights contradict legal definitions. One of the most striking aspects of Jamaican popular culture is that people with the least access to formal power in relation to dominant Jamaican society have been continually able to redraw the contours of citizenship, and to challenge the authority of an irrevocably colonial state. Some of the most dramatic claims have been made in relation to culture, when people assert their authority verbally, physically, and in dialogue with the main legal framework that grants people authority over cultural works: copyright law.

Copyright Law and Colonial Assumptions

Claims of ownership over Jamaican culture by popular music practitioners date back to the inception of popular music. What is interesting is how little those claims have relied on the specifics of copyright law—and, on closer analysis, how impossible it would be for them to use the law to support their claims. It is not surprising that people descended from an enslaved population might not find an easy relationship to property law, since until recently property law only included them in the system of property rights on the worst terms possible. In the realm of property in cultural works, Jamaican copyright law was written by its colonizer, and thus it is reasonable to assume it reflects an interest in culturally and economically subjugating the island's Black majority.[31] Even if this is not its stated goal, there's no reason to think its design and application would be aimed at developing local authorship and economic development among that population. After independence, copyright law was left untouched. Jamaicans who rely on that law presume, as the legal scholar Cheryl Harris says, that "definition from above can be fair to those below, that beneficiaries of racially conferred privilege have the right to establish norms for those who have historically been oppressed pursuant to those norms." Harris goes on to say that "reality belies this presumption."[32]

Although in 1976 the Jamaican government set up a commission to investigate revisions to the Copyright Act of 1977, as drafted by officials, it was never put into law.[33] Jamaica retained its English-authored copyright law until 1993, and the fundamentals have not been altered significantly since then. Subsequent revisions have mainly been informed by U.S. assumptions instead of British ones, but the law is still not designed for communities that were on the exploited side of colonization.[34] Jamaican copyright law until 1993 did not attend to Jamaica's role in a global media system: while the Berne Convention, an international copyright agreement, was first written in 1896, neither the United Kingdom nor Jamaica signed on until the end of the twentieth century. In fact, Jamaica joined the Berne Convention at the same time as it joined the Agreement on Trade Related Aspects of Intellectual Property (TRIPS), in 1994, which marked the first revision to Jamaican copyright since 1913. The 1994 act was passed so that Jamaica would be in accordance with TRIPS, as required by membership in the World Trade Organization (WTO). As before, not much about the law was informed by the specific needs of people on the island, and many basic features fit poorly with the realities of Jamaican musical practices in particular.

Most Jamaican popular music has developed through practices that contradict a law supposedly intended to structure the behavior of creators and consumers. This contradiction has not been discussed much, perhaps mainly because before and after the colonial era copyright law in Jamaica was unenforced.[35] Despite this lack of intellectual property "protection," music makers have not lacked incentive to make music and, indeed, have been responsible for developing national authorship and creativity on a massive scale, locally and internationally. This insurgent authorship has built Jamaica's music industry into the country's third-largest producer. Notably, its main era of expansion was in the 1970s and 1980s, well before Jamaica joined the TRIPS agreement and before the government began making some efforts to enforce copyright domestically. The wealth generated from one category of Jamaican music (reggae) has continued to be significant on a global scale: a 1995 UN study puts "worldwide income from [Jamaican-based] reggae music at not below 3 percent" of global music production—an impressive figure for an island with a population of around 2.5 million.[36] Music is a field of practice where Jamaican popular music practitioners have been disproportionately influential and successful. Despite this, Jamaican musical practitioners' relationship to law has rarely been analyzed except in terms of lack, failure, or disobedience.

The relationship between legally defined ownership and creativity requires more close attention. The terms of this analysis matter a great deal: foundational copyright concepts of "authorship" and "ownership," as well as "originality," that are enshrined in law are not recognized across all musical arenas. As Skatta reminds us, they are terms with different meanings in different cultures and creative communities. Copyright protection requires originality, but traditional legal definitions of originality focus on ways that new works are not connected to (or made up of) existing works. The more isolated a work is from its cultural context, the more likely law will recognize it as original. This is quite different from the way many Jamaicans perceive what is valuable in a musical work—and from how they use the word "original."

Another contradiction is that copyright defines fixed relationships between people and creative practices to sort out which kinds of activities are permitted or forbidden. But in practice, those relationships are flexible and contingent, and if we rely unquestioningly on such definitions as "author" or "owner," we will miss important dynamics of power. Copyright law's notion of the author is external to Jamaican practices, and arguments that rely on authorship unchallenged embody what Harris identifies as "whiteness": mistakenly assuming that "fairness can result from any rule, a property rule, or indeed any other rule, that imposes an entirely externally constituted definition of group identity," which in practice reproduces racial subordination.[37] The work to which copyright is assumed to apply is also an externally constituted definition; assigning legal power resides to creative acts at the moment they involve material writings or recordings.[38] This means that neither acts of improvisation nor individual or collective memory-based creativity are recognized as sources of value. However, since people with more power have more access to recording devices and techniques (including writing and musical notation), so copyright law's reliance on fixation shifts power and profit away from the majority of creators and toward elites. As we will see, this shift too is in line with coloniality. These characteristics of the law mean that even for those Jamaicans who would like to own copyrights or to claim recompense from what they see as money unfairly collected, the law is extremely poorly suited to the task.

Many creative practices have flourished in copyright's functional absence, shoring up poor Jamaicans' cultural and, to some extent, economic survival. Analyzing how Jamaicans have reworked their relationships to each other and the state can lead to a better understanding of the conditions for cultural and social autonomy and, along the way, provide some suggestions for how or if copyright law can serve the interest of creators from oppressed and colonized communities.

Neither Fixed, nor Works, nor Necessarily Individual:
A Living Tradition

The 1911 Copyright Act and its recent revision state that copyright subsists "in every original literary dramatic musical and artistic work,"[39] "fixed in writing or otherwise," and that "the author of a work shall be the first owner of the copyright therein."[40] So people called "authors" create things called "works." (Even the act's "joint authorship" provision assumes distinct, separable contributions by individuals.) The problems with fixation are outlined above. By allocating rewards to individuals, copyright concentrates financial return based on a particular individual's relationship to the conditions of its creation and on that individual's ability to restrict access to a work in exchange for a license. The focus on permission also clashes with key aspects of phonographic orality. Jamaicans have raised the practice of adaptation and reuse to a sophisticated practice, deeply embedded in Jamaican musical tradition and owing very little to copyright conceptions of ownership and permission. As well as permission for adaptation or reuse, the Copyright Act requires copyright owners' permission for any broadcast[41] or public performance of a work.[42] The public performance and broadcasting of musical recordings have long been an important aspect of Jamaican musical creativity. The law sees these practices as the public consuming works, not as an example of the public taking part in a collective creative process that is vital to music making.

The law concerns itself with the behaviors of individuals with little sense of shared culture or community. Yet a tremendous amount of musical creativity derives from shared cultural practices and the collective interests of communities. Within Jamaica, the specific communities that are at the heart of the music industry have (as will be discussed in the next chapter) particular collective interests in making music, which shapes their creative practices.

The law also presumes that there is a final product of creativity, known as a work, whose value can be understood separately from other works. But in practice, many forms of creative expression involve using shared cultural objects, phrases, or vocabulary that cannot be so easily separated. This is true in Jamaica and elsewhere, and more often true for communities on the wrong side of colonial power. Because copyright law focuses on the work—a fixed, discrete object—it defines the social relations of music making in relation to works rather than focusing on the social dynamics of creativity in which works may be an element of a larger creative practice. This conflicts especially with Jamaican traditions of phonographic orality and syncretism that rely on the reuse of preexisting music as the foundation for new musical interactions and recordings.

This aspect of the law also reinforces classed and raced inequality. By assigning ownership based on creativity in fixed form, the process of fixation and the technologies it requires (from writing to recording) become central to copyright's value. However, writing and recording skills are not always the same as musical composition, improvisatory performance, or memory skills. In poor countries, such as Jamaica, both writing and recording require a significant amount of social and material capital, and they are concentrated among a relatively small elite. Instead, a significant amount of creativity occurs in live performance. If ownership accrues to the person with the power to make a fixation, this can undervalue the contribution of other participants in the music-making process.

Contradicting Colonial Expectations

In the past twenty years especially, scholars, policy makers, and historically disenfranchised communities have also made ownership claims over cultural works to defend against their appropriation by dominant classes.[43] However, many cultural studies scholars and musicians have resisted defining ownership in market terms. In relation to Black cultural works, for example, Daniel Fischlin and Ajay Heble argue that "the expressive modalities of black culture have repeatedly had to struggle against processes of reduction and commodification."[44] Property rules, according to this argument, rather than according power to owners of culture, transform culture into "forms in which it could be frozen and sold,"[45] which can harm a living tradition of resistance and regeneration.[46] If this is the case, to effectively resist the appropriation of culture—or of the material rewards for cultural creativity—means refusing, at least to some extent, culture's commodification.

At the international level, there has been increasing pressure on countries like Jamaica to do what is sometimes called "harmonizing" of their intellectual property laws:[47] bringing them more in line with shared international standards. The WTO's primary justification for requiring the global harmonization of copyright and enforcement is that copyright provides an incentive to creators, who will be motivated to create more works through the promise of rewards extracted via the control of already-created works. WTO member states that fail to comply with copyright law can face trade sanctions.[48] The WTO's one-size-fits-all approach to intellectual property, in which copyright enforcement has only a positive relationship to cultural productivity, derives from the World Intellectual Property Organization (WIPO). WIPO sets the WTO's intellectual property policy, and its approach is epitomized by their 1997 assertion that the "development of national authorship and creativity cannot be set in motion without guarantees to the author of adequate remuneration for his efforts."[49] WIPO's assertion echoes the ahistorical approach put forth over ten years earlier: a 1981 WIPO and UNESCO (United Nations Educational, Scientific and Cultural Organization) study of copyright in the English-speaking Caribbean asserted that the "rejection of copyright would lead to the drying up of literary and artistic production."[50] Such a prediction contradicts the history of creative industries throughout the world as well as Jamaica's recent history. Despite being ahistorical and unempirical, assertions like these are surprisingly widespread.

In fact, Jamaican popular music's productivity and vitality contradicts many of WIPO's claims, but this fact has not led to a formal critique of WIPO in Jamaica. Other countries have made such critiques. Starting in the 1980s, a coalition of countries in the Global South began to demand that WIPO acknowledge that countries usually identified by the WTO as "less developed" might have specific intellectual property needs. In the Uruguay Round of multilateral trade negotiations over intellectual property that led to the creation of the WTO and TRIPS, nations in the Global South fought unsuccessfully for TRIPS to allow as much flexibility as possible for nations to determine the scope of protection. After this failure, they reorganized and successfully pressured WIPO to adopt the Development Agenda (DA) into its mission in 2000. Countries from the Global South argued that copyright law as traditionally defined by WIPO did not serve their interests: as net importers of copyrighted works, for example, they saw no immediate advantage in enforcing copyright.[51] The DA emphasized especially that copyright ought to respond to the specific situation of resource-poor countries and called for these interests to carve out alternate contours for copyright depending on local circumstances. Concurrently, communities, regions, and nations have begun to define different kinds of intellectual property rights based in specific situations. These movements reveal a desire for new legal instruments of intellectual property to represent the people and practices those instruments are ostensibly meant to benefit. In the mid-1990s, Indigenous communities in South America and India created a new internationally recognized category of intellectual property called "traditional knowledge" as a defense against multinational corporations who were profiting from Indigenous knowledge of plants. Multinational corporations were only aware of certain plants because Indigenous people used them, yet the law did not recognize Indigenous claims over their own knowledge: because it was held collectively by communities over time, it was not protectable under patent law (which recognizes ownership based on novelty, not tradition). Massive profits accrued to the corporations who made use of these plants, and little came back to the originators, until Indigenous communities fought back.[52] Alongside these struggles, a field of scholarship has sprung up examining the relationship between intellectual property systems and development.[53] One such work, by the anthropologist Boatema Boateng, offers a fascinating in-depth study of Kente cloth making in Ghana and describes copyright's poor fit with local creative traditions. Kente is a patterned cloth that is economically valuable and distinctive. Practices of Kente creativity situate ownership in master artists and, importantly, in their lineage—a lineage of blood and training, in which claims to ownership must be rooted in that lineage rather than in a contract or solely in the act of weaving, printing, or sewing a design.[54] In such ways do some creative practices situate authority and ownership in relationships that make copyright law hard to enforce or even irrelevant; the book's title, *The Copyright Thing Doesn't Really Work Here*, well makes this point.

Jamaica did not participate in the DA, which is not surprising, since the main actors in Jamaican popular music live almost as far from the world of Jamaican elites who might participate in intellectual property negotiations as they do from Geneva, where those negotiations take place. More recently, UNESCO has recognized reggae music as an "intangible cultural heritage" worthy of protection,[55] which could suggest other justifications for altering the legal context for Jamaican musical practices. To decide which exceptions, limitations, or other restructurings of copyright would be necessary or helpful for Jamaican people and musical practitioners requires sustained attention to the specifics of Jamaican creative practice and to the dynamics that affect who can make claims on their behalf. This book represents a step in that direction.

Accounting for Not Accounting for Copyright Law

The past twenty years have seen increasing numbers of empirical studies that interrogate the relationship between creators and copyright.[56] Many have focused on the technological challenges to copyright in the digital era. One reason is that the internet has rendered visible to industry and law ongoing practices of musical reuse and sharing, especially in hip-hop and dance music (which developed out of jazz and blues). The internet has also rendered everyday practices visible to industry and law in a widespread and intimate way.[57] Simultaneously, the internet and file sharing have weakened major industrial players' ability to profit from the control of material recordings as they had in the past, triggering a great deal of anxiety among powerful corporations like EMI or Universal, with armies of lawyers and lobbyists at their disposal.[58] Many of the practices causing concern predate the digital era but are more visible now. Whatever the reason, an ahistorical consideration of digital technology has pervaded discussion of copyright law in the United States and to some extent the Global North. Focusing on technology has often prevented deep engagement with historical or cultural contexts of creation. These empirical studies rarely investigate the ways creators see themselves and their creative activities in relation to broader historical and economic concerns and often do not situate their creative decisions in the broader context of the everyday life that structures how, when, and why they are able to create. They also tend not to carefully address the historical processes and institutions that predate the current technological and social era. A few important works have addressed these issues in relation to Jamaica, most notably Peter Manuel and Wayne Marshall's "The Riddim Method: Aesthetics, Practice, and Ownership in Jamaican Dancehall" and Jason Toynbee's work on phonographic orality.[59] But there is much more to be learned from a more sustained examination of Jamaican popular music's political and social significance, especially the specific ways it challenges legal frameworks of creativity and personhood. Some of the most fruitful work in this direction has been scholarship associated with the University of the West Indies at the Mona Reggae Studies Unit, especially that of Sonjah Stanley-Niaah, Donna Hope, Carolyn Cooper, and Erin Macleod. Their influence is especially strong in chapter 2 of the present work, where I focus on the lived experience of the street dance, something I explore ethnographically and put in dialogue with their insights about the complex ways people use music, their bodies, physical space, and technology to assert and negotiate power. Cutting edge scholarship has also been fostered by the journal *Small Axe*, which has in particular pushed the analysis of music to explore how music challenges fundamental mental and social concepts of time, authority, and the self. This book's analysis of specific challenges to colonial authority brings up material that engages with many contributors (and their ensuing books as well), such as

Katherine McKittrick, Phanuel Antwi, Louis Chude-Sokei, Deborah Thomas, and others cited below and in the following chapters.

This book is a theory-building work formed by ethnography. My approach draws a great deal on grounded theory, wherein I start first from my own experience, as a researcher and a whole person, with sites and people. This requires a rigorous analysis of my own positionality as well as attention to the richness of data generated by ethnographic methods. From both I derive insights that then find points of intersection with existing scholarship. My active engagement with the invaluable works of the authors mentioned above arises especially out of the discussions in those chapters where the fieldwork evokes their work. Another important contribution of this book is that it uniquely puts in dialogue ideas across critical copyright scholarship and ideas from Caribbean studies, popular music studies, musicology, and ethnomusicology. This dialogue also arises out of the fieldwork first, about which more below. This choice reflects my approach to theory as something that should be used to help understand the world as it happens, for which it makes sense to continually ground it in observation and example. This grounding and regrounding puts my research in constant dialogue with theory, to help make this work (and theory) more accessible across disciplines and beyond, including among the people whose lives theories often purport to describe or explain.

Ethnographic Methods

Ethnography is at the heart of this study. As a method of engagement and analysis, it demands that a researcher participate as much as possible in the daily life of a social group or set of groups. Ethnography grounds its theoretical insights in observations at specific but sometimes various locations over time. But ethnographic projects are not only windows into local knowledge and meaning. Since local communities are not isolated from the world, the focused approach on the everyday still allows a careful examination of the relationships that knit the local to the global.[60] While many people in the world are connected, we are not connected equally, and the value and meanings of those connections are not uniform. Situating analysis in a particular location and time prevents normalizing or reifying existing communities in their current moment and avoids too easily generalizing their experience in ways that may be inappropriate. Ethnography is enhanced by a historical understanding of the site of engagement—in this case, that has meant considering the history that shapes current engagement with Jamaican popular music, as in chapter 1, and by close analysis of culture, such as the musicological and textual analysis done in chapter 3.

Ethnographic methods are particularly useful for investigating the dynamics of Jamaican popular music. This is especially true given the oral aspect of Jamaica popular music—people quite often use recordings as part of a live, interactive, and collaborative performance that gives them meaning. An examination that focused solely on recordings would miss important aspects of the living experience of music. A further value of ethnography in this project is due to Jamaica's particular politics of writing and recording. The processes by which any aspect of life makes it into a written record is shaped by power. Written records are even more likely to be incomplete in communities where resources are scarce and the material conditions for storing written records are less than ideal. The same is true, with even greater inequalities of access, for audio recordings. To understand human interaction and meaning making, such material objects provide fascinating windows into moments at which those objects were made, and in some cases, we can speculate as to how they were used. However, they need to be contextualized in observation and engagement with everyday life.

In the service of this project, I conducted hundreds of hours of participant observation over the course of ten months, which included attending musical performances and observing recording studio sessions. I analyzed musical texts and recordings that circulate throughout the Jamaican diaspora and interviewed musicians, studio owners, engineers, and other musical practitioners. I also experienced, from day to day, the social, legal, economic, cultural, and environmental forces shaping everyday life in Jamaica. I experienced them from my position as a white academic graduate student from the United States, which shaped my engagements and interpretations in ways I will discuss below. While I was based in Kingston, Jamaica, for most of my fieldwork, I also made forays to Toronto and London.

Overall, I interviewed thirty-seven people involved in music at various levels, people who ran studios, producers, and sound systems. For eleven months in 2009, I lived in an apartment on the edge of the University of West Indies campus; I regularly took minibuses, official buses, and taxis and walked about town, most often to Papine Market around the corner from me, where I could pick up a coconut from the vendor on the corner and check out the latest mix CDs of local DJs from a pile spread out on a cloth on the ground. I did my best to engage in daily life both within and across gender, class, and racial lines. This left time for plenty of informal conversation, with people in shops and at social events, with attendees at clubs and street dances, and with taxi drivers (who about 25 percent of the time had a CD they wanted to play for me of music that they or a relative had made).

My social wanderings and participation in the business of daily life do not give me a full understanding of what it is to be Jamaican in these various spaces. There is also no sense in which I could say that I was pursuing an objective or disembodied understanding. But that was not my goal. My experiences were shaped by my embodied social presence. Rather than obscuring my subjectivity (an impossible and suspect goal), it was through learning to account for my presence that I was able to clarify the material and social forces that shape the experience of daily life. This included, as best I could, deducing how experience was shaped differently for me than it would be for someone else. Ethnographic analysis's strength is its ability to illuminate the meanings of complex social processes and generate or sharpen theoretical insights into them. Its validity draws on my position as a researcher to provide an epistemological basis for my interpretations. Just as a historian should analyze the forces that shape what is present or absent in an archive and what its contents mean in context, discussing my position as a researcher clarifies my interpretive process and the grounds by which I claim to know what I know.

Feminist and Intersectional Approaches to Research

As feminist and Indigenous methodologists teach us, the practice of research, as well as the product, is a political process. My position does replicate in broad ways the colonial relationship of academia to the Global South, whereby people with more power study those with less, often for the purposes of dominating them or profiting by the knowledge of them. This relationship is dramatized when the scholar is, like me, a white person affiliated with white-dominated universities that privilege white-defined ways of knowing. Knowledge gained advances, however indirectly, individual white people's careers and, at worst, can be used to exploit and dominate the subjects of study. It is important, both epistemologically and in my own commitment to feminist and antiracist practice, to understand the political dynamics that shaped how I engaged with people and how they engaged with me.

I worked on finding ways to subvert or minimize this overarching dynamic wherever possible. Of course, my participation in white supremacy is not wholly a matter of choice; I carry it with me wherever I go. I also had choices about how to engage with people I encountered, and they exercised choices about how to engage with me. Through these interactions, I found ways, discussed further below, to be as transparent as I could about my interests and effects; I tried to meet the terms for my participation that I could afford to meet and negotiate as clearly as I could what those terms might be.

My orientation toward transparency and accountability led to some interesting shifts in power dynamics on the interpersonal level, something that heightened my interest in how local and immediate social relations provide avenues for moments of agency. For example, in studios I visited repeatedly or stayed in for a long period, sometimes a (male) engineer would ask me to write something down by hand. I might be asked to write a session name or a song title on a CD. Although pretty much everyone can write, having me do this labor for them seemed to amuse them. It resembles secretarial labor, traditionally gendered as women's work and done for someone in a position of power. It may also have been a performance of prestige for other people to witness: I was never asked to write something down, that I can recall, when there wasn't another person around to see. On occasion, I helped write biographies or assisted with an artist's or engineer's press kits. When asked, I shared information about the music worlds I moved through, although most of the time people did not seem very interested in that. Thus, while we shared thoughts and observations and learned from each other, people found ways for me to work, in a small way, for them. While not a reversal of relationships in the global system of white supremacy, these interactions reflected a way to build relationships with the people I was spending time with and to demonstrate good faith. I cannot defend my or any white person's position in white supremacist society and, instead, must fall back on the incomplete but meaningful relationships I had with the people I met and worked with and occasionally for.

Racial and economic power dynamics were heightened and altered because I was researching popular music. While the music industry is exploitative along lines similar to those in academia (or colonialism), it is also familiar terrain for many Jamaicans, and one in which their expertise is recognized by many, especially on their home turf. A foreign white person interested in music was not an anomaly, and many people wished to engage with such figures for their own purposes. After some interviews, even after explaining I was a graduate student writing a book and that I would anonymize their contribution, we would talk for an hour, and then they would ask, "So what magazine will this be in?" These patterns suggested something about the expectations of those I interviewed, including hopes for what this could do for them. Given my already-explained and Institutional Review Board–required commitment to anonymity, I generally could only disabuse them of their hopes for fame and hope that they would still want to talk to me.

Another frame by which people understood my presence was the ongoing tradition of foreign women, white and otherwise, coming to Jamaica for sexual tourism, or in other words, to get a "Jamaican boyfriend."[61] It was a pattern discussed widely across Jamaica from jokes and cartoons in newspapers to my personal experiences of street harassment. These Jamaican boyfriends, sometimes called "rent-a-dreads," are discussed with a mixture of emotions and interpretations. On one side, foreign women have more money and more resources and can unknowingly be a significant source of income. On the other side, harm to a foreigner is more likely to excite the interest of the police or the press. Among poor Jamaicans, it was sometimes described as an act of power by men, whose prowess or desirability was enhanced. While I did not hear these jokes directed at me, in more casual interactions, I did regularly encounter the language of romance or sexual propositions or insults, mainly from non-elite Jamaican men, in public and private. Such gendered interactions like flirting often appeared to enhance the status of the man doing it regardless of whether it put me off balance or I took it in stride.

My position as a white foreign woman also may have improved my access, compared to that of an upper-class Jamaican woman or man. As Gray describes (and as I observed on occasion), the relationship between the poor and the middle and upper class is often one of "mutual contempt."[62] As a foreigner, I was exempted from that more intimate hostility. Some middle-class Jamaicans seemed to chalk up my interest in popular music to a voyeurism with which they were not entirely comfortable. In some cases, they were responding to the stereotype of white women who do not concern themselves with respectability in Jamaica, whether for lack of respect for a colonized country (the "spring break" attitude) or for the aforementioned purposes of sexual tourism. A more charitable interpretation of my interest came from the widespread acknowledgment that many foreigners love and are interested in Jamaican music. This also smoothed my entrance into musical spaces of all types. When I was in studio sessions or at dances, people were aware of my presence as an outsider and a minority but were not too surprised to see a white woman wanting to observe or participate in events. In more public musical scenes, I was often not the only outsider present, whether defined by gender, race, class, or nationality. All the larger street dances and the more well-known music events had a smattering foreigners in attendance. That said, my presence brought multiple layers of meaning: when I ventured into areas known by many to be dangerous or beyond the state's reach, my presence signaled the possibility that police would in fact take an interest if anything happened to me. My possible safety was intertwined with threats of state violence, given the often capricious and brutal practices of Jamaican police in poor neighborhoods.

While I did not usually feel I was in actual danger,[63] I found that people around me had various ways of testing my boundaries and asserting their control of our interaction. With men, this testing sometimes involved sexualized interactions. With men and women both, avoidance was also a tactic—this included not returning phone calls, moving and not keeping meeting times, and keeping me waiting in spaces where I was clearly out of place or not in charge. In such moments, I felt the exercise of local power as people controlled my access and, in some occasions, used my presence, visibly waiting at their convenience, as a marker of prestige. People made sense of me, as I tried to make sense of them.

Three realms of discussion suggested boundaries to be negotiated. One was talking about law, contracts, and legal rights: people often appeared anxious or uncomfortable when I asked about them—so I usually treaded lightly, asking these later in the conversation and inviting stories of experiences rather than generalities. The strongest boundary people preferred to maintain had to do with talking specifically about money. I was aware that my questions could raise suspicions that I could be a tax investigator or other agent of the state or a rival music industry player. In many cases, when I asked about money, people would be vague in ways that discouraged me from pressing them, often also altering their body language and voice in ways that suggested they were not comfortable with this line of questioning. Rather than press people and create resentment, I would attempt to respectfully negotiate this boundary and make note of its presence. Another set of boundaries had to do with my familiarity with Jamaican music. Quite often people I wished to learn from would test my musical knowledge or display interest in and approval of any Jamaican musical knowledge I displayed. It was helpful that, although not Jamaican, I have been a DJ for twenty years and am quite familiar both with DJ practices and with many aspects of Jamaican popular music practices. This knowledge helped demonstrate my commitment to the music (which seemed to be appreciated even though many white musicians, journalists, and record label owners do exploit Jamaicans while knowing and loving the music they make). One studio owner whom I only accessed by phone, at first, was suspicious and not interested in my research project but was intrigued by my DJ history. Once I told him about being a DJ, his tone shifted. Eventually he said I could come to his studio. When I arrived, after a bit of conversation that again touched on my own DJ experience, he asked me sternly whether I understood the meaning of the phrase "killing a soundboy." I got the sense that this was a kind of test. "Yes," I responded, "it's a metaphor. It comes from the soundclash, when sound systems are competing with each other." "Right!" he said emphatically. "It is a way of speech. It isn't really about killing." This interchange, as well as testing how much of an outsider or insider I might be to Jamaican musical idioms, also reflected a concern about the way upper-class Jamaicans and foreigners too often ascribed violence to the poor.[64] My hard-won professional knowledge of Jamaican musical traditions, artists, and genres aligned me with Jamaican popular culture, which is still looked down on by many local elites, and demonstrated a commitment to it over time. That knowledge eased my way into many musical environments.

I did not directly pay most of my research subjects for access to them, something that has often been an important way that poor people gain some benefit and also set the terms of engagement. I did pay a Jamaican expert, consultant, and research assistant, Andrea Lewis, who thoughtfully helped me engage with the local scene. In exchange for a fee, she expended considerable resources on my behalf, as well as giving me the chance to do work for her and others discussing aspects of the music industry, writing biographies, and doing other organizational and administrative labor. My participation at various levels and aspects of Jamaican popular music engagement and production was greatly helped by her labor, wisdom, and social connections, and we also became friends. I also did seek out people independent of her help, although I cannot be sure that her influence did not smooth (or otherwise shape) interactions even when she was not directly involved. After an initial struggle to make my own contacts, I found my research easier as time went by in Jamaica, as I negotiated for access to various spaces and conversations. These negotiations could be delicate, not so much because I felt unsafe but because there was little I could do to prove my good faith other than simply be present and do what I said I was going to do. The other facts I could put forth in my favor were the goodwill generated by my social connections, my knowledge and experience of DJ culture from the inside, and my previous work volunteering in a restorative justice project in the Jamaican prison system (which I would discuss if asked about my previous time in Jamaica). These facts became relevant especially in more private spaces where my presence required more explanation and there were chances for informal conversation.

An Instrumental Ethnography

I pursued this work in a narrower way than some of the wonderful ethnographies about Jamaicans' lives and music.[65] I do not investigate the full sense of how people involved in Jamaican popular music make meaning, but instead investigate a more focused question. I seek to identify the aspects of Jamaican popular music making that have the potential to be liberatory and to articulate how they challenge colonial definitions of citizenship and sovereignty. This book may seem narrow and possibly idealistic as a result, but its value derives from its unique combination of legal and cultural arguments to this particular question. It is intended to contribute to theory and provide inspiration for policy as well. That said, there are important questions this book leaves unaddressed.

One site of minimal focus is that, although my research practice is heavily influenced by feminist and intersectional approaches, I do not directly pursue questions of gender inequality within the popular music scene. Women's expertise in the Jamaican music scene is rarely visible in the control of musical technology, women's voices are a distinct (although powerful) minority in the music, and women's work in music is much more likely to be behind the scenes, organizational, managerial, and generally uncredited. There are, of course, notable exceptions in all these arenas, from the respected music studio I found that was run by a woman to the one female studio engineer I met (the only one I ever heard of working during my time there). Women's authority and expertise was most visible on the dance floor (especially the authority and expertise they had in their own bodies, at least in public). This distribution of presence and influence suggests a specifically gendered component to struggles over sovereignty and authority and to the exilic spaces in which they occur.

My choice to mainly set this aside is because to address it would first require addressing broader gender dynamics in Jamaican employment and representation. For example, women's underrepresentation may not result merely from a lack of social power on women's part, given the conflicted standing of popular music in Jamaican elite society. It may reflect one way that power deriving from within and from outside of colonial authority is gendered. The eyes of coloniality may read Black Jamaican men as less ame-nable than women to some realms of colonial authority. Jamaican women, according to the Gender Equality Report published by the World Economic Forum in 2013, take part in tertiary education at a rate of 2.29 women to 1 man and are employed in such occupations as "legislators, senior officials and managers" at a ratio of 1.45 women for every 1 man. Women's higher presence in offices and schools suggests there is room inside the system, al-beit restricted and exploitative room, for women. That room doesn't cor-respond with other kinds of security or power; for example, women and men do not receive equal pay for equal work (women received $0.64 for every $1.00 men received in wages): in 2018 women's unemployment rates were almost double men's, and in the political realm, women made up only 17.5 percent of Parliament. Women, for reasons listed above and many others, cannot possibly be said to have it easier than men do in Jamaica. On the other side, for women, especially poor and Black Jamaican women, the dangers of being seen as disreputable are likely higher, which means that exilic spaces are also gendered. Although women may be perceived as more civilized or civilizable (in accordance with white supremacist read-ings of threatening bodies), their position may be more precarious and re-quire constant discipline along colonial lines of femininity. Women are a minority in music, but the fields of Jamaican economic and social activity called "higgling" (a local term for street vending) are almost entirely con-ducted by women, especially by Black women from the lower classes. In many ways, the predominance of women higglers and informal commer-cial importers (ICIs) parallels men's predominance in popular music, a phe-nomenon worth further study. While higgling is also arguably outside and within Jamaican law,[66] the terms of women's participation differ from that of people engaged in music professionally in a way that reveals the contours of colonial gender roles. The exilic positioning of Jamaican popular music appears differently available to women than to men. This would be a fruit-ful line of inquiry for further work concerning the liberatory possibilities of subcultures and outlawry, places where women are often a minority.

I do not mean to minimize the many negative, unequal, or exploitative aspects of Jamaican popular music. Those aspects are not unique to Jamai-can music but function across various levels of Jamaican society.[67] As a society created out of massive violence, exploitation, genocide, and en-slavement, Jamaican social institutions are likely to reinforce those dynamics in all aspects of social life (although differently in different spaces). An illustrative example would be homophobia and antigay violence, a subject I address here because I do not address it elsewhere. This is an undeniable theme in Jamaican popular music, although its presence has waxed and waned at various times. Many outside Jamaica know only this about the music and about Jamaicans: that it is homophobic, that Jamaicans (at least the poor ones) are homophobic, and that homophobic violence is endemic. It is true that homophobia is commonly expressed, especially in popular music, and that antigay violence occurs often in Jamaica. But the question of violence in Jamaica goes beyond sexuality—violence is present in Jamaican life in many ways and includes the direct violence of state brutality, as well as the terrible violence of poverty, pollution, and neglect that ends or stunts many Jamaican lives.[68] I am not arguing that antigay violence is less important than other kinds (or that gay and lesbian Jamaicans do not experience antigay violence, in addition to all the other kinds). I do suggest that when prejudices exist in Jamaica, they may be visible in violent ways. Some have suggested that homophobia is equally powerful in elite Jamaican spaces; it is just expressed in elite terms or simply organized out of visibility. Rather than treating direct violence as an extreme and elite or institutional violence as "less homophobic," it may make sense to say that different expressions of homophobia are available to people without institutional power. As well, elites are not above relying on violence ascribed to the poor to enforce this prejudice. After a 2012 episode of homophobic violence on a college campus in Jamaica, the lower-class security guards were described as having backward attitudes and fired after public and international outcry, but such violence serves to discipline sexuality on campus just the same.[69]

The source of these attitudes, as well as their social function, is historically specific. Colonial states had a direct interest in policing Jamaican sexuality for the purposes of economic and social control. Thus, spaces of anticolonial freedom may afford some potential for a more liberatory vision of sexuality (an argument that some scholars of dancehall have put forth to varying degrees). Jamaican popular music practitioners do play with performances of gender and sexuality, both in their personal style that diverges especially from upper-class gender norms and in their dance practices.[70] It is not surprising that many of the most interesting critical approaches to gender and sexuality in Jamaica have come from scholars of popular music or are enacted on the dancefloor. This includes Nadia Ellis's insightful reading of dancehall's phrase "out and bad" and her playful, polysemic approach to tight-pants-and-makeup-wearing male sexuality in dancehall;[71] it also includes Donna Hope's unpacking of masculinity as performed on the dancefloor in ways that do not strictly conform to colonial norms.[72] Even the term "homophobia" and the identities it supposedly relates to—gay and lesbian in particular (the term "queer" had not made an entry into popular parlance when I was in Jamaica in 2009)—are themselves culturally specific. Who is to say that a sexual or gender binary is the right form for a decolonized Jamaican way of life? As the Jamaican scholar Carla Moore reminds us, in the bold and brilliant anthology *Beyond Homophobia: Centering LGBTQ Experiences in the Anglophone Caribbean*,[73] there is a danger in importing political and social categories forged in the Global North when they might erase or misrepresent other genders and sexualities that originate outside the colonial experience. I look forward to the field of alternative and decolonized sexualities and genders in Jamaican dancehall that I hope will flourish, which has begun with the book above and which does engage with some of the concerns raised here. In this book, I start from an examination of alternative and decolonized approaches to sovereignty and citizenship—concepts that include authority over self and community in material and cultural ways—as enacted against the social relations presumed by copyright law. The broader significance of Jamaican popular music lies in its capacity to redraw and resist, on many fronts, the coloniality of power— one thing requiring further investigation is the extent to which that capacity is gendered or sexualized. Still, sites of disobedience are always interesting for exploring the limits of coloniality. This disobedience is not only at the level of property but also reflects the socially disruptive role of Jamaican popular music over time: a role that has continually led to its being critiqued, decried, and banned from licensed and formal cultural spaces.

As a work rooted in ethnographic practice, this book has the capacity to contribute to both theory and policy. On the policy side, ethnography enables "the initiation of policy options that are at once more informed and more creative for having been grounded in a richer understanding of the historical and cultural processes of the people for whom they are designed."[74] While copyright polices have not, in fact, been designed for Jamaican people (but instead for idealized or colonial subjects), ethnography provides insight into how polices could be designed for them. This is another use of theory: opening up ways of thinking, understanding, and living that help people address the problems they face. Theoretical insights arising from this work and connections to theoretical frameworks put forth by other scholars are most often presented here alongside evidence about the material realities of daily life that are the test of those theories' applicability.

Chapter Overview

Chapter 1 outlines the history of Jamaican musical practices and situates them in Jamaica's particular class and race politics, attending to the role of copyright law in various eras. Specific musical traditions, institutions, and practices spring from the material and social conditions of poor Jamaicans. Those conditions precluded their ability or desire to participate in colonial notions of propriety or property. Resistance to these colonial notions takes shape against and outside the boundaries of legality and respectability, in interactive and participatory creative practices. Chapter 2, the ethnographic heart of the book, is rooted in accounts from street dances, a central creative practice of Jamaican popular music. These events occur at night, usually on the sidewalks and streets in a poor neighborhood, with people gathered around a sound system—turntables or CD players and speakers and a DJ. Using observations from street dances I attended, I illustrate the conditions that allow street dance participants to generate social, economic, political, and cultural power on their own terms in popular music. In chapter 3, I use the idea of musical conversation to outline the motivating factors and sociopolitical significance of phonographic orality in Jamaican popular music. The concept of conversing musically encompasses practices of symbolic and textual interaction in which participants engage with each other and with ideas and issues in cultural life by means of music. Closely examining the logic of Jamaican interactive musical forms, such as "answer tunes," reveals an attitude toward time, space, and identity rooted in less-colonial approaches to culture.

The concluding chapter draws together these ethnographically grounded observations to articulate the mechanisms that enable people to use music to circumvent coloniality. I intend these conceptual frameworks to be useful in further analysis of the potential for or actual existence of cultural autonomy. I also hope they may be useful to people in Jamaica and the diaspora, struggling for autonomy and liberation.

1 Voice of the People

Cultural Survival as a Musical Imperative

Popular music practice in Jamaica has been centered in the experience of poor Jamaicans. It is a syncretic practice with distinctive methods of technological engagement and a complex relationship to state power. The following history is not intended to be comprehensive. It is a history that illustrates how the cultural context for music making in Jamaica has engendered musical practices with certain characteristics that remain relatively constant over time. By setting those characteristics against the framework of copyright law, this history highlights how Jamaican musical practices reflect particular diasporic and sometimes anticolonial logics that challenge the categories of people, practice, values, and objects as defined by colonial authority. While by no means the sum total of Jamaican music's value or meaning, this discussion helps to explain why Jamaican popular music has been so vibrant, dynamic, and internationally influential. Jamaican popular music's clash with legally defined systems of cultural ownership reflects poor Jamaicans' ongoing struggle for cultural autonomy.

While music developed into a significant economic force on the island, in the first decades of popular music's development, the Jamaican government recognized it for its symbolism (when it recognized it at all), whether positive or negative. Apart from the broad outlines of copyright policy left untouched until 1993, state intervention in the music industry as an industry has more often come about as a response to that industry's growth rather than as a cause of it and is also shaped by a general hostility to or ambivalence about popular music.[1] Here I discuss the acts of the state from the perspective of the people in music that were affected by them, to the extent that state intervention was seen and felt. While the history of Jamaican economic policy in relation to music has yet to be fully written,[2] a history of the social dynamics among everyday people with implications for law aids in understanding what otherwise might seem contradictory or idiosyncratic state actions and inactions.

A Glossary of Musical Practitioners

For clarity, I offer a rough glossary of musical practitioners. These categories situate practitioners in relation to particular traditions and material relations. They are roles for people engaged in musical practice, in the sense of having technical expertise and artistic voice. It is important these categories not be reified as fixed relationships to rights or levels of creativity. For example, although I conceptually separate DJs from instrumentalists, the different terms do not denote different levels of creativity; nor do they define or justify a particular relationship to the ownership or ability to profit from the music they play. (As we will see, Jamaican musical traditions provide clear examples why creativity in particular should not be understood as more or less associated with any one role in relation to music.)

- Sound system: the technological apparatus for playing recorded music for a live audience. Traditionally turntables, amplifier, and speakers, later a mixer (to allow the simultaneous blending of two records) was added, and the turntables now have often become CD players, DJ controllers, or laptops.
- Instrumentalists: people who play traditionally defined musical instruments, such as the guitar, bass, keyboards, or percussion.
- Vocalists: people who sing, chant, or rap. Confusingly for those outside the scene, Jamaican popular music sometimes uses the term "DJ" to describe someone who chants rhythmic lyrics on the microphone to the accompaniment of recordings. I will use DJ as below and identify where people in the text are using this alternate definition.
- Artists: instrumentalists and vocalists.
- DJs: people who use prerecorded songs to create a live performance using a device like a CD player, turntable, computer, or electronic music controller. Sometimes called a "selector" by people involved in DJ culture (to distinguish from the DJs who are "chatting 'pon the mic").
- Soundmen: the operators (often owners) of sound systems on which DJs perform. "Soundman" is a title and a position of authority in Jamaican popular music (although not always respected by the Jamaican upper class, including those in government). A soundman can sometimes also be a DJ or an engineer himself, but the term denotes ownership or control and expertise with respect to the sound system. The term is gendered, in this case fairly accurately. Although

one of the first operators was a woman (Doris Darlington), female sound system owner-operators are rare and not well documented.

- Engineers: the technicians in recording studios or at live musical events who are in charge of the mixing board (a device that processes audio signals from turntables or instruments). An engineer uses the mixing board to adjust volume and other qualities of various audio signals simultaneous with live broadcast or recording.
- Dancers: While many audience members dance, I use the term "dancer" to describe someone known for dancing or who is paid or receives material reward for dancing.[3]

Although "audience" is not listed here, audiences, even when not dancing, also make complex and powerful creative contributions to music, to which other musical practitioners respond.

Pre-1954: Out of Many Musics— Diasporic Expression in the Early Era

Jamaica's precolonial existence was a site for the Arawak and Taino peoples, with their own cultural practices. However, this history is little recorded, and the Indigenous influence is rarely described (and even less studied) in relation to Jamaican culture. Jamaica-as-Jamaica began with white English colonizers and enslaved Africans, some escaped Africans (maroons), plus a small number of indentured servants and migrants from elsewhere. Thus, from the early days of Jamaica as a political and cultural entity, a variety of musical traditions and tastes were circulating. Colonial imperatives shaped the way music was shared or created on the island, but they could not control everyone's musical taste. While the colonial upper class amused themselves mainly with music reflecting upper-class English tastes,[4] the poor majority—comprising African-descended people plus a tiny middle class of Chinese, Indian, Lebanese, Sephardic Jewish, and other people of mixed descent—developed popular music informed by their own experiences. The sonic roots and tendencies in popular music arose from these realities of Jamaican life since its creation as a British colony.

A Syncretism with a Center: Sound, Religion, and Language

Early Jamaican musical practices combined instrumental, drumming, and singing practices that drew on multiple traditions, including African music;

traditions of such local syncretic religions as Kumina, Pocomina, and Revival; the culture of British enslavers; and those of the Indians and Chinese (who first came as indentured servants and whose children often became shopkeepers and later studio owners), as well as religious music—both British Protestant and various African traditions. As the first Jamaican popular musical genre, *mento* developed in the 1920s and relied on technologies that reflect the experiences of enslavement, diaspora, and African roots. Mento incorporates the banjo (of West African origin, via the American South),[5] the mbira or rumba box (also of African origin, a wooden box with flat metal strips that looks like a thumb piano but is large enough to sit on while it is played), a fife or pennywhistle (from the British military band tradition), and hand drums. These instruments accompanied witty lyrics covering topics drawn from everyday life. Mento was heavily informed by Trinidadian calypso, which at the time was a more well-known genre, as well as by the European quadrille, a nineteenth-century dance form. Confusingly, on contemporary musical recordings and in print media, mento was sometimes called "calypso," although calypso's instrumentation was usually rather different.[6] Notable songs from the early era reflect local realities, such as Lord Flea's "Linstead Market," describing a woman's struggle to feed her family, and many revel in the enduring pleasure of sexual double entendre, such as the ribald "Shepherd's Rod" or Hubert Porter's "Big Bamboo" ("I asked my woman what could I do / to make her happy and keep her true / She said the one thing I want from you / Is a little piece of the big bamboo").[7]

Despite the recurring bawdy lyrics in popular music, Jamaican musical practice has been shaped by religion, primarily because churches were one of the few places where young Jamaicans (mainly men and boys) could get musical training and have access to instruments. Instrumentation itself and the sonic character of music were shaped by what was available in churches. Popular music's lyrical content was also influenced by Christianity, with biblical phrases and parables a common theme. Some biblical language was paradoxically spread by the increasing influence of the religion or "livity" of Rastafari (many Rastas reject the term religion and use "levity," which can mean the oneness of all living things or a way of life in accordance with that life force).[8] Rastafari itself sampled and incorporated from the Old Testament in a syncretic spiritual practice. While various religious groups have fostered musical practices and made a varied imprint on Jamaican music, this study does not directly address Christianity and Rastafari's effect on popular music's creative forms and practices.[9]

Rastafari began in the 1930s with the worship of Haile Selassie, emperor of Ethiopia, as an incarnation of God, following his embodiment of certain predictions, including his successful rebellion against Italian colonizers. While there is no central text, as a way of life it generally involves rejecting the status quo (associated with white supremacy and colonizers) in dress, food, and language and is rooted in a militant, pan-African philosophy.[10] In its first decades, Rastafari embraced pan-Africanism as a global philosophical, political, and spiritual approach. Rastafarians also resolutely aligned themselves with the poor and disenfranchised and, in the early era, were themselves from that social stratum. This alignment plus their explicit rejection of colonial social norms—especially the embracing of Blackness and rejection of white supremacy—meant Rastafarians faced extreme hostility from the state,[11] including police forcibly shaving their hair, raids, imprisonment, beatings, and torture. Rastafarians were regarded by the upper classes as not at all respectable. From its genesis in the 1930s, Rastafari began to spread especially among the rural poor, and it influenced popular music in both form and content, especially as Rastafarians came into the city. Rastafarian musical traditions, which included drum patterns and the rumba box with its deep, warm bass tones, also exerted a sonic influence on the popular music that began to take on newly explicit form by the late 1950s and would later come to the fore in the reggae era.

The Jamaican class system shaped musical engagement in various ways. Because music was not recognized as a respectable profession or skill in the Jamaican formal education system (as it was considered not practical or morally edifying enough for the poor and not respectable enough for the upper-class schools), the island's musical talent has mainly come from the neighborhoods of the urban poor majority.[12] Jamaican formal education has not incorporated extensive musical training. Where it exists, music class historically focused on Western classical tradition, hymns, narrowly defined folk songs, and such instruments as the recorder (nearly ubiquitously referenced by interviewees as an example of a musical practice they learned in school). The primary exception—music education of orphan boys—is a striking example of how the urban poor seized and maintained cultural power in music.

In Jamaica's capital of Kingston, in the 1940s through the 1960s and beyond, the only places that had dedicated musical training programs were ill-funded institutions serving some of Jamaica's most marginalized populations. The Alpha Boys School, a charity orphanage for troubled youth run by Catholic nuns (with no government support), served as the home and training ground for a majority of instrumentalists who defined Jamaican music for well over a generation, some of whom are still performing today.[13] The only other music school on the island, well into the late twentieth century, was another reform school, the Stony Hill Reformatory for Boys. Music making's association with reform schools did not reduce its disreputable air among the Jamaican upper class.[14] Among musical practitioners, whether in reform schools or not, the majority of vocalists, instrumentalists, and dancers originated in poor communities.

In a visible way, class also affected the location and content of musical performances. Jamaicans have used the terminology of "uptown" versus "downtown" to delineate class since well before independence. This roughly maps onto residential patterns, in that many low-lying areas near Kingston Harbor (a not very scenic industrial shipping port into which many open sewers run) are inhabited by the poor, while the rich tend to live uptown in the foothills of the Blue Mountains. Many of the swankier hotels catering to tourists are similarly far from the hustle of downtown. Although instrumentalists mainly came from poor communities, many venues for live music were uptown, in hotels and at formal dances where someone could afford to pay a whole band. In general, Jamaican upper-class interest in live music was accompanied by a demand for music that did not reflect poor people's tastes. As local bands developed, paying gigs first mainly required they play "covers" (instrumentalists and singers replaying the songs) of light entertainment music, including some big-band jazz.[15] In a pattern that would continue throughout Jamaican musical history, whatever musical traditions were popular among the poor were not welcome in upper-class social spaces or state media platforms. This also meant any sonic references or influences that centered the poor were generally unwelcome; for example, Rastafarians and their musical influences were not welcomed uptown, and even Patwa, the language most associated with the poor, would be less often heard uptown (except in the most self-consciously folkloric performances).

Patwa[16] itself marks social location, although its significance changes depending on context. Despite its name likely deriving from the French "patois," Patwa has no French references but developed in response to the communication needs of Africans from various language groups abducted by English colonizers or living under them. A product of what linguists call creolization, it is closely related to English but grammatically distinct, drawing on Central and West African sources including the Twi language, preserved especially by the Maroons—descendants of rebel slaves who defeated the English army and negotiated land ownership by treaty with the English before Jamaican independence.[17] Historically, Patwa was excluded from Jamaican formal education and seen as unprofessional or disreputable.[18] But Patwa not only signifies Jamaicanness to non-Jamaicans: spoken in everyday life it often reflects identification with poor Jamaicans. Back in the preindependence era of Jamaican popular music, Patwa's increasing presence in Jamaican music in the 1940s and 1950s predated its institutional recognition as folk culture. Patwa's presence reflected both a shift in how singers identified themselves and which audiences they were trying to reach.

While language, lyrics, and instrumentation provide windows on music's meaning for Jamaicans, popular music was primarily intended to be dance music. Proper discussion of it requires attention to the bodily engagement with music and the places that legally, physically, and culturally influenced how that engagement took place.

Spaces and Technologies of Popular Music

While not generally welcome or represented in upper-class spaces, Jamaicans from the poor majority greatly desired music. While radios and record players reached the island by the early twentieth century, in 1950s Jamaica they remained relatively expensive (costing up to a year's wages)[19] and were mainly found in upper-class people's houses. Record players first reached the poor in shared social spaces where many people could gather around a single speaker or set of speakers, the cost carried by someone with a business or who was otherwise slightly more well-off than their neighbors.[20] Even radios were initially too expensive for most poor people, so in both cases, people engaged with these technologies not at home but in social settings. People began to develop ways to amplify these technologies beyond their initial design, building increasingly impressive speaker systems to broadcast the sound farther and more emphatically. An early innovator and dominator of Jamaican popular music, Clement "Coxsone" Dodd, described to the historian Garth White the transformation of personal audio technology into a social and commercial one: "We had a very big Murphy radio. . . . So what I did was bought me a Garrad changer; plug it into the radio, make and extension box from our room to the front of the shop. On account of that we had to stay open late, and my mother did a lot of business."[21]

Dodd would later build the Studio One, a vitally important force in the history of Jamaican music, but before that he, alongside his mother, Doris

Darlington, was one of the first DJs. Darlington (also nicknamed "Nanny," the name of a historical Maroon leader) owned a food shop and liquor store with space outside for people to dance, drink, and eat. Although in histories of sound system music, it is not often noted that a woman was a foundational DJ, Darlington played records on the sound system for dances when her son was off buying records overseas.[22]

Class politics also shaped musical participation at the level of the mixing and recording studio. Studio equipment was expensive; therefore, studio owners were mainly not from the poorest strata of Jamaican society, but, perhaps due to upper-class hostility to music making, they usually were not associated with the ruling class either. They tended to be from what might be called the lower middle class—such as shopkeepers in poor neighborhoods. For this reason, as well as the affinity between dancing, drinking, eating, and socializing, shops and commercial enterprises were vectors for the social enjoyment of music. Trojan, another major label, studio, and sound system, originated in a similar setting: Duke Reid, an ex-policeman, owned a liquor store and entered the music industry playing records in the parking lot. In poor neighborhoods, shop owners could afford to buy this equipment, which helped them attract customers. Thus, they invested in radios and expanded their capacity to include larger speakers with which to entertain more customers.[23] As audiences grew, Reid and others enhanced their sound systems further with turntables that played vinyl records, so as to better respond to audience tastes for particular tunes. As most recordings originated outside Jamaica, early sound system operators relied on their own and others' international networks to bring back music from overseas or flew over themselves on record-buying trips. The dances where these records were played were sites of intense competition over who could provide the best music.

Dancing was not incidental to the experience of the sound system. Musical events occurred in yards and driveways, primarily in the poorer neighborhoods, where one could take up space and make noise without being shut down by police. By contrast, upper-class people tended to engage with music in private venues and more often hired live bands, from whom they demanded very different music from that played downtown.[24]

The radio in Jamaica was the first embodiment of media technology use diverging between classes. When Dodd first turned on his radio to attract a local downtown crowd, he most likely tuned into broadcasts from Texas or Louisiana, not from Jamaica. Local radio, at first, did not much meet poor people's tastes; in fact, that was not its purpose. Radio stations on the island were foreign owned until later in the 1950s (and national radio did not begin until 1959), and their programming reflected what the colonial rulers saw as a "civilizing mission" rather than the tastes or experiences of the African-descended majority.[25] The island's poor majority mainly chose to listen elsewhere. Broadcasts from Florida, Louisiana, and Texas, as well as neighboring islands like Trinidad, fed Jamaican tastes in poor communities: Trinidadian calypso, U.S. country music, New Orleans jazz, big band, and rhythm and blues were the main sounds.[26]

The international reach of radio and the popularity of specific kinds of foreign music were supported by Jamaicans' migration patterns. The era immediately following World War II saw massive migration from Jamaica, as postwar labor shortages inspired the United Kingdom to offer colonial subjects free transport and jobs. The first ship to the United Kingdom arrived in 1948, laden with Jamaicans and their musical tastes and skills, who settled mainly in poor and working-class urban areas where a similar relationship to BBC radio existed as in Jamaica.[27] This expatriate community formed the basis of what would later become a sizable British-Jamaican community and a future market for Jamaican recordings.

It is worth noting that the comportment of poor people dancing to music was commonly identified as a challenge to social norms informed by coloniality. Jamaican social stratification enshrined (a mainly British-centric) white supremacy at the top of cultural expression. The coloniality of power also tended, in the rise of independence, to associate the small middle class often characterized as "brown" (rather than Black) as being the repository of good manners, deportment, and civility.[28] This set them against the Black majority of the urban poor, against whom social codes of deportment and civility were often weaponized. As they began to claim their own cultural spaces, they rejected the coloniality of Eurocentric social dancing, as well as the coloniality of copyright law.

Copyright: Providing Foreign Goods for Foreign Goals

The British government in Jamaica was not focused on copyright law. Since there was no local recording industry, and British colonial elites gave little respect to local music, enforcing copyright law simply meant transferring money from people on the island to copyright owners abroad. Overall, Jamaican popular music making was not recognized as an activity that accorded legal rights to those that made it—or perhaps it is more honest to say that the Jamaican poor were not seen as the kind of people who could be rights-bearing intellectual property owners. From before independence through the 1990s, a single entity on the island was responsible for managing copyright work for rights owners: the Performing Rights Society (PRS), a British organization that tracked who was performing copyrighted works (a practice that required a license, under the law). Before the rise of a local recording industry, the PRS mainly managed the rights to already-copyrighted music originating outside of Jamaica.

Copyright only protects works in fixed form, but since most Jamaican musical practitioners did not write music down, there would have been little reason for them to be interested in copyright law before recording studios existed on the island. In the meantime, Jamaicans began to develop traditions of musical engagement organized around relationships and interests not shaped by the requirements or assumptions of copyright law.[29] These traditions reflected oral traditions of sharing, engaging, repeating, and memorizing musical elements (to be discussed further in chapter 3). As dance events with recorded or broadcast music grew in popularity, oral musical traditions shaped how people engaged with recordings, giving rise to a whole new approach to musical engagement, which also did not follow the contours of copyright law.

The content and function of copyright law in Jamaica also limited its relevance and value to Jamaicans. Before and after independence, Jamaican copyright law was the same as the British Copyright Act of 1911, and it was not even revised (as it was in Britain) to keep up with developments in technology and practice. Even after Jamaicans started writing and recording their own music, this historic origin of Jamaican law made avoidance quite sensible on a number of grounds. Primarily, as a colony of Britain (until 1962) and with its history as a slave colony, the purpose of Jamaica's laws was not to empower or enrich Jamaicans on the island, especially not the poor and Black majority. But in addition, the basic tenets of copyright law rendered it a poor fit for practices in Jamaica.

The British Copyright Act of 1911 defined ownership of copyright as dependent on a work in fixed form (i.e., written or recorded in an unchanging format), to be owned by someone identified as "the creator or someone who caused the recording to happen," and the act specified that the work had to be "original." In the era before music recording was possible, it is unlikely that many Jamaicans wrote popular music down on paper. Most creative practices popular among the Jamaican poor were collective, collaborative, and iterative (revisiting and reusing the same musical elements repeatedly over time), as in any primarily oral tradition. The traditions of phonographic orality, arising from the particular class and racial and economic pressures Jamaicans faced, would have become difficult to maintain or would be deemed simply illegal had copyright been enforced.[30]

1954–1962: The Rise of Phonographic Orality

A key year for Jamaican music was 1954, when the local entrepreneur Ken Khouri founded Federal Records, the first Jamaican site of vinyl record production.[31] Had Jamaican popular music been centered on the productions of commodified recordings, produced by single entities on the island, and sold to the public, this would mark the beginning of the kind of industry recognizable to a colonial capitalist state. However, Khouri had been an importer of foreign music, and he created Federal Records principally to save himself the cost of import duties and shipping because he could press his own copies of foreign music to sell locally. Although Khouri had made single recordings without an imprint as early as 1949, these were more often one-off recordings of weddings and special events and not pressed for sale. For his new pressing plant, tourists were one set of customers,[32] and sound systems were likely another—poor Jamaicans were not likely to have record players or spare money for recordings. In fact, accounts disagree about whether Khouri or Stanley Motta's MRS records was really the first recording studio (although Motta does not seem to have had a pressing plant). Motta had founded MRS records in 1951. While there is disagreement about which individual studio was first, most accounts agree with the legendary singer Laurel Aitken that "[in the early 1950s] recording wasn't a business, it was live music."[33]

In fact, it took some time for the act of making records to be connected with the act of musical creativity in a studio. Well before Jamaica started creating much content for these recordings, creative practices sprang up around broadcast and playback technology. As new technologies of musical engagement emerged in Jamaica, they highlighted, and in some cases heightened, the cultural differences between how the upper classes and the poor understood music's purpose. This did not mean that no Jamaican upper-class people (or British people) enjoyed or supported Jamaican music but that institutions established by and reflecting state power tended to be hostile to music of Jamaican origin and that upper-class venues tended to be similarly hostile.

The Jamaican class system and its particular racial inflections also shaped who participated in the aspects of industry that required material capital. Khouri's role, as a Jamaican with Lebanese and Cuban parentage, reflects an ongoing dynamic in the music industry. Many members of ethnic groups that initially arrived in Jamaica as indentured labor (such as the Lebanese) remained a step above Black Jamaicans in the social, legal, and economic hierarchy. Lebanese and Chinese Jamaicans, while not recognized as white and historically discriminated against, faced less hostility than Black Jamaicans. Because they could differentiate themselves from Black Jamaicans, these ethnic groups could more easily take up social space closer to them than could those who might fear being mistaken for them (as some Black middle- or upper-class Jamaicans might fear being "tainted" by close association). As well, their connections to international networks of migration and trade could be useful for business purposes. On the other side, their ethnic identities did set them lower in a colonial hierarchy of respectability that also rejected popular music as disreputable by definition. This cultural and often geographic proximity helps explain the disproportionate presence of Lebanese and Chinese Jamaicans, as well as Sephardic Jews, in Jamaican music. Stanley Motta, of MRS records, was a Sephardic Jew, while the Chin family's influence in music also dates back to the mento era: in the 1950s, Chin's Calypso Sextet was a popular mento band named after Ivan Chin, who was not a performer but the producer, likely owning the expensive equipment used by the band to play and record. The Chin name is also found at the heart of some of Jamaica's most influential and longest-running record stores and labels, such as Randy's and VP Records. The interlocking dynamics of ethnicity, class, color, and race sorted out who could engage with music most easily at various levels of industrial and creative production. The changing musical technologies available to music makers both shaped and were shaped by these social dynamics.

Three Dynamics of Creativity against Coloniality

Technology in Jamaica often exacerbated the gap between colonial capitalist understandings of musical engagement and the way music worked for the poor majority in three important ways. First, the state entities that would initially control broadcast technology like radio (when Jamaican radio was founded in 1959) and television (founded in 1963) defined the acceptable content of music on those platforms, both by taste and by regulation. Second, upper-class cultural norms interlocked with state regulation to define acceptable practices of audience engagement with music. Respectable music audiences were expected to buy, listen to, or sedately dance in controlled settings to music that reflected acceptable cultural norms. In contrast, the urban poor appeared increasingly interested in dancing enthusiastically and expressively to loud music at night in public places. Third, legally validated processes of music making that relied on fixed notions of authorship, ownership, and consumership were at odds with the ways Jamaicans used technology to make music. They were especially at odds with the way Jamaicans used recordings as raw material for live performance or repeated studio reengagement—what Toynbee calls phonographic orality. The era leading up to independence crystallized these three dynamics.

Dynamic One: Popular Music as "the Voice of the People"

In the build-up to Jamaican independence in 1962, there was widespread public demand for Jamaican self-determination. At the government level, too, many saw culture as a force that would support and develop a healthy independent nation. People at various levels of Jamaican society recognized that mass media platforms would be crucial to promoting national consciousness. In 1959, the government founded the Jamaica Broadcast Corporation (JBC) and two radio stations, one "independent" but with the state owning the majority of shares and a second that was fully state owned. Norman Manley, the premier of Jamaica, argued, "[There are] special needs in the fields of self-expression, culture, information and entertainment that require a less commercial format."[34] In fact, both stations espoused a noncommercial, cultural mission.

The scholar of Caribbean radio Alejandra Bronfman characterizes Jamaican radio as having "diminished utility as an instrument of politics" due to "radio's relatively late implementation, the mountainous terrain, and continued control by elites wary of the boundaries between proper and improper English."[35] Radio's general utility may have been diminished, but the politics it retained were of the top-down kind. Although Jamaican radio programmers rejected a strictly commercial approach, they still relied on cultural hierarchies that valorized European, British, and American high culture. This still tended to exclude voices of the poor, although there were some changes regarding Patwa. This was especially due to efforts of people like the poet, playwright, and media announcer Louise Bennett, who fought in the 1950s and 1960s to have it recognized as a "nation-language" and who gained a foothold in Jamaican broadcasting from 1965 to 1982. This project aided in the acceptance of Patwa as folk culture. It was (and is) deployed by upper classes and politicians to evoke a kind of folk, or folksy, means of addressing the public. But advancement through upper-class institutions, to this day, requires mastery of formal English, not Patwa, and its presence is an uneasy signifier. As recently as 2005 (over thirty years after Bennet's Jamaican broadcasting shows ended and a year before her interment in Jamaica's National Heroes Park), over 50 percent of Jamaicans interviewed in a University of West Indies survey of one thousand thought "patois-speakers" were less educated, less intelligent, and made less money than standard English speakers.[36] This negative association reflects a continuing ambivalence about language seen as rude but also authentically Jamaican. While early JBC broadcasts include some works in Patwa usually cast as "folkloric" offerings, official independence celebrations mainly avoided sounds and music that were current among the island's poor majority, instead featuring military bands, sacred music, classical music, choral music, and quadrille dancing. In celebrating Jamaica's independent identity, "what the government did, and what the people did, were two very different things."[37] The nascent sound systems and downtown recording studios gathered their social power from popular culture's exclusion, reflecting the sounds and styles of the poor majority at a time when Jamaican identity was being defined. The era of Jamaican independence was the moment when the close relationship between expressions of authentic Jamaican identity and poor people's cultural production was solidified.[38] Popular music brought them together but through exclusion as much as through inclusion in official and government-supported platforms.

This movement of the music to the people also pushed back against changing cultural influences, such as U.S.-based music's growing presence on Jamaican radio. The soundman Prince Buster broke away from Clement "Coxsone" Dodd's Studio One sound system in the late 1950s to found a specifically pro-Jamaican-music and pro-music-of-the-poor system called the Voice of the People: "When I start making records, the chief idea was to start making Jamaican records, and push out that American thing."[39] Voice of the People perhaps more effectively fulfilled the cultural mission espoused by the JBC, by promoting music that was played by and sometimes written by Jamaicans.

SYNCRETISM WITH A NATIONALIST FLAVOR

As a colony comprising mainly people who came from far away, with very little (if any) influence of Indigenous people, the project of Jamaican identity building had to be syncretic from the start.[40] What was Jamaican was the particular way that syncretism was embedded in musical practice. It is clearer to say that Jamaicanness was evoked as a way of engaging with music, even music that did not originate on the island.[41] What made it particularly Jamaican was the way that phonographic orality facilitated Jamaican reuse of music originating elsewhere but with the insertion of local vibes, idioms, rhythms, or styles. In the genre of ska, the backbeat guitar technique (involving strumming on the upbeat of every measure) was perfectly suited for reinterpreting soul and rock-and-roll classics, as the guitarist could simply strum the same chords in a different rhythm.[42] Alongside songs penned by Jamaicans, the era saw continual releases of foreign pop tunes in a ska style. Ska interpretations of American pop music were equally as popular as Jamaican-penned tunes and could evoke Jamaican pride through asserting Jamaicanness against or in dialogue with preexisting tunes from afar.

Paradoxically, increasing emigration to England supported the wave of enthusiasm for music expressing Jamaican national identity. The expatriate community of Jamaicans wanted sounds from home, and because they worked in stronger economies, they could pay for recordings.[43] The expatriate community in England became the first important market for Jamaican recordings, both for soundmen who set up sound systems there and also for a public who could afford to buy recordings and the hi-fi systems on which to play them. By the late 1950s, a network of small, mainly white-owned businesses had developed in the United Kingdom that specialized in the wholesale importing and retail of calypso and Jamaican rhythm and blues.[44] Overall, their tastes still asserted specifically Jamaican knowledges, experiences, and methods of musical engagement.

Within Jamaica, the movement toward national (and anticolonial) self-determination also increased Rastafari's relevance to Jamaican popular music. Rastafari involved a cultural critique of everyday Jamaican life, in which music, food, and language itself were interrogated. The goal was to remove or overturn "corrupted" language and thinking that replicated a colonized experience and replace those terms with words reflecting the Rastafari worldview (for example, replacing "understand" with "overstand" because one should not see oneself as beneath the things you come to know or replacing the word for "police" with "Babylon"—drawing on biblical connotations of Babylon as corrupt). Notably, any kind of formal documentation including contracts could be referred to as "Babylon papers," reflecting a reasonable and historically supported suspicion of paper-based legal forms so often used to disenfranchise and displace Black people.

Rastafarian linguistic idioms became increasingly visible in musical lyrics, as did Rasta-associated drum patterns and sounds. A landmark musical recording illustrates the intertwining of Rasta musical identity and poor people's culture: the Folkes Brothers, under the direction of Prince Buster, released a song called "Oh Carolina" in 1958, which featured Rastafari drumming patterns that drew also on Kumina, a Jamaican religion with links to BaKongo West Central African traditions. Other sonic innovators like "Coxsone" Dodd (at Studio One) were also taking inspiration from the Rasta jam sessions in the hills outside of Kingston that melded jazz with African percussion.

But Rastafari and its influences remained most unwelcome on the radio and in uptown venues and were not included in their definition of Jamaican folk culture.[45] As well, the aesthetics and content of Rastafarian influence was explicitly hostile to the upper classes, police, and government. Rastafarians' presence, however contested, in popular music also oriented popular music toward the poor.

This rejection was also embraced by the fans of ska, who claimed the identity of rudeboy—a non-Rastafari term that described a sharp-dressing, hard-fighting youth often addressed in songs of the era. Here we see one of the earliest and clearest reclaimings of impropriety in Jamaican popular music—although many songs decried rudeboys and their rough behavior, they were also heroic figures precisely for their challenges to upper-class notions of propriety.

Although local musicians were increasingly producing recordings, it was sound systems rather than bands that spread local music across the island. The first generation of Jamaican instrumentalists were playing and recording ska in downtown spaces like Reid's studio, initially above his and his wife's Treasure Isle liquor store downtown on Bond Street. But most paid their bills playing in hotels uptown, nestled against the foothills of the scenic Blue Mountains or at tonier places like the Bournemouth Club on East Kingston's Bournemouth Beach, where bookers wanted jazz, calypso, and other music not associated with the poor.[46]

Upper-class hostility to popular music led many musical innovators to downplay their association with the music of the poor that the upper classes found "repugnant."[47] One illuminating example comes from the guitarist Ernest Ranglin, widely credited with inventing the ska guitar style. The recording in which he debuted this style ("Shuffling Bug") did not credit Ranglin. Rather than bemoaning his erasure, he explained in a later interview: "I didn't want to front it [claim authorship]. It was ghetto music and in Jamaica they used to put that music down." An author's credit could have hurt his ability to make money as a performer: "There were so many tunes

I was responsible for but I didn't go in front of them because I also had to be playing up at the society functions and the hotel dances, and there they would be looking down on me. Maybe I wouldn't get enough work."[48]

Like most Jamaican instrumentalists, Ranglin's day-to-day life depended primarily on playing music for upper-class audiences, who remained, at best, uninterested in or, at worst, actively hostile to poor people's music.[49] The coloniality of the musical economy prevented him from claiming public or legal ownership.

Dynamics Two and Three: The Sound System and Phonographic Orality

During the 1960s and 1970s, the small-scale businesses housing jukeboxes, radios, or turntables (owned by those at the upper margins of the lower class) grew in popularity, which necessitated larger speakers and more elaborate sound equipment—and thus the sound system was born.[50] The term "sound system" denotes a collective entity consisting of both the technology and the human beings who use it. The sound system's technological existence is as a collection of devices for playing back, amplifying, singing over, and manipulating musical recordings. Initially, sound system technology was a turntable (for playing recordings on vinyl), an amplifier, and speakers with which to broadcast the sound. But the sound system also provides avenues for creative input in a collaborative set of practices situated in personal interactions and in a broader community.

The soundman, sometimes called the "operator," is responsible for building and maintaining the technology; the selector chooses and plays the records. The term "DJ" is short for "disc jockey" but denotes having a personality on the microphone as well as skills with the records, speaking or "chatting" over the music using a microphone, and sometimes the DJ interacts with the recording itself by manipulating it physically. Later on, vocalists (still called DJs) mainly used the microphone to perform and hype up the crowd, accompanying the selector, who played and manipulated recordings. The technical skills involved in building, maintaining, selecting, and DJing developed into separate roles, each with their own creative input, although sometimes these roles overlapped with each other and with the audience.

Sound systems brought together the soundmen, DJ, producer, and audience in a collective creative practice. Bunny Lee described how "producers, including myself, would have to stay around a lot of sound systems to see what people were doing, which records, or bits of records, the crowds were reacting to."[51] Lee highlights the audience's integral role in the musical creative process as active participants in a cycle of sharing, judging, consuming, and influencing music production and performance. Negative audience response could suggest a reshaping of a tune or even prevent it from being released, while a good response benefitted the DJ, enhanced producers' and studios' reputations, and sent valuable feedback to producers and DJs that they incorporated into their creative decisions. The creative process was a social engagement that was reflexive and iterative, centered on the sound system.

Jamaican popular musical developed traditions that referenced this collaborative process. One such is the "lick back." "Licking back" a tune means restarting it from the beginning so that the audience can hear it again and the vocalist (if present) can restart his vocal accompaniment. The lick back also refers to the sound generated by the needle when the DJ spins the record backward on the turntable. Derrick Harriott, a Jamaican musician, described how it worked at sound system events in the 1960s. He had recorded a tune that "became such a hit that frequently the operator would have to lick it back ten times before the people let him take it off."[52] The audience demands the lick back. A DJ's skills evolved to include knowing how and when to lick back a track, which required carefully attending to the audience. Eventually producers began to incorporate the lick back sound into the recording itself, as an assertion of a tune's intrinsic value or to emphasize a particular element within a song. The interactivity was reencoded into a recording, ready for further interaction.

Sound systems existed to create these performative experiences, and the Jamaican music industry grew up around them.[53] With evocative names like Merritone, Voice of the People, or Kilimanjaro, they set up at dances and began to compete with each other at events called "soundclashes." At these dramatic events, rival systems set up in the same area, alternating tunes or sets of tunes, competing for crowd response. This competition was centered on the wit and originality of track selection as well as improvised vocal accompaniment. However, because performers improvised within the tradition of phonographic orality, their contributions mainly existed outside of legally recognizable intellectual property protections.

While these engagements took place at dances that were initially proximate to some other form of business (like Reid's liquor store), their growing popularity generated enough energy to become their own engines of creativity and small-scale economies. Starting from outdoor or semienclosed spaces alongside rum bars, sound systems moved to larger spaces, such as those controlled by lodges of fraternal orders like the Prosperity Club, an increasing number of dance clubs, and later "lawns," which were semienclosed and had larger capacity than the rum-bar-adjacent yards, streets, or parking lots. However, a primary mode of engagement remained the small-scale venues and driveways or lawns alongside houses in neighborhoods where sound regulations were not likely to be enforced.[54] This was more easily done in poor neighborhoods, which, as the music scene and industry developed, strengthened denizens of poorer communities' role as arbiters of popular music.

Rather than building up a local live music tradition that was later recorded, in Jamaica the process of recording and DJing largely predated or developed alongside bands and singers—and it did so within a new tradition of technological musical engagement. At first, local studios mainly recorded Jamaican versions of foreign tunes, reusing foreign-made recordings in the studio, with local vocalists singing over imported instrumentals.[55] This physically incorporated foreign recordings into the nascent Jamaican musical tradition. However, it did not take long for studios to hire local instrumentalists. Many instrumentalists and singers covered foreign songs, but over time they added their own compositions or mixed old and new, local and foreign, in a syncretic whole.[56] These new compositions and the growing number of Jamaican-trained instrumentalists were at the heart of ska.[57]

Ska continued the syncretic approach evident in mento but updated it with influences available especially via radio from the United States, including big-band jazz, U.S. marching band music, and an increasing taste for rhythm and blues. In its upbeat sound, ska instrumentalists showcased their virtuosity on the recordings, while DJs presented recordings to downtown audiences, often accompanied by a dancer or vocalist to demonstrate the latest steps and energize the dancing crowds.[58]

When the most concentrated sites and technologies of recorded music production—that is, recording studios—began to be built, most did not stray far from the poor urban areas where the musical authority was concentrated. The recording studios that dominated Jamaican music production for decades were most often located in poor neighborhoods: Studio One on Brentford Road, Prince Buster's studio and others along the busy but decidedly poor Orange Street in downtown Kingston. As long as ska was associated with the poor, it was not in demand in uptown venues. Both the relatively high cost of turntables (setting them outside the reach of most

Jamaicans) and the previous tradition of gathering around speakers to dance and socialize meant that ska recordings within Jamaica were directed primarily at soundmen and the dance rather than private homes and individual purchases. Early-era sound system DJs thus required little allegiance to the cultural concerns of the Jamaican upper classes. The poor majority's tastes influenced the sonic references, subject matter, and language in the music. The term "sonic reference" describes an audible recreation, approximation, or quotation of a sound one has heard before so that the listener makes a symbolic or emotional association between the memory and the current experience of hearing it. A reference can evoke emotional responses based on the memories one has had of hearing a sound before or based on shared musical knowledge between the listener and the producer or performer of the song. It also can function like a reference or citation in a scholarly work—making explicit a connection with a tradition, identity, or community. For example, as sound systems spread, Patwa's presence increased in song lyrics, evoking and strengthening a connection with the poor majority.[59]

PHONOGRAPHIC ORALITY IN THE STUDIO

The rise of sound systems kicked off a collective musical tradition that shaped the future of Jamaican music and continues to this day. Sound systems then and now challenge copyright law's reliance on a linear understanding of the creative process: rather than music being written first, recorded, and then broadcast, creative input occurs in a cyclical, reflexive way. In recording studios in the 1950s, instrumentalists' and singers' performances were often recorded live (without a written component ever having been generated) and etched directly onto an acetate, a flat disc of acetate that was softer than vinyl but could be played like a vinyl record (except that it would wear out more quickly).[60] The engineer in the studio was responsible for calibrating sound-recording equipment to get the best sound. The dancing audience's ravenous demands for music meant that many acetates were played out as soon as they were pressed.[61] Audience response could affect when (if ever) a recording would go to mass production and influence whether any further changes would be made to the song.

For mass reproduction, an acetate would be cut onto a metal plate (a master), which could then stamp the recorded information onto vinyl. However, since the demand for recordings came mainly from soundmen, who used records in live performance to "beat down" rivals, studios mainly did not focus on producing recordings for sale domestically. While popular audiences in Jamaica were crucially important to the creative process, they were not necessarily expected to pay for access to or control over individual recordings. The poor were mainly in no position to pay, did not have record players at home, and generally only engaged with music in social settings.

Copyright: Consolidating Creativity at the Margins of Law

Sound system culture shaped how Jamaicans thought about originality, about where creativity happened, and about how one could be remunerated. All of these were a response to the coloniality of life in Jamaica. While copyright law technically provided avenues for enforcing rights, it defined both rights and rights-bearing roles in ways that were impossible or deeply impractical for most poor Jamaicans. Even the relationship of Jamaica's first recording studio to copyright law bears this out: copyright compliance would have involved paying foreign copyright owners for the right to press their music to vinyl in Jamaica.[62] A recorded music's popularity as a performance medium rose in the 1950s, the initial gap between copyright law on the books and the (non)experience of law in action increased. At the same time, Jamaican popular music began to grow in popularity and influence within and beyond Jamaica. A striking feature of the Jamaican music industry during its formative decades, as we will see, is its ability to keep one foot firmly grounded in practices that subvert and contradict copyright law as well as that center poor Jamaicans' voices and stories. This relationship is not accidental.

This early era demonstrates how Jamaican class politics and economic structures limited copyright law's appeal and relevance for those most involved in music making. The one exception was the studios and those who ran them, who were the people who "caused the recording to happen" and thus, under the law, usually were the default copyright owners. This mattered somewhat for international music sales, where monitoring and tracking could in theory be more reliable. However, even internationally, local cultural contexts for Jamaican music abroad often kept Jamaican popular music off most mainstream media platforms and kept circulation underground: for example, British radio was not generally friendly to this music from a former colony. This underground circulation meant copyright law was unlikely to be enforced, since music use was not easily tracked. Even were it tracked, the Performing Rights Society, the only organization tasked with monitoring and collecting royalties, was based in England and not interested in Jamaican members. The ability to enforce and collect copyrights depended on one's ability to participate in the formal legal system and its institutions, but Jamaican popular music was not very visible to that system, whether in Jamaica or abroad.

1962–1970: Local Politics and Global Postcolonial Systems

Jamaican independence in 1962 brought to the surface the multifarious, occasionally violent, but also intimate relationship between the urban poor and the rule of law. This contradictory relationship is especially visible in the way Jamaican politicians made use of popular music in electoral politics. From the first postindependence election, both political parties exploited popular song lyrics in their campaign slogans. Clever politicians quickly recognized the value of music in maintaining a relationship with Jamaican communities through social, interactive music and dancing. Arguably the first dance space for the poor not located in a house, street, or business parking lot was Chocomo Lawn, founded in 1959 by future prime minister Edward Seaga, a rising star in the Jamaica Labour Party (JLP).[63] This former owner of West Indies Records made use of his connections to set up free concerts under the party's auspices. Seaga had previously helped ska artists receive airplay, and he had defused some of the government's resistance to ska music. He saw mento's and ska's popularity as a way of connecting to his constituents.[64] Jamaican popular music entered into a complex yet vital relationship to Jamaican politics.

Both the JLP and the People's National Party (PNP) rooted their power in poor communities and recruiting party members and rewarding them with government jobs or other resources.[65] These clientelistic relationships developed at the neighborhood level. Party allegiance meant that when a particular party was ascendant, its members (or their neighborhood) would more likely receive services like running water and paved roads. Since music was a major force especially in poor Jamaicans' identity, musical events and practitioners were an important power base and connection to neighborhoods. This connection took a darker turn as Jamaican politics grew more violent in the late 1960s.

In this changing social climate, ska began to mutate into a new genre called rocksteady. Sonically, rocksteady prefigures reggae more clearly than ska: a slower speed with an emphasis on the third beat in the measure, prominent bass lines and rhythm section while the guitars and keyboards recede further in the background.[66] The tradition of covering foreign songs continued, with a firm focus on American soul music, with occasional reflections of Jamaica's syncretic realities, such as "Always Together"—a Chinese folk tune, sung in Chinese, by Stephen Cheng, a Jamaican vocalist with Chinese heritage.[67]

Rocksteady's origin stories often emphasize how the audience's physical engagement with music and the social context affected its development. Bunny Lee, a pioneering producer, told the historian Lloyd Bradley how DJs responded to audiences' demands by creating what they called a "Midnight Hour slowdown session" in which a dancer's movements gave rise to the new genre's name:

> There was a guy named Busby in Kingston, he was a famous guy
> and him could dance. Whole heap of people used to follow him to
> the dance, but when he was in the dance, a whole heap of girls used
> to go crazy over him because him so good. When the Midnight Hour
> start up he used to stan' up and just rock steady. Literally. He used to
> call his dance "the rocksteady" and it was an announcer at [the
> Jamaican radio station] RJR that heard this and pick it up to go with
> the slower tunes. He used to introduce them by telling listeners,
> "Now I'm going to play you a brand new rocksteady," and other
> people used to talk about the dance like, "I see a guy doing the
> rocksteady the other night." The name jus' catch like wildfire.[68]

Other instrumentalists described audiences as complaining about ska's relentlessly upbeat pace and demanding that music "cool down," while some accounts describe an actual heat wave in 1966 as part of this sonic slowdown. Scholars of the era also suggest that rising political and social tensions, which spilled over into violence in the late 1960s around election time, led people to search for slower, gentler musical styles.[69]

These new dances and dance-oriented musical styles benefitted from musical structures that facilitated a dancer's interaction with the music: especially, repeating musical themes that help dancers follow a song's changes. But a specific feature, what science and technology studies scholars call a "technical affordance," in recording technology allowed this to happen. The first multitrack recording studios had a new ability: they could record on two tracks, usually separating the vocals and the instrumentals. Recording and playing the instrumental without the vocals was to become a defining feature of Jamaican musical practice—the riddim.[70] The instrumental track took on a life of its own: if a vocalist heard a song he or she liked, that vocalist could sing their own lyrics and melody over the same instrumental track. This practice was called (especially if done live) "riding the riddim."

Studios commonly recorded multiple vocals over one riddim and distributed records with the full song on one side and the riddim on the other, both to the public and to sound systems. In this way phonographic orality became embedded in records' material production, because anyone who had a record could sing over the instrumental.

In live performance—at a bar or, increasingly, at DJ-oriented events where sound systems set up and audiences gathered to hear them play— DJs lined up songs on the same riddim, one after the other, so even as the music stayed the same, a given singer could demonstrate his or her virtuosity in reusing the same musical element. Dancers could similarly recognize riddims' structures. Riddims are tools that allow for greater interaction—a listener's understanding of what was going to happen in the song could allow for carefully timed interactions, from dance moves to vocal interactions. Reusing riddims also added meaning for listeners over time as the riddims became associated with specific historical moments in which they had become popular. This dynamic interplay of musical references is central to how Jamaicans have historically constituted Jamaican identity through knowledge of shared culture.[71]

Riddims also gave rise to another type of recording called a "special" or an "exclusive." Since the instrumental track allowed for singing new vocals on a familiar riddim, soundmen began to commission popular vocalists to resing a customized version of a popular song (ideally the vocalist's own hit), in which the singer would reuse lyrics and melody but alter words to name the sound system. The vocalist received a fee, and generally would not record a special for rival soundmen in close proximity, as that would cheapen their value and demonstrate a lack of loyalty on the singer's part. If the singer or his song was famous, soundmen from far and wide might wish to commission a special, so they could capitalize on the singer's significance to enhance their own reputation. These specials were usually played at dances to demonstrate the soundman's clout: their exclusivity raised the soundman's status and impressed a discerning audience. In this way, a vocalist's fame and the fame of a popular song could generate multiple cash payments depending on a song's popularity and longevity.

In the 1960s, foreign audiences were also booming. In 1962, the white upper-class Jamaican Chris Blackwell (who would go on to work with Bob Marley), founded Island Records in London, to capitalize on the trend of U.K. audiences interested in Jamaican sounds. Some sources report that by 1963, fifteen thousand Jamaican records per month were imported to England.[72] Island Records, with its international base but local Jamaican connections, released what became Jamaica's first international hit: "My Boy Lollipop," sung by Millie Smalls, reached number one on the British charts.[73] Although "My Boy Lollipop" owed much to the sugary girl-group pop styles from outside Jamaica, such numbers reflected the potential crossover audience for Jamaican music.

Jamaican popular music was not accepted across all levels of society outside Jamaica—its cultural significance was shaped by the music's content but also by the symbolic meanings associated with Jamaica's colonized and racialized status and by the social structures that shaped who was able to hear the music in the new locations where it was of interest. Jamaicans in England, for example, tended to live in working-class areas of English cities. Social proximity, as well as the somewhat parallel experiences of an excluded and marginalized people, allowed Jamaican music to resonate with some working-class white British people. In a pattern that would continue, in England subcultures of white and mixed Black and white English youth, including such later subcultures as skinheads and punks, found value in Jamaican popular music. This value was centered in the oppositional content and sonic references that align the music with underclasses in a broader sociopolitical context. At the same time, English racism kept Jamaican music off the radio and barred all Black people from English bars. This kept Jamaican popular music closer to their home neighborhoods, at first in basement "blues dances" or house parties that were more under control of the community. Both subcultures increased demand for recordings that still circulated under the official radar.[74]

Postindependence Copyright: Old Systems Linger

Copyright law, notably, did not change after independence. This meant that the assumptions, interests, and dynamics it embodied were not oriented toward fostering local economic or cultural autonomy.

The 1960s increase in Jamaican-authored tunes could have meant an increase in rights ownership and benefits to the primary communities involved in music making. Both originality and authorship were a prerequisite for copyright to apply to a work, and it might have seemed that the rise of Jamaican-created musical recordings would increase local copyright ownership. But the explosion of Jamaican music production did not lead to a parallel increase in money for as many musical practitioners as one might hope. Within the letter of the law, the Copyright Act allocated ownership to those "by whom the arrangements necessary for the making of the recording . . . are undertaken,"[75] and quite often the first fixation of a song was in the studio with no underlying written composition.[76] This privileged studio owners as song owners even under formal law. While the labels may have formally owned copyrights, in most cases they did not seem to assert ownership of all the rights copyright defined and instead focused on controlling the physical master recordings to maintain control.[77] As well, sound systems' adaptation of supposed consumer products (audio recordings and record players) into creative tools, meant that within Jamaica, recordings' chief value was not as finished musical objects for a purchasing public but as elements in a creative process that generated money in other ways.[78] Domestic sales likely could not have generated much profit, even had sales been trackable in a formal way.

Tracking and enforcement of copyright law in the Jamaican context is thorny for a number of reasons that limited the value of copyright ownership in a traditional sense. Even after local recording took off in the 1960s, the Performing Rights Society (PRS), the entity tasked with enforcing the rights of creators and performers, remained apparently uninterested or unable to assist Jamaican instrumentalists and vocalists in owning copyrights.[79] One Jamaican government official involved in copyright reform diplomatically suggested to me that the PRS historically "did not go out of its way to capture new artists."[80] As far as collecting royalties from the primary broadcasters within Jamaica, the sound systems, their location in mainly poor areas added to the unlikeliness of PRS intervening, even on behalf of those locals who could have been positioned as copyright owners. Not only were poor neighborhoods seen as dangerous by most upper-class people, but the logistics of tracking and monitoring musical engagement in the streets and yards of poor neighborhoods would have been difficult and followed by the equally daunting question of how one would convince soundmen to pay the fees. At the international level, well-connected people who profited from the marketing of Jamaican music abroad had little incentive and no infrastructure to seriously redistribute that wealth back to Jamaica. In Jamaica, the lack of local infrastructure and the poor fit between creativity and legal forms meant that copyright remained irrelevant to the poor majority.[81]

For musicians and vocalists, copyright ownership was not as immediately helpful as money in hand. There is ample evidence in histories of Jamaican music that artists were generally not aware of copyright law or the possibility (however unlikely) they could benefit from it.[82] Although this is identified as a great loss to Jamaican rights holders, creative practices did not conform with the precepts of copyright ownership for many musicians. Virtually the same instrumentalists played on tunes in rival studios' tunes, and the band was identified usually with the sound system, studio, or producer, with the exact line-up shifting from song to song. Instrumentalists were paid according to the number of songs they could produce in a studio session or paid wages for time in the studio, while the copyright usually resided with the studio owner.[83] As well, working performers whose daily bread and butter came from entertaining audiences uptown were leery of claiming authorship of music associated with "the ghetto," as ska guitarist Ernest Ranglin described above.

There were advantages for artists being paid a wage or for time spent in the studio; it was a more certain calculation than the possibility of royalties in the future (especially since not every song generates royalties). However, artists did have an understanding that the popularity of a song ought to benefit them, if they could find a way to enforce it. This enforcement may have depended less on law than on social obligations asserted at the local level and in ethical, rather than legal terms.[84] Many accounts (as well as my own interviews) reveal an expectation that if a song did well overseas, a producer ought to share profits, as a matter of justice, although the mechanism and expected amount was often unspecified. Historically this expectation was sometimes met, although how often is unclear. While by no means a utopian equality, there is evidence of some sense of mutual or community-defined obligation.

As foreign audiences began to expand in industrialized nations and the colonial center, they engaged with popular music surrounded by more robust institutions for copyright monitoring and enforcement, and where more people—even Jamaican expatriates—had cash to pay for recordings. While the methods of social engagement in places like the United Kingdom still meant royalties were less likely to be trackable, there was a significant increase in the possibility of royalties for copyright owners in Jamaica. However, the experience of social exclusion or marginalization, at a physical and cultural level, also affected the circulation of Jamaican musical recordings. Jamaicans had always carried the music they loved alongside them, as sailors, economic migrants, and members of diasporic families. While in the earlier era this mainly meant recordings of American rhythm and blues, country, and soul music had circulated in Jamaica under the official radar (and with no payment of import fees), in the 1960s Jamaican-made recordings circulated along these widening routes, including increasing expatriate communities in England, Canada, and the United States.[85]

As Jamaican music gained in popularity abroad, pirate reproducers often stepped in where legal distribution networks failed to reach. Few Jamaican artists could have negotiated—or local labels afforded—a distribution agreement that brought their music to as many places as unlicensed transportation and even reproduction could reach. Radio in the United Kingdom and Canada did not generally play Jamaican music either: smuggling, in the service of sound system culture, spread the music.[86] Broadening audiences made it easier for artists to tour and enhanced their reputations so that artists might negotiate better deals with labels, promoters, or other powerful actors in the industry.

As is usually the case, many factors worked against royalties "trickling down" to the majority of musical practitioners.[87] The coloniality of the law and social conditions surrounding it meant royalties mainly accrued to more powerful middlemen and women in the industry. For the most part, studio owners paid singers and instrumentalists a wage or a one-time fee for recording, and they simply charged directly for sales of records as any other product.[88] The power, information, and resource imbalances that made copyright less relevant for the Jamaican majority are the same ones that disadvantaged Jamaicans and other colonized peoples more generally in an increasingly global market.

1970s–1984: The Reggae Era and the Materialization of Resistance

Reggae music in the 1970s expressed more directly a broadly Afrocentric spirit of resistance. Anticolonial resistance movements in the global South, antifascists in Europe and the United Kingdom, and punk scenes in the United Kingdom and beyond embraced reggae as the first postcolonial music genre, arising from a diasporic community and asserting explicit resistance to the old colonial order.[89] Jamaican recordings, and increasingly singers and instrumentalists from Jamaica, traveled to far-flung places to reach audiences already familiar with the music, doing so mainly through gray-market, bootleg, or pirate distribution.[90]

Reggae was a new genre, with recognizably different rhythms and different arrangements than audiences had heard before. But the earlier music did not simply vanish. Recording techniques that had become prevalent by 1970 emerged from the development of multitrack mixing, where different instruments could be recorded separately and layered together afterward. As well as cutting, filtering and layering tracks recorded specifically for a song, one could do the same with any recorded sound, incorporating it more deeply into a new song or version. Reggae songs incorporated lyrics, bass lines, melodies, and drum patterns from the earlier genres, reinterpreting them alongside new sounds and references. Riddims, those instrumental versions of songs, continued to recirculate with ever-evolving vocals. Increasing sophistication of studio recording and reproduction technology developed phonographic orality further. When a recording was reused, not only could vocals and instrumentals be separated, but also shorter snippets or separate tracks could be separated and reused. In the same way that DJs would select a particular song (or part of a song) to elicit a desired crowd response, a producer could now select a musical excerpt (a bass line, a lyrical interjection, a three-second drum roll).

Reusing familiar sounds or collections of sounds facilitates an interactive and social musical experience, drawing together musical practitioners—instrumentalists, voices, and dancing feet—into a coordinated but flexible moment of interaction.[91] This reuse also contributed to a common culture of shared knowledge and experience, similar to how the musicologist Ingrid Monson describes this working in jazz: "condensing social and cultural relationships both in time and over time through invention and musical allusion."[92] In Jamaican music, these practices made use of verbal quotations, musical quotations, and prerecorded selections (later called "samples") from existing songs, commercials, radio, TV, and film.[93]

Reggae's Shifting Political Valence

By 1970 reggae music was emerging out of ska and rocksteady. Sonically, the music slowed still further, bass lines became more prominent, and the rhythms moved farther from the soul- and rhythm-and-blues-influenced ska and rocksteady. Still associated with the poor in content, in its main sites of production, and in enjoyment, reggae lyrics took on a more explicitly political tone in the global context of rising Indigenous and anticolonial movements. Desmond Dekker's 1969 "Israelites" embodies this transition, using the biblical language of enslavement (the enslaved Israelites) to highlight the struggle of people who "get up in the morning slaving for bread . . . so that every mouth can be fed." Notably, this tune became a hit in England as well, resonating with Jamaicans and working-class white audiences. However, the specifics of colonial inequality began to be more explicit as time went on. A few years later, many songs' wording would be even less metaphorical: Peter Tosh (of the Wailers) sang: "Everyone is fighting for equal rights and justice. Palestine is fighting for equal rights and justice. Down in Angola. Equal rights and justice. Down in Botswana. Equal rights and justice. Down in Zimbabwe. Equal rights and justice. Down in Rhodesia. Equal rights and justice. Right here in Jamaica. Equal rights and justice."[94] The song delineates a global colonial system organized along racial lines. In general, poor Jamaicans were well aware of nations in Africa and beyond that were gaining legal (if not economic) independence from colonial oppressors. The music reinforced and spread this knowledge, especially through Rastafari's pan-African and anti-imperialist influence. This content also affected how Jamaican political parties resonated with popular music—depending on whether they aligned more with global capitalism or global anti-imperialism. This choice became increasingly relevant as Jamaican political parties were interested in popular music for very local purposes: as a way to enhance parties' increasingly close and violent relationship with poor urban neighborhoods.

In the 1970s, both the JLP and the PNP recruited disaffected young men from poor communities, armed them, and sent them to violently disrupt opposition party rallies and meetings. Poor neighborhoods aligned with one party or the other developed into "garrisons" or "garrison communities."[95] This militaristic term evokes the inhabitants' function as political parties' de facto armies, whose own neighborhoods became battlefields. Interneighborhood factionalism regularly exploded into murderous violence, peaking around election time, with each party decrying the other for its unruliness and violence. Thus, neither party avoided what tragically became powerful (though not unique) features of Jamaican domestic politics: factionalism, patronage, and party-based violence among the poor.[96] Police and even the army intervened on occasion (and continue to do so), but not in ways that would make poor communities likely to find them a neutral force, as they have been similarly tied to particular parties or politicians or other local but nongovernment authorities.

Social Power through Exile

The connection between clientelism, violence, and outlawry is complicated by the importance of local authority figures, sometimes called "dons" or (only partially euphemistically) "area leaders" or "community leaders." These figures were points of contact between local politicians and the neighborhoods, often distributing resources promised by one party to the neighborhoods that supported them.[97] Embedded in poor neighborhoods removed from the scrutiny of the law, dons were not obligated to differentiate between legal and illegal business (whose boundaries were already blurred by politicians). Dons used their access to resources to provide support for their communities, which could include paying for water, school fees, and providing food, as well as underwriting recording studios.[98] In this way, their social power derived not from state power but as much from their ability to operate outside it, to do what politicians could not do, and to build a base of power even more directly with the urban poor they lived among.

Obika Gray has described exilic spaces as physical and discursive and imaginative sites of interaction that are in some ways outside of colonial power and created partly by the failure of colonial institutions to fully define and control the lives of colonized people.[99] His work on dons and "outlaws" illustrates how the Jamaican government's failure to provide basic needs led to these figures gaining power precisely because they were not affiliated with government authority or "respectable" society—their very disreputability combined with their ability to provide material resources gave them a legitimacy that in some cases politicians had to seek the support of.

The role of dons illustrates how many benefits and resources that people elsewhere might associate with a government (including access to running water or paved roads, as well as jobs) were, for poor Jamaicans, based primarily on personal relationships. Personal connections with influential figures, including illegal or extralegal actors, could be at least as reliable, and perhaps more responsive, to address poor people's needs. These connections were fostered also through music: in fact dons and politicians both sponsored street dances and other musical events. Future prime minister Edward Seaga not only ran musical events at his venue called Chocomo Lawn, but later (in the 1980s), blending illegal and upper-class authority, he claimed the nickname "One Don."[100] The urban poor's cultural authority and even its "gangster" tendencies shaped the look, feel, and practice of politics.[101]

This dynamic was also reflected in Jamaican political parties' use of particular musical content, in that different parties tended to rely on different musical tendencies. The JLP was oriented more toward free-market policies, was friendlier to the United States, and was less invested in ideologies that valorized the poor than was the PNP. The JLP candidate for prime minister, Edward Seaga, as mentioned above, organized concerts at his venue but notably avoided presenting Rastafarian artists or bands. In contrast, the PNP, espousing a socialist agenda and more likely to use language that endorsed setting lower classes on top, was also more likely to incorporate themes and images of Rastafarianism into their social events and campaigns.[102]

After the PNP victory in 1972, popular music made further inroads into official culture. The two national radio stations began to play more local music content, but most still avoided the new sounds of downtown. This meant radio, while playing some promotional role toward the songs played on the air, continued to lag sound systems as engines of popular music. Gussie Clarke, a producer, asserted, "The radio were never going to play roots music [reggae]. . . . Because of this, the sound systems get big again. Bigger than they were in the sixties. People were flocking to the dance to hear *new* records. . . . the sound systems were the only place to hear them."[103] As sound systems remained the dominant local institution supporting Jamaican popular music, they kept musical energy rooted in communities whose interests and tastes were set outside and against those espoused by elites.

DUB: CREATIVITY CONTRADICTING COPYRIGHT

As sound systems pushed sonic experimentation in public performance, this experimentation in the studio created a genre called dub that further subverted the social relations of industrial creativity that colonial copyright continued to presume. Sound engineers created dub music with the mixing board, using skills developed in the process of audio production and processing. Engineers like King Tubby, who had long been technical experts at improving sound recording quality, came into recognition as artists in their own right. His studio (located downtown in a poor neighborhood called Waterhouse) became a hub for artists pushing the limits of song and audio structure. Artists like Tubby and the wildly experimental Lee "Scratch" Perry turned the mixing board into an instrument for creative manipulation, shifting the tradition of phonographic orality into another technological site. Dub transforms the instrumental version of a song into a musical framework against which a sound engineer manipulates the mixing board and various effects to create a new musical experience.[104] An engineer might add an audio effect (like an echo), drop in selections from the vocals or other recordings, alter the volume and other sound frequencies (like the bass or treble), or otherwise manipulate the broadcast or audio recording. Dub only had a small window of popularity in Jamaica in the 1970s, but it reached a wider audience outside of Jamaica. Much of dub's creative approach has spread through the circulation of records and techniques between Jamaica and England (and the United States as well). Its greatest influence has been in audio manipulation techniques pioneered by dub producers, which have been widely influential in many genres.

The technological skills and expertise inherent in dub music are not well recognized by copyright law. One contemporary music critic commented, "One of its major principles is the denial of the right of the musician to control completely his own output."[105] The critic does not appear to see the engineer as a musician but only as an interloper in a creative process that starts with instrumentalists. But even beyond that, the statement only makes sense if one assumes that musicians in practice had that right of control, something that has never been fully true.[106] In many creative contexts musicians have not wholly or even partially controlled their output, if by that we mean the circulation of recordings. Copyright law in Jamaica had no history of according such a right to poor Jamaican musicians, in particular. Still, it is not hard to see a kind of authorship in the person of the engineer instead of the composer or the instrumentalist. The great dub albums of the era name the engineer—for example, Lee "Scratch" Perry, King Tubby, or Errol Thompson—regardless of whether they wrote the music or played the instruments. However, most listeners and fans (and makers) recognize that dub is something that is done to existing music, not the act of a sole creator. Dub music highlights the existing ruptures in such formal legal relationships and the cultural logic that underlies them, in practice and in sonic form as well. By removing some sounds and tweaking or altering others, dub opens up a conversation about the origins of sonic meaning and the means by which it reaches our ears. Dub music's power lies in its unfinished nature, its sonic gaps evoking the ruptures in time and knowledge created by the colonial experience and refusing to be stitched up.[107]

FOREIGN AUDIENCES IN AN ERA OF ANTICOLONIAL MOVEMENTS

In the 1970s many Jamaican popular musicians looked abroad for inspiration, especially to global anti-imperialist struggles. Channel One, a studio that opened in 1975 and quickly gained a respected name in reggae, named its studio band the Revolutionaries (although they also recorded for other producers under other names)[108] and released songs like "Che," "Angola," and "PLO," which linked these struggles to a global resistance to the forces of Babylon. People outside Jamaica involved in revolutionary struggles also found reggae music to be an inspiring soundtrack and musical influence. International interest in reggae grew apace in the 1970s, catapulting Bob Marley in particular to stardom. This "rebel music" was well suited to the era's Indigenous and anticolonial movements. In the United States, reggae crossed over into a broader counterculture, radicalized by the Vietnam War, which meant that in 1978 Marley could sell out Madison Square Garden in New York. Another key dynamic in foreign audiences' delight in reggae was that, although reggae had a threatening sonic symbolism for the Jamaican upper classes, people in the Global North were less bound up in the colonial anxiety of respectability. This took on a particular dynamic in the United States, where U.S.-based Black communities were generating their own musical styles that were to varying extents initially read as threatening (from blues to rock 'n' roll to soul). Compared to the voices of Black people from within the U.S. borders claiming their space, reggae's pan-African symbolism was less threatening for white audiences in the United States. This meant countercultural elites, the poor and Black people outside Jamaica, and many anticolonial activists could identify with reggae in a way that was not as possible in Jamaica.

For the most part, Marley's fame grew without the assistance of major multinational record corporations. The fluidity of association between artists and producers, and the confusing or arcane realities of copyrights for various master tapes, discouraged most multinational companies from investing in Jamacian artists, including investing in promotion. However, for artists who did achieve a global reach, colonial power was still instrumental in shaping access to the broader world. A key figure in Marley's success was a white upper-class Jamaican, Chris Blackwell, who with great marketing savvy capitalized on the growing taste for rebellious symbolism among middle-class people outside of Jamaica. Blackwell had founded one of the first labels not associated with a sound system, a fact that demonstrated his connections were more to institutions outside of Jamaica's ghettos—it was his international connections that helped establish Marley via support outside Jamaica—since Jamaica's upper-class minority was mainly still hostile to the music of poor people ("sufferahs").[109] Predictably, Blackwell came to own the rights to much of the music Marley played.[110] While the Marley family did establish themselves financially in Jamaica, other Jamaican performers did not easily replicate this success. Some reggae artists did achieve fame and some fortune, especially on the wings of global movements of anticolonialism and anti-imperialism that latched onto the first popular music coming from a recently independent, colonized country. But for the most part, their successes did not alter structures of legal ownership and authorship that tended to favor upper-class and white actors over the poor and Black people. Marley and others had to claim authority rooted in audiences outside Jamaica (especially outside the Jamaican urban poor) before Jamaican upper-class institutions would bend to them even a little bit. While not diminishing their powerful impact on global music, without structural changes, such individual successes did not lead to a more supportive industry or uplift poor Jamaicans in a structural way.

Copyright in Reggae: More Authors than Owners

In the reggae era, the dynamics of a colonial legal and economic system still rendered copyright law unavailable to the majority of musical practitioners and most useful and valuable to elites, whether inside or outside Jamaica. The 1970s saw a series of international conventions for multilateral enforcement of copyright, but Jamaica did not join them. These conventions coincided with growing concerns in the Global North over artistic works reproduced in countries where copyright laws differed (including the countries in the Global South). Some have argued that Jamaica's refusal to sign was based on advice from American "experts," who persuaded the Jamaican government to legitimate the plunder of local music for foreign exploitation and reproduction.[111] But this argument does not address the possibility of local *losses* due to royalty payments overseas, owing to overseas ownership or the possibility of covers and samples requiring overseas payments. In fact, much of Jamaican-originated music circulated outside of legal scrutiny, and most often only became visible once upper-class people within and outside Jamaica owned it. Music exports were largely informal and not tracked at the national level while official music venues and radio, where recordkeeping might have been slightly more systematic, still focused more on foreign than local productions.[112] Even if Jamaica's fantastically high productivity of music meant it could be a net exporter of copyrighted works, copyright enforcement might have resulted in a net loss.

The colonial infrastructure of copyright in Jamaica continually undervalued Jamaican creators in any case. Even as reggae boomed internationally throughout the 1970s and 1980s, the PRS did not increase its representation nor appear particularly motivated to ensure that royalties reached Jamaican performers. In fact, it would prove to be very difficult to craft an effective copyright law. In 2009, when I interviewed a participant in the government attempt to revamp copyright law in the late 1970s, he explained, "There was never a complete understanding of precisely what was involved in operating effective copyright legislation." And he went on to note, "The infrastructure necessary for copyright legislation was never put into effect." The new Copyright Act, then, was passed but never enforced.[113] Jamaican history suggests that the law depends on the local situation, in which many social and institutional factors influence copyright's relevance.

As in earlier eras, the immediate concerns of living in poverty and power relations with the studios often outweighed more far-reaching goals. As the vocalist Dave Barker said to the historian Lloyd Bradley: "We wasn't used to this copyright thing. . . . Even if you had a family member here [in London] . . . who told you about it, there was so much crap you had to go through to attain some sort of recompense." As well, most artists had little experience with royalties but were paid for labor they did in the studio or onstage, something much easier to track. Recording more songs or getting more performances was the only clear way to earn more money. "What most of the artist would do . . . was to go, 'Oh eff it,' just leave it and go record somewhere else. Because they still have the way of thinking that said if you want more money you got to record more song."[114]

Local social relationships also discouraged many from claiming copyright: such claims might be the source of conflict. Barker reminds us that artists "didn't want to fall out too badly with the big-time producers."[115] Studios also needed to maintain friendly relations with their artists, to maintain access to a wide pool of talent and to benefit by association with artists' reputations as well. Especially if an artist was internationally famous or locally respected, he or she would revisit the studio, demanding more money or other support in exchange for their contribution to the studio's fame and the money the studio might be getting overseas. The vocalist U-Roy describes a positive relationship with Duke Reid, saying, "He [Reid] was giving me some money all right at that time, and we have an agreement that, when everything is kind of cropping up I'm going to want a little house out of my royalty. And he did do that. I used to go to him for any money I want during the weekend for running my house."[116] U-Roy uses the word "royalty"; however, as he tells it, U-Roy's method of receiving payment is informal, unlike the regular distribution described by formal rights management systems. Such informality suggests a more personal or community-based set of norms and expectations around payments. These narratives were not confined to history, either—in my 2009 interview with CM, a producer who has been producing in the studio since the 1980s, he told me he didn't own any copyrights. He said, "I don't get songs released that I really have control over." He then told me of one song he said he produced with an artist that went on to do well internationally: "The other day, I was reasoning with him [the singer], and him say, 'OK, I never really sign up for the publishing for this, so it's really yours.'" I asked CM, "Did he come to you?" And his response was: "Well, I would say, we come from the same community. We grow up together; my sound system was really one of the first that play the sound and develop the artist so that relationship growing in the music and him as a man coming up, [having] a record distribution and knowing all about this copyright and publishing ting, I tink even that is enough fi (Patwa: "to") show him that well. . . . [He made a noise like sucking his teeth and tilted his head, raising his eyebrows.] Make [CM] a piece of the pie, too! Cah [because] he has been successful over di years!"

The rationale CM gave me for why this artist came to him with money for a song that was doing well overseas was not rooted in legal rights but in history and social relationships. It is also not clear if this was a one-time payment, an assignment of formal royalties, or something else. Investigating the song in question does not simplify this picture. I tracked down eight different versions of the song CM named all coming out within one year of each other. The music collectors' site Discogs.com did not list CM's legal name or another associated name in the credits anywhere; it credited the singer as producer on one version and as coarranger on another. Four of the versions have a label name that is the same as the singer's last name, with two spelling variations on the singer's name. Spotify and Apple Music list the song on a compilation under the artist's name released by a different label. Riddimguide.com (another online source) lists the song as being by the artist but also identifies the riddim as one that was released at least twenty-two times by various labels and producers. Riddimguide lists the artist as the producer of the version named by CM, which is one of the two oldest. As is common with Jamaican popular music recordings, the closer you look and the deeper you dig, the less clear its provenance. This reflects both the range of people who may be involved in creating and the constellation of people who have the power to get their name attached to anything officially having to do with a recording.

It is extremely hard to reliably calculate the economic value of informal payments. The value generated is also intertwined with nonmonetary value embedded in the reinforcement of social relationships that allow people to help each other survive in sometimes desperate circumstances. Some interesting research, less specific to music, suggests that poor Jamaicans rely on mutualist and collective understandings about the distribution of wealth and that social norms of mutual obligation extend beyond the music world.[117] There is some evidence that many parties appear bound in a network of mutual obligation, the more so the closer together they are in terms of location, culture, and length of relationships. U-Roy's "royalties" and CM's "piece of the pie" represent an alternate system to copyright law in terms of how, when, how much, and to whom recompense is owed for what kind of musical labor. That said, in the music industry as well as in daily life, it is important not to romanticize the decidedly unequal relationship between powerful studio owners and poor artists.

Absent evidence about the reliability of informal payments, it seems likely a good degree of uncertainty persisted in this informal system. But uncertainty is also a major factor in music industries where copyright is enforced. The moment of negotiation over licensing occurs before a song has been commercially released, and no one knows whether a song will make money for anyone at that stage. This means artists cannot rely on copyright as a source of certain income. For labels, if their roster is big enough and their holdings deep enough, they can spread the risk, but few individual artists can afford to do so. Even if a song eventually generates royalties over time, still more time passes before they are distributed to the copyright owner. This delay between recording and receiving royalties may often be insufficient for a poor person's survival. For artists with plenty of energy and not much else, it makes economic sense to build their reputations and enhance social connections by performing and recording as often as possible, collecting one-time fees at the point of performance and recording. This focus on constant performance may be a factor in Jamaicans' impressive musical productivity.

Reggae's increasing international popularity did lead to some Jamaicans making their fortunes off foreign audiences eager for Jamaican sounds. Often they would establish themselves within a formal copyright system outside Jamaica, a pattern still followed to some extent today: Jamaicans who reach a certain level of fame often join collecting societies like ASCAP (American Society of Composers, Authors, and Publishers), BMI (the U.S.-based Broadcast Music Institute), or the PRS (as above, the UK-based Performers' Rights Society) to capitalize on the better infrastructure for monitoring the sale or use of recordings outside Jamaica. In the 1960s and 1970s—the reggae era—this was effective in limited and contradictory ways. Not every Jamaican artist was big enough or connected enough to collect money outside Jamaica. To move effectively among the more formal and foreign copyright regimes required skill and connections, which meant participation in the international music scene was structured along unequal lines. Because those regimes were not in effect inside Jamaica, Jamaican music could flourish on its own terms in ways that copyright enforcement at the time would not have allowed. It is impossible to judge different regimes' overall productivity. The much wealthier United States and the United Kingdom have larger markets, better infrastructure, and more resources, and whatever scheme artists used (within or outside copyright) would generate more money in those places than it would in Jamaica. For poor people within Jamaica, it would not have been as effective to rely solely on copyright in such an unequally accessible international system as it was to keep connections to local practices.[118]

Changing technology also contributed to musical engagement outside of copyright's purview. By the late 1970s, cassette tapes lowered the costs for recording and for copying music, increasing its informal circulation and further developing these practices beyond the view of copyright law enforcers.

1985–1993: Global Sounds, Local Authority

In the 1980s Jamaican practices of phonographic orality were carried to the United States by Jamaican émigrés like DJ Kool Herc and played an important part in developing U.S. hip-hop, similarly centered on live interaction with recordings.[119] By 1985 these U.S. sounds and styles had cycled back into Jamaica and were reincorporated into the genre dancehall. Dancehall combined the digitally generated and sampled sounds and more minimal production style of early hip-hop instrumentals with Patwa vocals and Jamaican musical references.

Shifting Focus of Musical Imagination

Alongside changing sonic patterns and practices, music's content also shifted. Moving away from the global and Afrocentric focus of reggae and 1970s Rastafarianism, dancehall focused more on local Jamaican experiences. Scholars suggest some interlinking reasons for this shift in content. First, the increasing numbers of economic migrants in the United States increased expatriate Jamaicans' desire for connection to their island home.[120] Second, Prime Minister Michael Manley government's inability to follow through on its projects for the island discredited its language of socialism and pan-Africanism—and this discredit was echoed in musical shifts towards nihilism and individualism in popular music and in popular culture more widely.[121] These failures can be ascribed as to the depredations of the International Monetary Fund (IMF) against the Jamaican economy, as well as a "strike of capital" led by foreign investors hostile to the prospect of socialist islands near Cuba. This geopolitical tension also included political and social upheaval in Jamaica as elsewhere. While too complex to be discussed closely here, this era in Jamaica can be characterized by the further collapse of state authority on the global stage (often paired with outbursts of state violence against the urban poor). Political violence (often associated with elections) in the garrisons, including violence perpetrated by the police and the army, continued to shape Jamaicans' daily life. Equally violent economic policies also increased in the 1980s, especially via Jamaica's first 1977 loan from the International Monetary Fund (IMF) during the global oil crisis, which brought with it stringent austerity policies. These policies drastically reduced access to basic needs and exacerbated economic precarity in Jamaica. Dons increased their involvement in the drug trade as local politicians could not provide what people needed, which meant that guns and the global drug trade increasingly used Jamaica as a foothold to the Caribbean, the United States, and beyond.

In that context, many Jamaican musical practitioners turned to new ways of constructing an identity based on the harsh realities of life in the "yard" (the Jamaican ghetto).[122] The ongoing presence of homesick or nostalgic Jamaicans abroad reinforced an interest in more Jamaican-centric content,[123] while the challenges a hostile world raised to the hoped-for rise of African independent nations also perhaps weakened the faith in pan-African narratives as the 1980s went on. While not necessarily nihilist, the lyrics, at least, more often reflected an interest in individualist and short-term pleasures, such as sex and intoxication, money, and competition within dance music itself (against other singers or sound systems). As will be discussed further, it is important to remember lyrics cannot be understood in isolation from the context in which people engage with music: popular music remained a social practice that was engaged in collectively.

The change in content did not end Jamaican music's global popularity, although it did correspond with a change in its significance and its audience. Dancehall's spread did not follow explicit Afrocentric or anti-imperialist politics but instead was part of a more general rebellion of youth culture, reaching as far as Zimbabwe and Japan.[124] Riddims circulated with dancehall recordings, spreading phonographic orality to new places, as people learned to participate by "jumping on the riddim." This spawned new recordings from all over the world, in which local DJs and vocalists incorporated sonic references from Jamaican music. Lyrics reflected this new reality, such as those below (accompanied by a rough translation) by the popular Jamaican dancehall vocalist Cutty Ranks, in his song "The Stopper."[125] International fame was increasingly part of Jamaican musicians' lexicon of success:

> Mi ragamuffin' and mi international (I'm poor/tough and internationally known)

> Say galang Cutty Rankin' gwaan go kill them with the culture (People say to me: go on, Cutty Ranks, use Jamaican practices to dominate other DJs and sound systems)

> London Paris, and even California,
> Down a Japan or me gone down a Africa
> Down a New Zealand or even inna Canada
> Yes, Cutty Rankin a go kill you with the lingua (my lyrical skills will defeat others in musical competitions)

Despite dancehall's global reach, foreigners engaging with Jamaican popular music continued to culturally respect its Jamaican source, including often singing in an approximation of Patwa. Some, seeking inspiration or symbolic stamps of Jamaican approval, traveled to Jamaica to record and collaborate with Jamaicans. Consistent with the tradition in Jamaica, many foreigners would pay one-time fees rather than negotiating copyrights for the possibilities of royalties.[126] Jamaican vocalists and producers became markers of prestige within a global musical network, but they still required validation by the urban poor in the street dance to maintain their relevance to the culture. Once recognized, Jamaican vocalists could capitalize on their recognizability, commanding fees for simply providing a few words or phrases to a song. Foreign musical practitioners, as well as foreign record buyers, began to arrive in Jamaica as part of this increased global popularity. Japan's Mighty Crown sound system, founded in 1991, developed their skills in the Jamaican idiom to the extent that they eventually won soundclashes in Jamaica and developed a Japanese market for Jamaican music.[127] These distant audiences in turn inspired Jamaicans to engage even more with a global network of listeners and performers in their lyrics and with audiences when on tour.[128]

Phonographic orality remained central to dancehall's creative style. Locals and foreigners alike relied on referencing long-standing Jamaican musical works in order to claim membership in this musical tradition; artists in the 1980s reused riddims as much as thirty years old. Phonographic orality also allowed the integration and diffusion of new tunes into a shared musical culture; the first dancehall song to use digitally generated instruments, "Under Me Sleng Teng" (1985), had over a hundred versions in Jamaica and countless more abroad and ushered in a new era of electronically based riddims.[129]

In the 1980s, the Jamaican government undertook a wave of deregulation and privatization, and radio was no exception as the government allowed private broadcasting access to the airwaves. This led to the first non-government-owned radio station, seemingly less concerned with civilizing than with profit. Irie FM, the first all-reggae station, gave much greater opportunities to local artists who desired airplay. Deregulation meant that four islandwide stations dominated the airways through the 1980s, in addition to smaller regional ones (whose broadcast was somewhat erratic). There were various influences on radio stations' play lists, including "payola," a term describing producers' presentation of gifts and money to radio DJs for playing their records. Although radio was overall more friendly to poor people's music than it had been earlier, a 1980s music industry study reported that many artists felt that getting their songs aired required substantial influence with radio DJs.[130] Deregulation may have removed or weakened some cultural gatekeepers but it increased the role of financial influencers in what was played on the air. This financial influence may have had a different effect than the cultural programming directives previously in place. While not a neutral gatekeeper, payola as well as the commercial stations' broader programming directives likely allowed more poor people's music on the radio, compared to what had gone before. Similar to U.S. radio in the early era of rock 'n' roll, racial hostility to Black music was pitted against the willingness to take money in order to play it.[131] While by no means egalitarian, payola ironically brought in a mechanism that did allow some pushback against narrowly culture-based rules against airplay.

Copyright during a Global Music Boom

Although music's content and structure changed between the 1980s and 1990s, copyright law did not. Nearly ten years of global popularity had made more people inside and outside of Jamaica aware that there was money to be made from music, which likely increased pressure on the Jamaican government. On behalf of Jamaican performing artists, however, the PRS's approach to enforcement remained lackadaisical. While in 1984 the PRS reported that in cases where they could not locate artists who had earned royalties, "50 percent of net distributable revenue is voluntarily paid [fund established for performers" the music researchers Krister Malm Roger Wallis could find no evidence of such a fund.[132] Such a discrepancy between the stated function of an artists' rights agency and what it seemed to be doing reinforced local expectations that formal institutions mainly provide ways for foreigners or upper-class people to profit from poor Jamaicans. Rather than reexamine mechanisms of collection (or redefine copyright in ways that might better match local practices), the Jamaican government's main response was to launch campaigns aimed at educating and transforming local musical practices to better conform to copyright law.

In 1991, for example, a government education campaign called All T'ief is T'ief ("All theft is theft") attempted to emphasize and simplify ownership of copyright. Through radio spots, posters, and official events sponsored by the government, the campaign attempted to reach the public. This campaign gained much of its moral urgency from the past experience of many musicians, when songs became international hits but left poor Jamaicans with little to show. However, the campaign did not address the mechanisms of power that left many Jamaican creators without copyrights to own in the first place or the PRS's unwillingness to collect on behalf of those that did. In addition, it did not engage with the primary ways that profit from music accrues to people in Jamaica. In general, a small number of mainly upper-class Jamaicans and people overseas have made the majority of profit from Jamaican music, but a great many do so legally, as owners of copyrights. Rather than theft in a legal sense, ongoing dynamics continually tilt the ability to own copyrights away from the poor. Alongside the imbalance of power between poor Jamaicans and those whom they sign contracts with, those groups have a differing ability to take on economic risk, which means that poor artists are likely to take cash in hand in exchange for copyright ownership (if they get anything at all). Those risks incentivize people with structural power to use contracts as a method of intimidation and control rather than transparency and empowerment. None of these are problems that copyright enforcement in itself, or the language of "theft," understood in a legal sense, is equipped to address.

Many people were (and continue to be) sympathetic to the idea that the profits from Jamaican music had wrongfully accrued to a chosen few. However, the mechanism of copyright has little to do with how or why that happened. It is also unclear whether Jamaicans saw this campaign as describing their own creative practices of reuse of riddims, which copyright law would flag as illegal, or thieving.

1994 to the Present: New Contexts for Old Social Forces

Although undeniably a force (if not the only force, other than tourism) that puts Jamaica on the global stage, Jamaican popular music has continued to trouble the upper classes. Deregulation and the rise of new media platforms has led to non-state-controlled stations that do, to a varying extent, play Jamaican popular music. Irie FM, launched in 1995, debuted an all-reggae format that was hailed by musicians and pundits alike as a tremendous step forward for Jamaican music. Irie FM became quickly enmeshed in a symbiotic relationship with the Jamaican poor and with street dances. However, the station's allegiance to popular music often brought censure from upper-class and government authorities. Meanwhile, government radio programming continued to avoid or have ambivalent relationships with the music associated with the poor. In a recent restructuring of radio stations, reggae music made the cut, but dancehall's presence was drastically limited, citing the same kinds of concerns that used to be aimed at reggae and, before that, ska.[133]

Wherever they were broadcast, lyrics portraying experiences and attitudes popular among the poor continued to spur condemnation in such bastions of respectability as the *Daily Gleaner*, Jamaica's national newspaper. After the latest restructuring of the largest radio conglomerate, the RJR media group (which owns five stations), dancehall artists saw themselves excluded yet again. Discussions of this organizational change rehashed the same critiques of popular music that have been made since the ska era. Popular music still regularly generates outrage from ministers, government officials, professors, and others criticizing it as degenerate.[134] For every advance in the local and international scene, there seems to be a countermove aimed at limiting the flourishing of Jamaican popular music: just one year after the dancehall artist Shaggy won a Grammy in the United States (and a few years after Shabba Ranks had won twice in a row), the government introduced new regulations on sound levels in public via the Noise Abatement Act. This law gave police further reason to crack down on popular music in the streets, the very place that nourished the Grammy-winning sounds.

These dynamics are never unchallenged, and especially, the past twenty years has seen increased interest coming from an institution most associated with the upper classes in Jamaica: the University of the West Indies (UWI), whose Reggae Studies Unit has been enshrined within the Institute of Caribbean Studies for twenty years. However, these inroads are not untroubled and are continually shaped by resistance and backlash. Carolyn Cooper, the founder of the Reggae Studies Unit, pointed out in a recent speech at UWI that her initial vision was an International Reggae Studies Institute that would stand independently as a global beacon of scholarship but that its incorporation into UWI required its paring down to a "research unit" within a parent institute. Its limited scope, she suggested, was due to continuing unease about its presence. As I listened to her talk, I recalled a dramatic letter to the editor published in the *Daily Gleaner* in 2009 that specifically condemned academics for lending dancehall unwarranted credibility by pursuing it as a subject of scholarly research.[135]

Despite the undeniable social and economic power of popular music in Jamaica, government and official institutions seem unable to account for it on the terms most often used by practitioners, which leads to strange and interesting silences. In 2013, one researcher observed a public presentation to the Jamaican government on the entertainment industry in Jamaica and noted that "although sound system owners, operators and selectors had been part of public consultations that informed the presentation, the report to parliament included not one reference to a sound system. They were simply not mentioned."[136] It is likely that sound systems are still too rooted, culturally and practically, in ways of life (copyright violation included) that are incompatible with formal state recognition.

The continuing lack of formal institutions to foster and develop Jamaican musical talent reveals the Jamaican government's continuing unease with music as a respectable occupation or site of advancement. This is not only a difficulty in dealing with creative practices but also, many suggest, an unwillingness to celebrate poor, Rasta, and Black people. MB, a respected producer I interviewed, was blunt about the continuing failure to convert the Jamaican global superstardom of Bob Marley, Shaggy, and a few others into broader prosperity for Jamaican artists. He told me, "We [Jamaica] did not capitalize on all the superstar thing that we had. There is Bob Marley, there is Shaggy, but we did not know to convert all of that excellence and achievement and motivation. A lot of that is a racist and a class thing. Bob was a Rastaman and from Trenchtown [a historically poor neighborhood] and ting."

In our conversation, MB's language slipped between past and present, between 1980s Bob Marley and 1990s global pop star Shaggy. This slippage reflects the ongoing nature of the relationship of the Jamaican state and upper classes to poor people's music across the decades. This reality limits the possibilities of meaningful policy-based change and is a key reason why copyright law has been difficult to define and enforce.

New Technologies and Laws, Old Practices and Prejudices

The section addressing this era contains more of my own observations, both based on my fieldwork in Jamaica in 2000, 2009, 2011, and 2014 and before that as a fan and DJ of Jamaican music. It is an era of tremendous technological change, and the one in which a wider discussion of music-making technologies and copyright law came to the fore. Many legal and technological discussions of these issues focus on the rise of the internet, file sharing, and digital sampling. However, it was clear in my experience with Jamaican music as a DJ and a listener that the anxieties around ownership and control of music in the digital age had previously existed or been redefined by Jamaicans with nondigital technology. I was curious about the continuities between earlier practices and current practices, especially as the music had already demonstrated immense popularity, productivity, and creative influence while engaging in practices that industry observers believed would destroy—or save—the music industry.

Any observer or participant in Jamaican music now, as a buyer or an event goer, can see that the Jamaican tradition of using prerecorded music as a main source of raw material for creative performance has continued. While riddims written or played on synthesizers and drum machines made less use of local instrumentalists or samples, riddims themselves have remained the basis for musical involvement. When in recording studios, not only did I see producers pulling from stacks or lists of riddims as they decided how to work with an artist, but on occasion an artist would stride into the studio and demand that the producer "give me the riddim" of a hot tune or a historic tune. I never observed a discussion of royalties or licensing in relation to this practice. Recording studios still draw on hundreds of shared riddims and samples, including riddims derived from foreign songs.[137]

As Jamaican sonic exploration has ranged more widely over the past twenty years, foreign interest in Jamaican popular music networks has also increased. This has expanded into satellite Jamaican popular music scenes, from Japan to Germany, alongside places with more Jamaican presence like the United States and Canada. One example is the Germaican Records label based in Leipzig, Germany. In the mid-2000s they even opened a Kingston office that lasted for several years. Via Germaican Records, German pop-dancehall bands had Jamaican vocalists sing over their riddims and even enjoyed some popularity in Jamaica. The German reggae singer Gentleman has said he "calls Jamaica his second home" and spends significant time there, although his official residence is in Cologne. Other Europeans, like the Italian vocalist Alborosie, have relocated to Jamaica to live, at least for a time.[138]

In terms of genre, dancehall continued to dominate Jamaican music in the 1990s, although older genres also retained pockets of local and foreign support.[139] U.S. and European pop and dance music influences also continued to be important and have been incorporated into Jamaican musical practices through imitation as well as reuse of recordings. Especially in the 1990s and 2000s as the internet has expanded the musical landscape, sonic references have incorporated even farther-reaching musical styles: popular tunes have involved sounds like Indian tabla drums or other foreign instrumentation, as well as completing the circle of influence by revisiting hip-hop, initially arising out of Jamaican phonographic orality in New York City.[140]

When I arrived to live and do research in Jamaica in 2009, it was well after compact disc technology had arrived on the island, but earlier formats were still in use. In older, more established studios, floors and tables were usually piled high with tapes, vinyl records, and CDs, alongside computers with regularly updated databases. Newer and smaller studios tended to hold a well-stocked hard drive and much less nondigital formats as well as an occasional pile of CDs. Nearly all studios visibly contained accumulations of Jamaican recordings from over forty years, reflecting a rich musical history available to the ongoing traditions for reuse.

These traditions are audible and observable as well, and I saw how DJs, dancers, and audience members engaged with music at nightclubs and especially street dances. The urban poor continue to be the arbiters of musical style and popularity, as well as the model for what a Jamaican "star" looks like. Upper-class Jamaicans and white faces (or Chinese—as prevalent as whites in Jamaica) are still rare among popular vocalists, dancers, and instrumentalists. Upper-class Jamaicans remain better represented in studio production, management, distribution, and promotion.

Digital technology has, since the 1990s, begun to lower some class-based barriers to studio production and distribution—although more so for the middle classes than the poor. Home studios have proliferated, continuing and extending traditions of musical reuse as new technology enables cheap duplication, sampling, and editing. These changing technologies of musical reproduction again highlighted the gap between local practices and the presumed interests and values of copyright. First cassette tapes, but especially recordable compact discs, became new media for circulating popular music. Because they allowed individuals to cheaply reproduce audio recordings at increasingly high quality, these new technologies increased the ability of members of the public, even the poor, to consume and reproduce music.

Reproduction technology led to new and underexamined roles in the world of Jamaican popular music: the semilegal or illegal middlemen and women who could make and sell copied music. Because Jamaican popular music was much more centered on songs and riddims than on albums, what got made most often were (unlicensed) compilations of whatever was hottest in the street parties or of songs and artists understood to be classics. Little scholarship or reporting has been done on the role of cassettes in the public consumption of music, but by the CD era, it was far easier to purchase a compilation CD of music from a hawker at a traffic circle or by a gas station than it was to find a record store selling music legally. The sound systems' priorities shaped the production process so that music was released to the public via street dances and nightclubs long before mass production of a recording was even considered. To stay on top of what was popular, one had to find someone who could access a recording that might not ever make it onto an officially licensed album or only if it was demonstrably popular among the public in other ways. The speed and unofficial circulation of music made informal CD sellers an important node in the network of Jamaican phonogram circulation. Needless to say, these sellers and manufacturers were not licensed and were occasionally subjected to crackdowns and confiscations, although this did not appear to limit their presence much.

In twenty-first-century Jamaica, phonographic orality continues to disrupt many dominant assumptions about social engagement with music. At many street dances, I observed collaborative, interactive creativity between the DJ and the audience. I saw how shared knowledge of emotional attachments to music and its social context disrupted a linear approach to time, where the old could be valuable as the new. In addition, the interplay between different recordings illustrated the dialogic value in reusing music and fragments of music, one that was important in a way that could not be encompassed by simply adding the value of two references together. In 2009, one street dance experience, recorded in my field notes, included all of these moments in one.

At the beginning of the night, the DJ was playing mostly American R&B and pop, familiar songs to all but nothing wildly popular with the audience. As the crowd began to filter in, he began to switch to different kinds of music, songs that referenced earlier Jamaican musical history—especially songs from the early 1990s—the era when Jamaican dancehall music reached global popularity.

It was older music, and the content and sonic qualities were very different than the smooth, slick, bright layers of 2000s hip-hop and R and B. I felt the music was signaling its Jamaican-ness through its inclusion of songs and samples from an earlier era. The audience members around me had seemed to know and like the R and B well enough, dancing and nodding along, but they responded more energetically to the change in sound as it shifted to recordings crafted and popular in Jamaica. At a certain point the DJ brought in another song that had been a hit in the 90s—probably around the time that most of this late-twenties crowd had first started to hear popular music. In response quite a few people waved their hands in the air and imitated gunshots (waving "gun hands" in the air and shouting "blaow blaow" to imitate the sound of a gun fired in the air in appreciation). At this audience outburst, the DJ "pulled up" the record for the first time that night, spinning it so that it ran backward for a moment with a distinctive sound and dramatic gesture, arm raised high. He then restarted the song. The DJ also spoke over the microphone, boasting about his knowledge compared to other DJs—while demonstrating his access to and familiarity with classic tunes. The audience's energy continued to build, and then when the DJ hit what felt like the first peak of the night, played a more classic-sounding tune, but an update of an old song—it actually combines an instrumental that was first recorded in the 1970s and remains wildly popular, with Bounty Killer, a currently respected vocalist, singing new lyrics on top of it. That felt like the DJ was bringing it up to the present, since Bounty Killer was big in the industry at the time.[141]

Many aspects of this performance style date back to the early sound system era as described above by Bunny Lee and Derrick Harriott. The DJ's musical creativity demonstrates values that do not fit with the strictly commodified and bounded understanding of musical recordings as finished works. The DJ used turntables, microphone, and sound effects (sometimes simply adjusting volume, treble, and bass levels) while drawing on knowl-edge of the audience's expectations and likely experiences. He had also mas-tered interjecting live performative elements, and most important, he demonstrated great skill in strategically juxtaposing songs to create a nar-rative and interactive musical experience, which reflected an awareness of popular news and controversies of the day, as well as of Jamaican musical history and the audience's collective memory. This extension of Jamaican performance traditions, and the new ways that Jamaicans built economies of reputation and performance on them, fit poorly with copyright law's con-tinuing focus on fixed, individualistic control of recorded works.

Copyright Post-TRIPS

Copyright was officially revised when Jamaica joined the TRIPS agreement in 1993 and its new Copyright Act was passed in 1994. But this should not be construed as the government finally coming around to copyright's uni-versal beneficence. There were strong external pressures to join. Interna-tionally, the WTO and international trade organizations have become increasingly interested in intellectual property enforcement (not specifically related to music). Most importantly, the WTO requires members to sign this agreement as a condition of receiving other trade benefits and includes en-forcement and monitoring as part of its obligations. This pressures WTO members irrespective of their specific needs and interests. While there are some variations at the domestic level, TRIPS still relies mainly on familiar concepts of fixed individual ownership, originality, and exclusive rights.[142]

Despite the TRIPS mandate, the mechanism for enforcement in Jamaica has remained hazy. One example of how slowly such enforcement works lies in the compulsory license instituted in the Jamaican Copyright Act of 1994. The Jamaica Association of Composers and Performers (JACAP) was formed in 1998 as a response to the historically ineffective PRS. But as of 2010, JACAP had not collected any royalties for this license in Jamaica. Its direc-tor asserts that collection of royalties has begun internationally, due to mu-tual agreements with foreign rights management organizations.[143] Many members continue to be dissatisfied with JACAP, which reported in 2010 that it spent 52 percent of its budget on administrative costs.[144] This may explain the reportedly low numbers of Jamaican producers registering their works. Enforcement is a thornier problem that cannot be solved by policy, however carefully crafted. In one conversation with a producer, running a small but popular studio with numerous local and international production credits under his belt, I raised the subject of JACAP and received an out-pouring of frustration that hinted at various complexities regarding formal and informal permission and ownership. "What is JACAP all about?" he demanded.

> I went to JACAP with one riddim that I redid; the riddim wasn't mine originally. When I went to JACAP, they tell me, "Oh, it is impossible to register these songs because you have to get permission from the people who have the riddim originally." Now, that is really stupid. You understand what I'm saying? Because what if the person who had produced that riddim has died? How are you going to get a paper from that person? What you need to do as JACAP, you need to have this in file to say, I can check to see who the riddim is originally; then you as JACAP supposed to have some information, so you would know who is the organizer. Or then, it wouldn't be the riddim you are registering; it would be the songs. Instead of saying, "OK, you need to get a letter." It's bull! For me, I get a lotta songs I didn't even register as yet.

This producer's commentary only hints at the can of worms opened up by investigating ownership of songs or riddims that are already made. The image of the dead producer here, while possibly relevant to the example (although a legalist response might simply suggest he seek out their heirs), more productively works as a cipher for the nearly unanswerable question of copyright ownership—not because nobody will claim it but because it is likely that multiple people have or will claim it if it is seen as something valuable. Add in the fact that paperwork tends to be nonexistent or contra-dictory (as any slog through Discogs.com regarding 1990s dancehall will tell you) and that the principles by which ownership are accorded are not agreed on by everyone, and you have a tangle of confusing claims that mean many want to steer clear of or idealistically want JACAP to settle.

Such tangles help explain why, within Jamaica, copyright has remained largely irrelevant to practices of collaborative or flexible authorship, espe-cially the reuse of recordings and riddims. However, this situation may change when it comes to the interests of foreign copyright owners. One 2007 example shows that foreign copyright holders have attempted to interfere in local Jamaican musical traditions: The U.S. hip-hop artist Ne-Yo's song "Independent Woman" was widely available online with an instrumental version, as well as several "remixes" that incorporated various U.S. sing-ers and rappers. But when the Jamaican artist Vybz Kartel added vocals over the U.S. instrumental, the combination of Jamaican content with a U.S.-originated tune became hugely popular at Jamaican dance events. I heard it at least twice a night at five different dances over the course of three months, to ecstatic response including comments by others regarding the tune's high quality and popularity. Ne-Yo's record label (EMI) eventually demanded that Kartel destroy all copies of his version.[145] This demand would have been extremely difficult to enforce locally, although it might be possible in relation to formal and international networks of distribution, like iTunes, which could be reached by the label and has the power to remove a recording from its library. While local access might not be too badly affected, copyright enforcement could limit Jamaicans' ability to circulate the Kartel version internationally. This would make copyright enforcement a disadvantage to Jamaicans practicing their traditional method of musical engagement. In addition, if EMI could embed copyright enforcement in technology that Jamaicans use, it could foreclose on their creative practices automatically, perhaps even in the studio process.[146]

The relatively recent instatement of a compulsory license for reuse of recordings might improve the situation for more Jamaican musicians. A compulsory license could prevent the kind of haggling that slows musical circulation and could shift costs to soundmen or others better able to pay royalties. JACAP's above-mentioned ten-year failure to collect royalties suggests that the trouble may lie outside the realm of copyright policy and instead with the institutional conditions in which the law must operate. The compulsory license also differs from musical practices outside of Jamaica, which could lead to more conflict at the international level where Jamaicans remain at a disadvantage.

Still, the majority of Jamaican musicians express dissatisfaction with their ability to make a living. While not arguably that different a concern from the majority of other Jamaicans in similar socioeconomic standing, the language of copyright holds out hope to many that it could be an engine for remuneration of local creators. In response, the Jamaica Intellectual Property Office (JIPO) has launched several educational campaigns that focus on theft or piracy but do not address the significant power imbalances and creative dynamics that have shaped how copyright (does not) work in Jamaica or that serve to disempower poor Jamaican creators. In terms of legal prosecution, government attention has apparently focused on unauthorized sales of CDs and DVDs or unauthorized duplication and sale of CDs and DVDs. In three years of copyright disputes on record at the JIPO offices not a single case exists of copyright infringement in the creative process of performance or studio recording.[147]

For the majority of Jamaicans involved in music copyright has remained external to their daily considerations and practices. The attraction of royalties is dimmed by the difficulty in making or collecting them, while other career-making resources remain based on what creatives can control—their bodies, skills, and personality in live, real-time activity. As we will see in chapter 2, musical performers primarily use recordings and performances to enhance their reputations, producing music quickly and performing it often. Vocalists depend primarily on payments for live performances or for custom recordings for advertising shows or studios.[148] Engineers and producers are paid for studio time; instrumentalists are paid for performance or studio sessions; all can become "personalities" whose endorsements are commercially valuable. Thus, Jamaican musical practitioners capitalize on Jamaican music's global reach as well as its local power. However, the means by which they develop the skills to do so are still mainly self-generated.

Conclusion

This brief history describes several aspects of Jamaican musical practice that reflect its unique position at the nexus of local needs and official exclusion. It reveals how Jamaican popular music is continually situated in poor communities. In poor communities, popular music developed in the creative spaces of the dance, the studio, and the sound system. In particular, sound systems' phonographic orality has subverted both the individualistic and linear frameworks for understanding creativity. Musical practices in traditions of syncretism, repetition, and phonographic orality have contradicted many assumptions in the law. Within these creative spaces, which I explore in the next chapter, the urban poor, although never isolated from coloniality, have found it possible to express themselves as members of a public that could not be fully recognized within state-defined understanding of proper citizenship. Instead, their practices have continually embodied social relations that are poorly defined by industrial capitalism, with clear legal and categorical separations between creators and consumers, and with clear boundaries around creative works understood as separate objects whose value comes from their differentiation.

The social relations between the rich and the poor in Jamaica, between recording studio and musician, and between communities and individual musical practitioners all limit copyright's ability to shape or reward most aspects of Jamaican popular music on the island. Copyright law is in fact an intensely symbolic project, regulating how people may legally interact with works of cultural expression—as if the act of interaction is not itself a kind of cultural expression. Copyright embodies a legal logic with its own embedded cultural assumptions about the nature of creativity and the location of value in creative works. It is embedded in a legal system that recognizes rights and claims only if they conform to practices and communities defined without respect for local methods of creative engagement.

Every Night It's Something

Exilic Authority in the Street Dance

· ·

In 2017, Global Directories, the Bermuda-based company that makes telephone books for Jamaica, commissioned several Jamaican artists to design work for the covers of its telephone books—the national residential telephone directory and the Kingston–St. Andrew telephone directory serving the metropolitan area around the nation's capital. Each artist was tasked with celebrating an era of indigenous Jamaican music. For the Kingston–St. Andrew book, the Jamaican artist Lennox Coke was asked to represent dancehall culture. He designed a detailed and entertaining scene of a street dance, including a man holding a microphone, standing next to a DJ, flanked by enormous towers of speakers. In the foreground, men and women danced together and alone, including a woman with her backside to the viewer and a woman bent forward in front of a man leaning back, pelvises near but not touching (a frozen image of a popular dance move), and a woman dancing alone, one arm up over her head, back arched. All the women wear short, tight skirts or shorts that reveal their bodies' shapes; the men appear in colorful clothes, and many wear gold chains, all display what one journalist described as "aspects of dancehall 'bling.'"[1] The telephone book's publication of this cover was met with immediate backlash. A group called the Jamaica Coalition for a Healthy Society decried the cover as inappropriate. After public debate (with many sides being put forth), the telephone book company apologized for offending anyone and released an alternate cover "for institutions such as churches and schools."[2]

This drama shows street dance's simultaneous importance and disruptiveness to Jamaican society. Nobody could deny the scene's indigeneity. As the artist, Lennox Coke, pointed out, "This image is not strange to us. We have street dances. Whenever Jamaicans get a chance to play music, there will be dancing. And the comments about the skimpy attire? On the street in Jamaica, people walk in this attire, even without going to a party."[3] And yet the image was still deemed threatening enough that the company had to provide an alternative.[4] As described in the previous chapter, this hostility to

Jamaican popular culture and to poor people's embodied engagement with it is a feature of Jamaican society derived from its colonial history. This hostility explains Jamaican popular culture's limited access to formal media platforms.

While there is a middle class alongside the ruling class of Jamaica, the gap between the poor and those above is very great, and the middle and ruling classes often align, especially in relation to norms of respectability and propriety. In the discussion below, I generally address the upper classes together, except where specific interests make their differences relevant. This class dynamic gives the street dance a different kind of cultural significance from, for example, a recording studio. Some recording studios do exist in poor neighborhoods—many legendary studios are downtown—and they are not wholly middle-class places by any means. Studios are, in some ways, sites of the concentration of financial power alongside musical and technological power. They are not, however, the site of cultural authority for Jamaican popular music, since popular music must be "tested" in the street.

Given the ongoing and structural hostility to poor people's cultural practices, it is striking to see how much cultural authority has remained among these communities that are generally excluded from the upper levels of society. Even when Jamaican music has gone international, its visual and audible references remain aligned with the voices and interests of Jamaica's urban poor. This was true in the reggae era (albeit with a pan-African twist) and remained true through dancehall's rise as a global music genre.

Skin color, language, and deportment continually demarcate class along racialized colonial lines, but attending to Jamaican popular music reveals an interesting dynamic within Jamaica compared to outside. While lighter-skinned and middle-class Jamaicans are disproportionately represented among dancehall's most international stars (most notably Sean Paul, one of the most internationally popular dancehall singers in the United States, the United Kingdom, and Europe), this international bias has not translated into the same kind of popularity at home; nor are such artists necessarily major influences in the music's development. The majority of Jamaican dancehall artists (including Sean Paul) who make it big outside Jamaica still preserve aspects of cultural expression that are not automatically comprehensible to outsiders, such as Patwa lyrics, despite the hegemonic power of English in the global pop realm. In fact, international dancehall acts from outside Jamaica (including from Japan, the United States, Europe, and beyond) regularly affect Patwa to fit in. What explains the ability of poor and

Black Jamaicans to define the terms of engagement with dancehall, even as it has become an international phenomenon?

As I investigated what it was that kept the music focused in this way, I, like many, saw the sound system as a key institution in popular music since its inception. As discussed in chapter 1, the term "sound system" describes both the combination of technologies for playing recordings in a live setting (turntables, CD players or laptops, a mixer, microphones, amplifiers, and speakers as large as the soundmen can afford) and the men who control those technologies—engineers, DJs, and roadies. Sometimes described as "mobile discos," a sound system can be set up in a matter of hours in a space that becomes a site for community musical engagement. Scholarship has not overlooked the sound system's significance.[5] While sound systems are a distinctive and important feature of Jamaican popular culture, focusing on sound system technologies and the people closest to them (the soundmen) does not reveal much about their relationship to communities or social groups. Most information about sound systems focuses on those with more capital, since speakers, amplifiers, and turntables have remained relatively expensive in Jamaica. Looking a bit more broadly, the historian of Jamaican music David Katz (for example) has identified "sound system culture" as "the perpetual arbiter of Jamaican musical taste."[6] The word "culture" points to a wider array of people and practices than the technology alone, but how should one differentiate it from other cultures? If culture is a product of a community, what community makes sound system culture? To understand what defines sound system culture, we have to look at how sound systems are put to use in a social setting. Observing sound systems in practice, we can see specific legal, cultural, architectural and geographic conditions that have tied sound systems and the music they make to the Jamaican poor. As Coke's art reminds us, the essence of dancehall music is not in sound systems by themselves but in musical experiences involving people at particular moments in time and space. Focusing too closely on the technology and its immediate controllers (DJs and the like) does not fully reveal the social meaning of the music that sound systems have played and influenced. The street dance, controversially enshrined on the cover of the Kingston telephone book, is the Jamaican tradition that has continually brought the sound system and poor communities together.

Street dances have been a feature of life among the poor in Jamaica since at least the 1940s. At these events, people gather at night, on the sidewalks and streets in a poor neighborhood, around a sound system staffed by DJs and engineers and among other people dancing, modeling, selling food and drink and other consumables, taking photographs, and, increasingly, recording video. The wide range of activities at the dance reveals them as important sites for personal and community advancement along creative, economic, and social lines, defined by the specific location in poor neighborhoods and among poor people.

As we will see, these means of advancement at the street dance do not take the form that the political and economic upper classes in Jamaican society generally recognize as legitimate or desirable. These alternate means flourish mainly because street dances occur in spaces controlled by the urban poor, which means they are also at the margins of law: they violate or, at least, strain property law's allocation of power to exclude and control access. This control is based mainly in the physical realities of street dances: the occupation of a public street, the emission of loud noises for many hours, and the circulation of illegal or unlicensed products, including musical recordings. Look closely at street dances and you can identify the limits of legal definitions of property, propriety, and even personhood. You can even see the contours of a different kind of citizenship.

I spent sixteen months doing fieldwork in Jamaica, mainly but not exclusively in Kingston, the capital. It is also possible to attend street dances outside the capital city. More than one Jamaican said to me, "If you get five Jamaicans together, there will be a sound system." And many times, I passed through a smaller town at night to see a tower of speakers with people clustered around it on a side road off the only main road in town. While my insights here come primarily from Kingston, the dynamics I identify exist across street dances; they will be shaped by variations in the features that I identify as constitutive. It would be interesting to examine how the higher presence of tourists in cities like Montego Bay affects street dances' exilic capacities. Such questions can only be answered by clearly identifying dynamics at play in a specific locale first, which here I do in relation to Kingston proper.

In Kingston, I attended twenty-three street dances, as well as various other sound-system-based popular music events and popular music events not based on sound systems. I have formulated the central arguments below from those experiences. The events share several dynamics that are central to understanding the relation between law and musical practice in Jamaica. The dances I attended multiple times included Boasy Tuesday,[7] Passa Passa,[8] and the island's longest-running dance, Rae Town Old Hits. I also attended popular nightlife events that did charge admission but were not in nightclubs. Including both street dances and this outdoor-indoor nightlife, popular music events flourished every day of the week in Kingston, from Hot Mondays to Boasy Tuesdays, Wedi Wedi Wednesdays, Bembe Thursdays, and Dutty Fridaze.[9] These events—street dances and street-adjacent dances—inform my observations, although I also attended some nightclub events and some more exclusive "uptown" events like "all-inclusive" parties, where, for a substantial fee, one could enjoy music and unlimited food and drink in a high-security setting well away from the hustle of downtown. I also attended several music festivals and music competitions.

Descriptions interspersed in this chapter are from my field notes and give impressions—sights, sounds, smells, and feelings—pretty much as they occurred to me at the time of my experience. They describe moments that gave me insight into the social meaning of the street dance. I provide the descriptions here as I wrote them in order to reveal the seeds of my own meaning making in the moment. I have since reflected on these observations in the context of further research, but for the reader, these descriptions provide some epistemological accountability—you can see what I found meaningful and what made an impression on me. While in some cases my responses may be different from those of other people in these moments, my analysis should provide insight into the dynamics that produce different responses from differently positioned people. Some attendees may not notice the smell of the gully or be struck by the size of the speaker towers; others may see differences in clothing styles or dance moves that I miss. These differences do not weaken my analysis, but they raise a question: Do the dynamics I infer from my observations help explain those different responses or different observations? If my interpretations are reasonable, they will.

I observed some characteristics that held across the street dance and to some extent the street-dance-adjacent events. Most of these related to participants' use of land, buildings, recordings, and their own bodies and the class and color of those involved. Since I was especially interested in how and when poor and Black people made themselves visible and were able to define the terms of visibility, by making observations across different spaces, I could see how parameters of visibility shifted. Street dances were at one extreme (and there was variation within them as well), and private, expensive, all-inclusive events in remote and heavily guarded locations were at the other. I observed that street dances' capacity to facilitate poor people's cultural authority depended on the social and material context, with the law's influence on poor people's power coming rather distantly beyond that, most of the time.

Street Dances as Exilic Spaces

On paper, street dances could appear marginal to Jamaican society: illegal or semilegal, free admission, outside, in poor neighborhoods. But street dances are anything but peripheral to Kingston daily life or Jamaican mass media. For regular reporting on street dances, you can turn to national television, Jamaican-oriented shows on international channels, Jamaican radio, the national daily newspaper (the *Jamaica Gleaner*), tabloids, or commercial radio. Celebrities are made and broken there; drama abounds, from the domestic to the military. Street dances also affect urban life in material ways: they can bring money into a neighborhood or disrupt an early morning commute. Their sonic presence in the city is a force to be reckoned with. In 2009 (and by many accounts, for the previous twenty years), their presence could be felt almost every night: after the sun went down, their speakers' boom could be heard across much of Kingston, even from the hills of the Blue Mountains overlooking the city. This duality—of being ever present and yet still not respectable—is at the heart of street dance. Their cultural and social importance is, paradoxically, strengthened by their presence at the margins of respectability. This marginal location allows them to bend or avoid the rigidly defined roles and behaviors that structure how people act, dress, and interact in uptown spaces. Because Jamaican respectability is tied to coloniality, it cannot ever really foster the flourishing of poor Black Jamaicans. Instead, these communities have developed their own incomplete centers of cultural power in sites outside state control.

Social spaces that allow power to arise from socially marginalized communities like the urban poor are what the Jamaican sociologist Obika Gray calls "exilic spaces." These spaces' power derives from the particular relationship of the Jamaican state to its people. In colonial times, the state's basic function was to dehumanize and forcibly extract value, and indeed life-force, from the Black majority on the island and redistribute it to white British elites in Jamaica and Britain. Although many involved in the state's functioning postindependence are themselves Black and none are officially British, many of its basic institutions (including copyright law) have not changed much from colonial times. The coloniality of power means citizenship is differently available to people based on race and class grounds. However, the postindependence Jamaican state has also not had the resources to enforce its power directly, either through military or police force or through institutions of mass inclusionary discipline, such as schools or other public institutions. The end of colonial sponsorship meant that the state became more dependent on Jamaican people's recognizing it as an authority. However, because the state and the Jamaican elite remained culturally oriented toward whiteness and British culture, its own legitimacy as a ruling system in a majority-Black nation of Jamaicans has been unstable: its authority is inconsistent, flexible, and parasitic.[10] This means the postindependence Jamaican state had to rely, in part, on forces outside its own establishment to help order society. The state's legitimacy depended less on extracting labor and instead on extracting cultural legitimacy for its own power.

This instability of state authority has had two results: most Jamaicans do not see the state as something to be relied on in an institutional way, and marginalized Jamaicans draw strength from exilic spaces and outsider status.[11] Gray's work has mainly focused on how crime and gangsters, or dons, have risen to be these alternate centers of power in Jamaica. Dons, in particular, base their legitimacy precisely in the state's inconsistency and failure. This is true in a more general way for communities of urban poor. People who cannot meet the requirements of respectability that are defined in relation to colonial standards of class, culture, and color must rely on exilic spaces to shore up a sense of identity less dependent on recognition by colonial power. In a sense, they redefine citizenship as Jamaicans in a way that goes beyond a relationship with the state.[12] In this analysis, exilic spaces are not only resistant and are not simply antistate; they draw on identities and practices that originate outside the colonial order. Exilic spaces arise from a "parallel process of cultural formation in the ghetto," where "whole areas of shared customs among the poor existed beyond the reach of state predation."[13] The location, "the ghetto," is a crucial aspect of what makes the space exilic, in that it is not only the site of state neglect but also the site where the poor have some measure of authority over the space.

The street dance provides fertile conditions for the shared customs among the poor to flourish beyond state predation: from creative practices to economic and social institutions, these social scenes allow for a range of social relationships unrecognized by elites. In particular, this cultural flourishing in the margins of law has shaped the ways Jamaican musical practitioners attained financial success. Practices of musical engagement, including DJing, singing, rapping, or speaking through a microphone attached to the PA system and all the other activities that together create this event, define and reinforce identities that are not fully dependent on the coloniality of power. Music in the street dance is mainly not owned in a fixed, exclusive way. Rather than exclusively licensing copyrighted material, most people enhance their reputation through the dance and charge fees or other recompense for their labor, while others sell associated goods. Exilic aspects of street dances foster social relationships of creativity, community, and economic interdependence among the poor, which are not easily compatible with the social order defined by the upper classes.

A crucial aspect of exilic spaces is their relationship to law. The Jamaican state's role, as discussed elsewhere, is primarily one of absence or negotiation. This is both because of the historic unease that government has had with popular music and the inconsistency and neglect (as well as sporadic violent intervention) marking the government's precarious authority. Street dances regularly transgress: traffic law prohibits people convening in or blocking roadways,[14] zoning law has historically restricted the use of public spaces for commercial or entertainment purposes, and the provision of food and drink generally requires a permit (including a fee and training) from the Department of Public Health. Many people were serving food or drinks at the events I attended, and while I was reluctant, as a white foreigner, to ask people directly about permits since I believed this would make them feel unsafe, I did not observe any permits posted (as would generally be required). In several cases, the practices looked to be in violation of some of the requirements. Flouting of these laws is not at all confined to street dances, but the confluence of technically illegal economic and cultural practices is striking.

While earlier regulations purported to limit loud sounds in residential areas, Jamaica's 1997 Noise Abatement Act went so far as to render illegal the majority of street dances and many semicontrolled musical events involving amplified sound. Although initially not much enforced, it has in the past ten years been enforced with increasing—and increasingly bemoaned—severity.

Similar to noise and other zoning regulations, strict enforcement of copyright law would disrupt street dances' communicative and interactive practices. Copyright law's text-based, hierarchical, and individualist framework for creative practice does not allow for the kinds of musical and textual interrelationships that characterize popular music in the dance. Such communicative and interactive practices build relationships and shore up poor communities in ways that allow them to depend less on a social order structured by colonial hierarchies of race and class.[15] Overall, the street dance offers a refuge within which people can violate laws and licenses regarding drug use and the sale of food, drink, and property rights (both physical and intellectual). The extent to which it can function as a refuge depends on many laws not being enforced.

Challenging Geographic Respectability

Attending Boasy Tuesday, I saw how street dances redrew notions of respectability centered on the downtown experience. While not in as notorious an area as Passa Passa, Boasy Tuesday also challenged hegemonic boundaries around property and propriety.

When I arrived in the autumn of 2009, I quickly learned that Boasy Tuesday was "the hottest dance in town." DJs on local radio broadcasts named it, local tabloids discussed it, and several of my Jamaican contacts mentioned it as "the place to be." An acquaintance (later a friend) who lived in the neighborhood described its rapid rise in popularity and how it attracted people from beyond the local area: he could see them walking by his house every Tuesday night. The dance occurred in a neighborhood of Kingston called Ken Cot, which is marked at the main road heading in to its interlocking streets and gullies by two large commercial bakeries that employ many people in the area. Before heading over at night, I investigated the neighborhood in the daytime, on foot.

Field notes excerpt #1

Walking through in the morning, the smell of bread filtered over the streets. Behind the bakeries, the neighboring streets are paved unevenly and full of potholes. One or two-story houses faced the street, with dusty but carefully kept front yards (when visible); some houses sit behind walls. On some streets the walls were too high to see over, on others they are knee- or waist-high. At 9:00 a.m. a lone coconut seller stood beside his cart piled high with coconuts, machete leaning against the wall. Restaurants, bars, and auto body shops, identified by hand-painted signs or murals depicting food or cars, were interspersed with homes. Other businesses infiltrate the homes themselves: I saw some houses with a narrow door with a window cut in it where a resident could lean through to sell soft drinks and phone cards from their kitchen. Later in the day, I walked past Ernie's, a well-known natural fruit juice shop run by the son of a local Rastaman, who did a quiet but steady trade in the afternoons, closing, as most Rastafarians' shops did, before sundown. In the roads' lower areas, bits of trash piled up in the gutters, although trash bins encased in lockable metal cages also sat in front of many front gates. Coming nearer to the nighttime location where the dance occurs, I noticed a gully alongside the road, open and unfenced, a trickle of dirty water and more trash gathering in it.[16]

The gully is a productive location for examining the dynamics of exilic spaces. A gully is an open storm drain that functions like a sewer, usually lined with concrete and often clogged with garbage and debris. While Kingston does have sewage treatment plants and some enclosed sewers, these exist alongside a network of open gullies that run sluggishly into Kingston Harbor (except during the rains when they can turn into mini rivers, although still rather sludgy). While Kingston has within it all the elements of a modern city (including tall buildings, office and industrial parks, commercial industry, and the like), gullies mark the incompleteness of infrastructure in the Global South even in a nation's capital. Gullies are not confined to poor neighborhoods in Kingston, but their presence is definitely more felt there. Especially because people in poor neighborhoods do not have as much space indoors to retreat to or socialize in, the gully is a regular visual, at times audible, and odorous part of life in poor areas. Depending on the level of rain, they may be dry or have slow trickles of water; during heavy rains, they channel rushing water (and garbage too) out of the urban area into the sea. When I was in Jamaica in 2009, a rising star in the dancehall scene named Mavado had taken up the image of the gully. His (2007) song "By the Gully Side" had taken the island by storm, following which he claimed the name "Gully God." Mavado's music and persona triumphantly reclaimed the image of the gully, a physical feature of the environment previously conceptually linked to waste and poverty in the public mind. This illustrates how social power works for those at the margins who can call on exilic space. Mavado could mobilize the authority generated beyond the "respectable" world to transform the gully's very repugnance into an indictment of the society that created it. In a public act, Mavado publicly set himself against those hierarchies by defiantly embracing something rejected by the powerful. Since Mavado, other artists have also claimed the name "Gully" (the most famous being Gully Bop), and the dance-centric singer Elephant Man released a song and an associated dance by the choreographer ICE that was widely popular called the "gully creeper." The presence of a gully marks the physical location as a site beyond the control of elites, a site where people not bound by elite norms of behavior are in charge. In this way, it marks not a public space or a private space but a local space, specifically a space controlled by the urban poor.

The power of this exilic claim (and the control over the space) may not be equally available to all. For example, I did not find women artists who claimed the gully in the way that men did, and the terms of respectability, as discussed above (and below), appear to work differently for men and women. There is one notable exception to women not claiming the gully that suggests that gender does shape particular exilic spaces' capacity for autonomy and shapes access to wider media landscapes. In the early 2010s (after my primary fieldwork but when I returned to Jamaica), I learned more about the "gully queens": a local name for a group of people that reached international fame in different circles than did Mavado. Gully queens identified as gay men and/or transgender women who had to resort to literally living in or near gullies (when dry) because homophobic/transphobic families and communities had driven them out of their homes. Their reclaiming of the gully has not been an avenue to validation within Jamaican dancehall scenes—which allow a certain level of experimentation with performance of gender but in many contexts do respond harshly to people publicly identifying as gay or trans. In 2014, Vice channel produced the first documentary about this community, *Young and Gay: Jamaica's Gully Queens*,[17] in which several gully queens suggested that upper-class gay or trans people had some leeway to live their identities but that poor communities were much more often untenable for poor gay men and trans women who could not or would not hide their identity. While the gully is in some ways claimed as a refuge, it is also discussed as an unpleasant last resort (or "hell" according to one gully resident)[18] within which they do their best to survive. In researching gully queens in scholarly and journalistic venues, and in my time in Jamaica, I found little evidence that the gully queens have been able to convert notoriety into local power as powerfully as Mavado the gully god. At the same time, gully queens have been the subject of numerous foreign documentaries and articles of various levels of respect and fetishization (overall generally positive and to some extent sympathetic) in such media as the *Huffington Post*,[19] *Vogue*,[20] and *The Travel*.[21] Most of this foreign interest was likely kicked off by Vice channel's 2014 documentary.[22] Some foreign press and activism has been tied to supporting the local needs of the gully queens via direct-aid charities like JFLAG and other organizations. Unfortunately it appears the increased interest has been in some cases followed by police raids on the gullies that even the most sympathetic foreigners had not the resources or the proximity to prevent. (Homosexuality is still illegal in Jamaica, although recently the prime minister has suggested this might change.) The experience of the gully queens does suggest the liberatory limits of the dancehall exilic space as it is currently formed; in some ways, its contours locally may still rely on older colonial norms of gender and sexuality. It is also interesting that queer women and trans men are not shown living in the gully or claiming visibility in the same way. This suggests that masculinity is particularly bound up in the exilic space of dancehall culture. (Doing something that could be read as stereotypically masculine appears to not be addressed as a public transgression in the same way.) It may be that the gully itself can function as a different kind of exilic space for the gully queens, with its own affordances and limitations—a question that deserves further study.[23] This feature of urban planning is simultaneously unhideable (as an open storm drain) and disreputable, and different subgroups among the urban poor have made use of that fact in different ways.

Disrepute is a social and double-edged (at least) fact. It is one of the social and cultural structures that shaped how I or any other participant was able to participate or access information about street dances. Participation in street dances and traveling the streets of Kingston revealed how laws, walls, and private security are not the only things that structure accessibility. Alongside these, (dis)reputation also created social boundaries, lending a certain kind of exclusive force to the street dance and the communities from which they spring.

Passa Passa provides a good example of how local history and geography shape the kinds of power that dominate in the dance. Within the geography of Kingston, Passa Passa takes place on the edge of Coronation Market and Tivoli Gardens, an area demarcated by old and well-known social and political boundaries. Coronation Market is one of the oldest and largest in Jamaica and, reportedly, the Caribbean. However, its commercial importance and historic significance did not mean people found it safe. In fact, the middle- or upper-class students and faculty I spoke with at the university carefully instructed me on how to remain safe at Coronation Market in broad daylight if I should venture there. Interestingly, they spent less time discussing concerns about my safety while attending an outdoor, unlicensed dance that only begins after 3:00 A.M.[24] I took this to mean that either the dance was associated with scandal first, and violence came rather lower on the list, or else that my interest in the dance meant I was beyond reason with respect to safety. The question of safety hinges on the other major significance of Tivoli Gardens, the urban area where Passa Passa takes place.

Before Passa Passa, Tivoli had been best known as a quintessential garrison community,[25] a site of poverty and partisan violence. As discussed in chapter 1, garrisons are heavily armed neighborhoods linked by a system of patronage to a political party.[26] Tivoli Gardens was originally the site of Back'o'wall, a neglected area that became a haven for Rastafarians marginalized by Jamaican society in the 1950s. Then prime minister Edward Seaga demolished Back'o'wall, forcibly and brutally dispersing the Rastafarians who lived there, and established a public housing project there for supporters of his party. That neighborhood partisanship developed into armed competition between neighborhoods associated with different parties. Violence that erupted initially over elections spilled over into other kinds of violence as neighborhood leaders took advantage of their position to get involved in businesses like the drug trade.[27] These other meanings of Tivoli still became relevant in my times in Jamaica, when taxi drivers or colleagues, as well as news reports, would advise that a trip downtown was not safe due to upsurges in partisan tensions around election time.

Only in the past ten years has Tivoli developed a new claim to fame from an internationally famous street dance.[28] While this has redrawn the local geography, especially for international visitors and others interested in popular music, the older boundary still shapes who comes: on a local level, Tivoli and Passa Passa were still discussed as dangerous and not respectable areas for, especially, local middle-class and upper-class Jamaicans. My foreignness exempted me from the anxieties about respectability that local middle-class Jamaicans (especially Black and brown ones) might have had. Even still, when I would mention to Jamaican college students at the university where I was going, they often sounded shocked and professed emphatically that they had never been and would never go there. In fact, all the markers of neglect and distaste that are discussed negatively in media and in spaces of upper-class Jamaicans also serve to demarcate these locations such that elites cannot enter and be at ease. Attending even when times were relatively calm did not remove the lack of ease that outsiders might feel in the space.

This insecurity also feeds an insecurity among upper-class Jamaicans in relation to popular music. Although wealth and connections are undeniably useful for accessing the financial aspects of music making, such as paying for studio time and making deals at the international level, access for upper-class Jamaicans to the social sites of music making could be more complex. One middle-class vocalist described how when he first went to a recording studio, "the people would look at somebody from my background as if to say why am I necessarily here, why am I necessarily doing this, . . . when I already come from a background which is kinda secure." He described how the physical and social environment could also be intimidating, when you were trying to break into the music scene, because a common way in was to catch the interest of a producer, which involved waiting around outside a recording studio. Since most studios were in poor neighborhoods, this location and social scene around it shaped accessibility:

> You had to be one of the guys outside waiting for a producer hear or see or debut you. So you are out in a yard for the whole day six hours bleachin' in the sun with maybe twenty niggas . . . like yourself thinking, "Wow, am I gonna get a chance to sing today or see the producer today?" That in itself is intimidating, especially when you're around a lotta cats that you don't even know . . . or may not—or don't have a background like you. You may feel like a outcast or you may feel like—not worthy! You may feel like, wow, you know, these guys don't want me around. You know what I'm saying? That's a big intimidation for a lot of cats, you have to overcome. That's the first thing I saw, not necessarily as a hurdle, but something to . . . something to . . . to . . . digest and overcome.

This person, who would have been described to me as "brown," spoke to me not in Patwa but in what felt like a more uptown Jamaican accent. He did use some Jamaican slang like "bleaching," which in this context means something like "hanging around in the hot sun." Interestingly he also used what might be identified as African American vernacular English, as well as the term "cats," which I never heard anyone downtown use. He also used what would clearly be a racial slur in the mouth of a white person, and which still made me a bit uncomfortable hearing it. His description of an experience uneasily navigating class dynamics was echoed by layers of language that reflected the shifting linguistic allegiances of that continual negotiation, shaped also by my presence as a white foreign woman facing him.

Several performers from middle-class backgrounds talked to me about the "trickiness" of being from uptown and working in a downtown environment, and when interviews touched on this subject, their language became more qualified and hesitant, and their body language and expression conveyed some discomfort or embarrassment. This discomfort of talking about it highlights how being of the upper class could culturally disadvantage one in the eyes of the Jamaican popular music public and creative community. My middle-class interlocutor told me: "I had to record myself initially because most producers wouldn't know me—they were like, 'Who is this uptown cat?'"

Sonic Respectability

The visual and social traits of uptown people that make them welcome in elite spaces, mark them as less welcome, or at least not automatically worthy of respect, in Jamaican popular music scenes. Within this locally controlled space, it is possible to redefine propriety against the social norms that dominate more formal social environments. Alongside reclaiming geographical features like the gully and centering dark skin, daring and colorful fashion, and Patwa accents, this redefining of propriety occurs in the medium of sound, which has cultural significance in itself. Upper- and middle-class Jamaican social mores have historically discouraged loudness of all kinds in upper-class spaces, where it has been associated with danger and vulgarity. In my travels through upper-class areas, both semiprivate and residential, I rarely heard music playing. Upper-class shops tended to have quiet music and more often foreign pop, while the downtown markets throbbed with sounds of competing, blown-out speakers set at doors or by the roadside. Neither the epically loud sounds nor the lively, interactive audiences of street dances have been welcome in areas more closely and aggressively regulated by law and colonial social mores of respectability.

Although Jamaican laws on paper restrict noise in all residential areas, these laws are enforced idiosyncratically or not at all in poor neighborhoods. As mentioned earlier, the most recent Noise Abatement Act of 1997, required volume reduction after 12:00 A.M. on weekdays and after 2:00 A.M. on weekends (though permits for later performances can be obtained on certain occasions).[29] While further research would be necessary to track how, when, and where enforcement has taken place before and after the 1997 act, in 2009 it was clear that street dances continued to ignore this law in sufficient numbers to dominate much of the night's soundscape in poor parts of Kingston.

Bodily Respectability

The social norms that define proper behavior within and across class in Jamaica also contradict many aspects of musical engagement. Homemade "flamethrowers" involving a can of hairspray and a lighter to shoot burning spray skyward, screaming, energetic dancing (especially dancing that involves the lower half of the body), and other methods of taking up space are much more evident in nonelite social spaces. As would be expected from a system shaped by coloniality, emphasis among the upper classes is on restraint and reserve, especially in relation to things associated with being "uncivilized." In upper-class neighborhoods, I became used to encountering public postings of dress codes in shopping malls, banks, and hospitals, which often included directives on behavior that emphasized restraint as well.[30] One evening when I attended an expensive nightclub, I was struck by the muted colors of people's clothing and hair in contrast to the street dances, but as the night went on, I was even more struck by the fact that I had a hard time telling if people enjoyed the music—physical response was so mild that, even as someone with DJ experience, I struggled to read the crowd's response. This was especially true after I had spent several weeks becoming familiar with styles and comportment in the street dance, which was set at a different baseline.

Even the physical affordances of the street dance allow for creative expression on different terms. One street dance organizer who had to move his event to an indoor location described how that limited dancers' ability to express themselves, as they "could not do some of the things they did outdoors, as that would be destructive to the building."[31] Jamaican dance moves are often extremely athletic and acrobatic. I regularly witnessed dancers climbing atop ten-foot-tall speaker towers or hanging upside down from light posts. These acts added to the dance's (and the performer's) notoriety and spur performative creativity as dancers attempt to outdo each other. The ability to engage with the performance space's physical structure requires flexibility in its regulation that may transcend the laws of property—as well as, seemingly, of gravity!

Traversing the Public and the Private

The anthropologist Lisa Douglass observed that in Jamaica "accessibility is a form of power."[32] The physical aspects of the area where street dances have occurred signal the social status of the people there. In general, wealthy areas in Kingston appeared somewhat like armored enclaves, with thick, tall, blank, and undecorated walls, except for occasional signs advertising the presence of aggressive dogs and armed security.[33] This privacy and blankness to public view demonstrated control over outside access that is backed up by the state and by privately funded power. In the absence of reliable state authority, the visibility of privately funded sources of security widened the gap between rich and poor. The rich could rely more on the state and invested directly in personal safety. By contrast, in the streets where Boasy Tuesday took place, I observed more permeable physical boundaries. Walls tended to be more symbolic demarcations of space than actual barriers to sight or entry: a knee- or waist-high cinderblock affair, beyond which a yard and the front of a house might be visible. The relative visibility of many houses from the street (with low walls or fences obscuring part of the view), the mix of residential and commercial activity (often in a single house), smaller (usually one- or two-story) buildings, and inexpensive construction all signaled a less wealthy neighborhood.

The absolute poorest urban areas had uneven zinc sheets shielding most living spaces, and the houses themselves were not always finished. Such houses might lack running water and require outdoor spaces for washing and bathing. As well, the extreme heat, exacerbated by metal roofs or walls, kept many people outside in shaded areas. In these places, privacy was somewhat afforded by a zinc exterior wall, but there was much less privacy within. People were also more crammed together, so the zinc walls sometimes created the feeling of hot metal tunnels within which people moved as efficiently as they could. The slightly less poor areas, where people could afford relatively solid homes, had fewer high fences and walls between residences and the street. This difference in walls suggested that class might involve different relationships to property: boundaries between private and public, as well as between residential and commercial, appeared more blurred.[34] This blurring was even more dramatic when I returned at night to Boasy Tuesday, organized by the Fire Links sound system.[35]

Field notes excerpt #2

At 12:30 a.m. on a Tuesday night/Wednesday morning in January 2009, I walked through the streets of Ken Cot with a friend who lived in the neighborhood. Far fewer people were visible than in the daytime, and the majority of them were young and male (late teens to early twenties). At this time the bakery smell had dissipated, overcome by the diesel fumes of traffic. I could smell the garbage rotting in water of the gully running alongside the main entry road. The doors and gates facing the streets on the way to the dance were tightly closed, in contrast to earlier. Streetlights only intermittently cast dim circles of light through which skinny feral city dogs wandered singly and in packs. From blocks away the bass boomed, raising the hairs on my arms, prefiguring the feeling of enveloping sound to come; as we rounded a corner we were joined by other people in twos and threes, and down the road I could see two massive black walls of speakers, perhaps twice as tall as me, on the sidewalk on the right side of the street. On the sidewalk, some vendors were selling bottles of beer out of coolers and buckets, while other sellers set up in the front yards of houses lining the street. The music poured out of the speakers, the bass already heavy and vibrating our chests. The smell of hot oil wafted over us as we walked past a thin dark man with short dreadlocks in a cap, setting up a fried-fish stand. Later, I saw another man moving through the crowd, balancing piles of snacks and cigarettes on his head, held together with a wire, from which he would tear off a bag of peanuts if you paid him a few Jamaican dollars.

As the night went on, the crowd deepened, attendees facing each other across the street, until the crowds grew thick and began to converge in the middle. Alongside the right-hand speaker wall, a raised stage held several DJs behind a large table holding CD players and a mixer. One of the DJs exhorted the crowd through a microphone, and a cluster of other DJs, soundmen, vocalists and local celebrities, male and female, crowded the stage, dressed in the latest fashions. The clothing was bright, hair colors too, and the DJ's voice occasionally overpowered the microphone into distortion, with the bass thundering along underneath.

By 2 a.m. the whole street was packed with people in their most outrageous outfits: lots of neon and matching accessories: hats and scarves and belts carefully coordinated or clashing. I saw a group of women in skintight leggings with strategic slashes and asymmetrical hair the same color as the leggings, posing and chatting. A videographer snaked through with a power cable tethered to the sound system: his camera shone a bright light forward that people stepped and jostled their way into, but it was almost too crowded for him to step back and get a full-body shot of anyone. The crowd undulated as people pushed towards the video light, parting only reluctantly to allow cars through at occasional intervals, and once to allow a stream of young men on expensive motorcycles to roll through revving their engines.[36]

It was easy to see how at the dance, the boundaries of the social space overlapped and transcended private property even further: people spilled over from the sidewalks to the lawns or spilled out onto them from their homes. Houses' private yards were visible to all and available to some for dancing and watching as well. Crowds redefined the public road as a space for performance, enhancing their reputation, creative expression, romantic and sexual flirtations, and socializing. These blurring boundaries challenge laws defining public space by blocking the flow of traffic in public streets.

Even more so than Boasy Tuesday, Passa Passa also blurred public, private, and commercial space. It did so largely through its close relationship with Coronation Market. In 2009, I came into Passa Passa with some friends at about three thirty on a Thursday morning. We knew there was no point in going too early, so we had spent time at a sound system event run by the well-reputed Stone Love, a private event with a cover charge.

Field notes excerpt #3

At 3:30 am the wide but mainly carless and empty expanse looked quite different from what I'd seen as a busy market thoroughfare in the daytime. The street was wider than Boasy Tuesday's more residential avenue, and provided more room for dancing en masse, but as we came in it felt slightly more exposed, as the crowd was not yet full enough to fill it. The sound was no less deafening, coming from even taller walls of speakers lining the road on both sides. By 4:30, a lively crowd filled much of the worn and potholed street from both sides, where some of the shop fronts turned their blank and dusty windows to the street of Tivoli Gardens. I watched groups of people break out in dance routines to songs in waves that spread across the crowd. Others stood and watched, or rocked back and forth on their feet. As the night turned into morning, farmers and merchants from far across the island trickled through the area in trucks, vans, or even pushing a cart or two, bringing their wares for the daytime market—shopping begins at 6 a.m. I think? As the sky lightened, truck drivers resignedly or cheerfully carrying eggs, melons, greens, or peppers wound their way slowly through clusters of dancers.[37]

Passa Passa participants repurposed aspects of the market as impromptu props, stages, or backdrops for dance or posed photographs and performances, and participants in the market crossed over and through the dance.

Authority Outside the Law

Passa Passa, like many street dances, reconfigured public and private space, as well as social power and authority. The absence of visible markers of order and the social distance asserted by middle- and upper-class Jamaicans from Passa Passa did not mean these downtown spaces lacked order. Despite upper-class people describing these places as sites of "lawlessness" and "anarchy" (echoing the way American and British music industry executives and music lawyers talked about Jamaica as a whole), a social order existed, but it depended on a different set of relationships between people and institutions than lawyers or executives were able to recognize.

During the street dance, it was possible to observe these different aspects of social order. The most noticeable authority in the moment was the authority of the sound itself—what Julian Henriques has called the "sonic dominance" of the sound system, whose audible power enfolds the bodies of people within reach of the speakers and overpowers other senses.[38] However, sonic dominance is only possible in places that allow loud music to be played, which is shaped by other social forces. One such social force was that of the neighborhood itself—its geography, reputation, and how one expected to enter it shaped who felt most at home. This could be offset by the reputation of the dance; for example, Rae Town, a long-running "oldies dance" on a Sunday night, was in an extremely poor neighborhood of rather bad repute, but the dance was so well known and beloved that many people still attended. The garrison community of Tivoli's reputation included locals (to some extent), but even so, many people feared to attend, despite Passa Passa's international fame. Another social force was the authority of those who made the music happen—the sound systems and the dons or other shadowy authorities in the neighborhood who funded and protected the events.[39] Many people discussed with me or each other how the leader of the garrison community valued its positive contribution to the community and helped keep the peace.[40] Interestingly, in 2010 I saw this narrative of authority contested, in formal media venues, by the founders of Passa Passa, who demanded (and received) a retraction from the *Jamaica Gleaner* for its assertion of a connection between them and the local don.[41] Even taking that denial at face value, the numerous direct violations of law that the dance embodies suggests that formal law was not defining the terms of engagement. As the majority of people involved are from the local community and the street dance is rooted in the urban poor's interests and identity, authority derives from those local conditions and relationships.

When I was in Jamaica in 2009 and 2010, there was an upswing in enforcing the 1997 Noise Abatement Act.[42] I observed police forcing soundmen to shut down their systems on several occasions. However, on other nights, the same dances ran until four in the morning or later without incident— even when the police came through. It was striking that at this time (and even more on earlier occasions when I had been in Jamaica), when police appeared, they did not always enforce the law. Once in 2009, at Boasy Tuesday, I recognized the same police officers who had shut down the event on a previous occasion. This time they simply drove through the crowd slowly in their battered-looking Toyota compact car bristling with automatic weapons, without enforcing the act or stopping the music. Nobody—not the DJ, the soundmen, the vendors, nor anyone in the audience—looked particularly concerned about police presence apart from a few cannabis smokers casually tucking their hands behind their backs. It appeared they felt reasonably secure that they would not be arrested—in other words, they felt the law did not completely define police behavior or that police discretion was in this case on their side. When I asked my companions about why or when street dances were shut down for noise, several people suggested rival sound systems make complaints to shut each other down. Such testimony suggests that people assume law enforcement is shaped by local concerns and rivalries. It was not clear the extent to which people were personally familiar with individual police officers or whether that played a role in police discretion. Another salient factor would be the threat of collective resistance and even uprising should the crowd judge police as overstepping their bounds. While I have not heard of such explicit resistance occurring at street dances, at times whole neighborhoods have risen up against police, and on occasion the neighborhoods have been apparently better armed. Although the most common spark has been election-related violence, there is a long history of conflict in which the police have not always won.[43] At a recent event in Tivoli, the same area in which Passa Passa occurs, many in the community rose up in arms against the attempted extradition of a local don who was wanted by the U.S. government. A multiday armed standoff ensued. In this case, however, the police and army together—with U.S. Army helicopters reported overhead—finally did capture Christopher "Dudus" Coke, and they also murdered over eighty local residents.[44] This brutal event and the curfew enforced by the military eventually led to the shutdown of Passa Passa, although its last official event was in 2012.

Before the military incursion (notably, with the urgency of U.S. pressure), there had appeared to be a kind of standoff between the forces of state violence and exilic authority. In 2009, it was striking, as a foreigner, to see police—still menacing, with automatic weapons and stony faces—making their presence known but not actually enforcing the many laws being broken in front of them by hundreds of people. For example, no food or alcohol licenses were displayed by sellers, and even more striking, given that cannabis is illegal and not decriminalized in Jamaica, the common presence of smokers, even hawkers of cannabis—often carrying forearm-sized branches of the plant in large bundles—never appeared to excite a response even when police were present. I never saw a police officer address any vendor of food, beverage, cigarettes, or cannabis, despite regular, if temporary, police presence. In several cases, cannabis vendors strolled quite casually past police cars driving through a crowd. Such moments suggested the street dance's negotiated authority.

At Passa Passa, I never saw police do this kind of slow, public intervention/nonintervention. This provided an interesting contrast to Boasy Tuesday, which is in a less notorious neighborhood. In times of local unrest, Passa Passa has sometimes shut down entirely, due to concerns about spillover effects of violence from within Tivoli Gardens, especially around election times. But at the events I attended, police were less visible, and neither the presence nor absence of police appeared the final arbiter of order. It may be relevant that Passa Passa is the most famous street dance in Jamaica (and possibly the world).[45] It's possible that this international interest makes local police less interested in intimidating the crowd, since upsetting foreigners or scaring them off could result in bad publicity for the police as well as for the community. The international interest could also perhaps turn the other way: once the United States expressed strong interest in extraditing Coke, Tivoli Gardens, and thus Passa Passa, could no longer stand. The dynamics of police intervention appeared influenced by a variety of local and international factors, depending on the event and the local context. Evaluating the probability would also require attention to the specific people involved in law enforcement: as a small country, nearly every official and officer is linked by family, neighborhood, or other social connection to people they are likely to regulate. This adds another layer of contingency to state response: personal relationships often appeared to undercut or reshape policy decisions unless there was substantial pressure from an external power. This contingency reinforces Gray's characterization of the Jamaican "parasitic state"—while in some cases the state could enforce its priorities on citizens, it also happened that the state was dependent on citizens' existing relationships. In the case of the street dance and the Jamaican music industry, quite often it appeared that nobody was interested in the police looking too closely at what was going on, not even the police.

In the relative absence of a particular state actor's direct attention, a law-centric approach to authority would assume authority resides in property owners or (in the case of public spaces) regulations like zoning and traffic law. However, street dances often appeared to ignore these rules and shifted authority, responsibility, and vulnerability from the individual to the collective, specifically the people occupying the space. When a street dance redefined public spaces, no individual owner was easily responsible for what happened in it; nor was there any one entity that could completely control what happened at the dance—even were a sound system to shut down its equipment, that choice would have been gauged against the possibility of angering the audience. By contrast, a dance indoors gives the building owner a greater measure of control and responsibility for what happens in the space. This responsibility means an owner would also be a potential target for law enforcement with more to lose than any individual at a street dance (although sound systems have more to forfeit than the dancing crowd). The relatively free flow of entrance and exit and the lack of formal control at street dances allows for a wider variety of activities to take place. This variety includes unlicensed or illegal practices, as well as moments of creative risk-taking and of stylistic rebellion against dominant cultural forces. As well, being tied to a venue with a legal presence makes one more visible to enforcers of copyright law. The law requires that venues where recordings are played must pay a fee to the Jamaica Association of Composers Authors and Performers, the organization that manages the performance rights of copyright owners (which includes rebroadcast of phonograms in public). The more established and visible the venue, the more likely it would be the target for collection. The farther one is from formal institutions and respectable spaces, the more insulated one is from these collections. Such collections could possibly benefit the Jamaicans, including those among the poor, who own copyrights. However, in practice, it would be important to investigate the advantages gained by participating in exilic creativity, compared to those gained by waiting for royalties to trickle down.

Because street dances are sites where locals redefine their practices against those embodied in the law and against social norms associated with upper-class values, they exemplify an exilic space. Most importantly, the specific transgressions of law that street dances create directly contradict a social order that prioritizes formal property rights and the regulation of behavior in relation to property and propriety—two social institutions that are at the heart of colonially defined order.

An Alternative Economic System

Street dances are an important economic hub not just in the world of music but also in the neighborhoods in which they operate. The musical experience cannot be separated from all the other people present, by choice or not—including the residents who may be in their homes or selling soda out of their front yard. While sound systems do not charge admission, sound system crews can get a percentage of alcohol sales that occur all around the dance. Sound systems generally convene and advertise a dance and provide speakers, DJ equipment, lights, engineers, and DJs. Videographers play increasingly important roles in Jamaican music-oriented economies.[46] Alongside generating informally taken videos, documentary and news footage (discussed further below), street dances are now sources of DVD recordings of edited highlights, which can be streamed online and, in some cases, monetized. (Note that monetization on YouTube or other mass commercial platforms might run into trouble as YouTube's automated copyright enforcement will not exempt Jamaican musical traditions from being flagged as violations.) As well, the circulation of "mixtapes" (actually mix CDs) put together by, generally, a different category of DJs than those playing at the dance, have operated in symbiotic relationship with the music circulating at the dance. Mix CDs usually featured the hottest tunes, depending on street dances to determine which tunes are hot, and also gave people who did not go to street dances a chance to hear what was current. These were not licensed compilations in the legal sense, with little information on them beyond the name of the DJ and occasionally the name of the CD series. The most up-to-date ones could not be bought at the island's few record stores but instead were sold by people (not the DJs or the producers of the mix CDs) standing outside at gas stations or in open-air markets, often displaying their wares on a small table or even a folded-up tarp. Their provenance was unclear, although they must have been mass produced at least at a small scale; their illegality meant it was difficult to find information about who made them. But everyone agreed (and my observations supported) that they came out every week with all the latest tunes that were big in the dances, embedded in and reinforcing a local musical circulation outside of copyright law.

At the dance itself, within the neighborhoods, whole mini economies spring up. As Glen Bartley, the organizer of Dutty Fridaze, put it: "Even the man that clean up the floor deal with the Red Bull can!" Collecting empty cans isn't recognized as a formal job but as something a local person can do and redeem cans for cash at recycling centers.[47] More recently the Canadian scholar and music journalist Erin Macleod interviewed a government representative for Rae Town, a poor area in Kingston that has hosted Rae Town Old Hits street dance since 1982, who admitted, "The fact is, this is the only time a large number of women and men can do a little hustling and earn something honestly for the whole week."[48]

The relationship between alcohol and the dance goes back to the foundation of Jamaican musical events: one of the first studios and sound systems began as the front-yard entertainment for a liquor store that profited from attendees drinking while they danced. For the most part, money at street dances was not tied to exclusive control over musical works but rather depended on these ancillary sales. Because these events lay outside of formal systems of legal regulation, they facilitated more informal moneymaking by a wider (and poorer) population. Similarly, selling cannabis was not usually so visible elsewhere, so the sellers' seeming confidence and undeniable visibility in this very public place suggested that the social order here was defined by something other than formal law. This more diffuse and small-scale economy among the local community of the urban poor distributes income rather differently than would a royalty received by a single owner of a copyrighted work. A royalty is uncertain, and if any is due, it will not come immediately and is dependent on local and international reporting systems and collectors. As well, copyright owners in general tend to be more middle- or upper-class, so the overall flow of royalty income accrues to them and is not dispersed among the poor communities that contribute so much to the music's creative force.

Some international corporations have invested in street dances, paying organizers to post advertisements or selling their products directly to the crowd. This support appears also structured by coloniality: the major sponsors are international brands like Guinness beer or the Digicel mobile phone company, which are less concerned about being associated with lower-class Jamaicans. These foreign entities are not dependent on colonial notions of respectability and instead can capitalize, to some extent, on street culture and build their brand on it. Some sponsors supply free products to sound systems or even local vendors, in this way following the logic of the music makers who do not charge for access to the music but instead seek to build their name and credibility at the street dance.

These economic activities redistribute money in the community in ways that are significantly more diffuse and immediate than are the potential royalties of copyright that could accrue to individual musical practitioners. But another kind of value that street dances help generate—reputation—has both social and economic effects but need not rely on the licensed exchange of commodities.

A Reputational Economy: The Currency of Currency

While the role of reputation is not easily accounted for in standard music industry economic analyses, Jamaicans involved in popular music demonstrate a sophisticated understanding of social status and the material and social advantages of one's reputation in various contexts. Street dances are notable media events. As noted, Jamaican TV and radio news report regularly on street dances (sometimes from the scene), and events occurring there form part of Jamaican mass media discussion. Newspapers treat the street dances as newsworthy events: photographers may be detailed to report on the hottest dances' fashions and gossip. In addition, newspapers encourage "citizen reporters" to submit their own photographs to the editors, who may publish them in print or on the website. Because street dances mainly occur downtown, in poorer neighborhoods, their newsworthiness subverts the colonial disrespect that the poor often face in elite Jamaican society. While the dances are not always praised, they cannot be ignored. And on occasion, they gather enough respect locally and internationally that they begin to change the terms of discourse. The national newspaper—in letters to the editor, opinion pages, and the occasional editorial—has regularly expressed concern about and disapproval of street dances, declaring them sites of immoral behavior. This has not stopped street dance organizers from talking back: in 2007 one of Passa Passa's main organizers argued for its official recognition as a site of authentic cultural experience for tourists.[49]

Such arguments have not tended to be successful because the contradictory values nurtured in exilic spaces do not find an easy presence in formal government initiatives. Even when there are ambitious plans for the government to capitalize on Jamaican popular music as a kind of "entrepreneurship" (a term used enthusiastically in a 2013 government cultural policy document grandiosely titled *Towards Jamaica the Cultural Superstate*),[50] gestures of inclusion have often been incomplete or fraught with silences. For example, one observer of a 2013 planning meeting following this cultural policy announcement, aimed at discussing rezoning public places, noted, "Those in attendance (that I could identify) included academics, researchers, Dancehall promoters, radio hosts, interested members of public, and government officials. Noticeably absent were artists and local, Black, working class, or poor community members. Given the government's best efforts to ensure the meeting included all groups affected by the issues at hand, the absence of artists seemed to frustrate officials and left open questions regarding what local communities would do in the event the zoning plan came into effect."[51] This sponsored event did not seem able to welcome the people who most situate Jamaican popular music and its creative practices along exilic lines: artists in their creative practices and the community members whose homes and streets create some of the local boundaries within which these exilic moments flourish. The state appeared uninterested in the idea that local community members might have some claim over the dances and the benefits generated by them.[52] And yet street dances provide a good deal of economic value for many poor people.

Alongside music, money, and goods, street dances generate and define another value, one more important to artists and sound systems: the currency of reputation. Reputation depends on the constant circulation of music and information. Although money and material goods in poor neighborhoods are often redistributed at a small-scale level, reputation is a more complex currency. It is not a characteristic or resource belonging to an individual that can be hoarded over time. This sets it apart from concepts like social capital. One cannot invest in one's reputation in a finite way or through wholly private or personal action. Reputation requires that knowledge be circulated among other people in order to be valuable. Being known can positively or negatively affect an individual, but it cannot be an individual's product or responsibility. Without others to do the knowing and to circulate the knowledge, reputation is meaningless. Nor can it be built up through simple transactional exchanges—it is rather embedded in a fluidly defined community through ongoing social relationships.[53] David Graeber's anthropological theory of value suggests that in some communities there is a practice of "timeless commitment"[54] that generates value between people; this echoes what I saw in Jamaica. Reputation plays a vital role in the economic and cultural dynamics of musical practice, with financial and social effects for various practitioners. Graeber also warns that relationships of timeless commitment can slip into patronage and exploitation, dynamics present in Jamaica as well. What I observed was that the extent to which Jamaican dancehall participants could flourish derived from their abilities to successfully control the context in which their reputation circulated. Reputation's value is not universally recognized but instead changes based on the context.

Reputation-building's circulatory energy was evident the night I attended a dance with one of my interlocutors, a twenty-five-year-old woman vocalist with several local and internationally popular tunes at the time.

Field notes excerpt #4

At around 11:30 p.m., we waited at the bar for the music to pick up. Like everyone else I could see, she was carefully dressed in casual but stylish clothing. She wore a tightly fitted button-down shirt open at the neck, new-looking jeans and large sparkling earrings. She was petite and curvy, her close-cropped hair was bleached neon yellow and fire engine red, and her impeccable makeup and delicate features lent her a glamorous and slightly doll-like demeanor. We stood among about seventy-five people clustering at the bar, in the restaurant hosting "Mojito Mondays" in its parking lot. This was at the time a relatively new event that several people told me to check out. Rolling her eyes in mock frustration, she described to me her hectic nighttime schedule. "Tonight it's Mojito Mondays and maybe Hot Mondays. And there's so many dances later this week! Sometimes I just want to stay home . . . But . . ." as she trailed off, she shrugged, giving a dazzling smile. As she spoke to me, a photographer from a local newspaper came to snap our picture, which I saw the next day in the "out and about" section of Jamaica's second-largest newspaper.[55]

In the photograph of the woman artist and me that circulated in the local newspaper, we both publicly demonstrated our association with one of the new and popular dances, enhancing our reputations as people in the know about what's hot in Jamaica. The vocalist's need to be visible was constant and urgent: she must regularly be seen—and seen looking good—at multiple events of sufficient prestige to enhance her career. Her reputation required staying current through circulating her image at events like Mojito Mondays or at least circulating knowledge that she was there. My reputation was enhanced by showing both my knowledge of where to go and my willingness to go there, as well as my proximity to a respected artist willing to be photographed with me in a public setting. This could help me gain access to more people and places within the music scene.

Reputation also has gendered dynamics. Mojito Mondays occurred in a more uptown location than most street dances I knew and included many more foreigners and middle-class Jamaicans. I never experienced a woman offering to meet me at a downtown event, and I rarely saw women music performers downtown (although some were in the audience). The increasing popularity, in 2009, of street dances outside of poor areas tracked street dances' growing international reputation, as cameras and smartphones became more accessible to share images and sounds across global media networks.[56] Like reggae music before it, it appeared that the cultural practice had to become popular abroad for the Jamaican upper classes to start making space for it. Still, the newspaper documenting us there rather than at Passa Passa gave our visibility a more uptown flavor, which might be safer for a Jamaican woman for whom a bad reputation could potentially have worse repercussions (personally or professionally) than a Jamaican man.

Not only musicians but also audience members built reputation through participation in street dances. The high level of energy that dancers devoted to their own visibility on camera revealed the urgency of this constant engagement. I remember this pattern from across several downtown dances at around two in the morning (which was usually when the street dances started to gather force), as the audience began to thicken. There was still room for multiple crews, and the energy was rather diffuse because the crowd was not (yet) packed together. Some more formally organized dance crews began to appear around three o'clock, notable first for their brightly colored matching outfits. Usually all male, occasionally they would have one woman, but I saw no all-female or equally gender-balanced dance crew. Women in the dance crews tended to dress similar to the men and less often in hyperfeminine or body-accentuating clothing that non-dance-crew women attendees sported. Both women and men tended to be on the younger side in the crews. (Those in their teens and twenties were very visible; thirties and forties, less so but still present.) Fashion appeared especially important to dance crews: they all sported elaborate hairstyles, often bleached, dyed, shaved, and braided into intricate patterns; sparkling jewelry, often including massive neck chains or pendants; other accessories, like hats, scarves (multiple), belts. At the same time, many attendees exerted similar levels of effort, so I could not be sure a fabulous-looking young man was a dancer until he began to break out, alongside others, into impeccably performed, synchronized dance moves. The dance crews' slick steps occasionally degenerated into a full-on scrum for central position in the area illuminated by the camera's attached spotlight.

Krista Thompson has insightfully examined visibility and the history of the "video man" (a role increasingly common in street dances that is sometimes associated with the sound system and sometimes freelance videomen—always men—who usually had a higher-end camera and often a bright light to illuminate the crowd) and the photographer in Jamaican street dances.[57] My observations here reinforce her account that people in the dance act like the video light is important and sought after and that participation in videography can have material consequences. Thompson traces how gender, race, and class all structure how videography is important to different people at the dance and what effect that importance has. Its rewards are not equally available to all, and it incentivizes participation in raced and gendered ways.

The battle for the video light can be ferocious and has, in some cases, even led to arrests,[58] which suggests that reputation is important currency. Most of the resources circulating at the street dance are provided to participants based on their standing; outsiders and newcomers are forced to pay for things that insiders and stars have thrust upon them. For example, vocalists, dancers, and "mogglers" (models) are usually unpaid, attending to build their reputations by being seen, yet their dedication is like a job in itself.

The category of mogglers was new to me when I arrived in Jamaica in 2009. "Moggle" is a Jamaican Patwa term derived from the English word "model." Several interviewees mentioned "moggling crews" as a feature of street dances. It appears a gendered category: mogglers are groups of women with striking, fashionable, and coordinated visual appearance, usually in very tight, body-accentuating clothing. For the most part, my observations suggested they tended to be slenderer and younger than the average woman in the audience. Some people recounted that mogglers were invited to grace dances with their presence, lending prestige and glamour to the occasion and (reportedly) sometimes receiving payment or getting free drinks. Moggling is not dancing but can involve striking poses dramatically in order to be seen in the dance. Although several interviewees mentioned that such women were hoping for professional modeling contracts, I was not able to find any accounts of this having occurred. Similarly, some aspiring designers and stylists may have hoped to gain renown from being a moggler or being associated with them, although I could not tell how the stylists' names would be known, and it was not clear to me how or if that had happened.

People clearly believed that if a person could enhance their reputation, whether through dancing, moggling, or performing, they could increase their chances of being hired to perform elsewhere, to get free entrance or other perks, to be paid to endorse a product, or to become a TV or radio personality. This connection seemed especially strong for singers; since recording studios are closely connected to sound systems, making a good impression could potentially lead to studio time or a stronger association with a particular studio. If a performer should become famous, those relationships can reverse: sound systems may cajole, barter with, or even pay a local celebrity to lend his or her presence to an event. Much of Jamaican musical practice is highly competitive. There are often winners and losers in a particular moment, whether in competition between rival sound systems or when dancers compete for attention and try to avoid mockery. Reputation is both the reward and part of the ammunition in this competition.

A heightened reputation can ease one's path not only among music fans but also in the halls of immigration officials who have the power to decide whether a Jamaican should be allowed to leave the country at all. Artists applying for the right to go abroad and work may be looked on more favorably if they can provide evidence of a lively local career. As one promoter put it: "When Dutty Fridaze is up (generating news and DVDs), the work permit [for artists to go overseas] is easier."[59] The street dance's local authority casts a shadow visible even to employees in the U.S. embassy. This is another example of how people involved in music turn reputation into economic value without using copyright. When I interviewed a prolific producer in 2009, he described how he had produced many songs for popular artists and not received any royalties; however, one of the famous artists "got me a visa so I could go a foreign."

Copyright and the Street Dance Economy

Most artists I spoke with did not describe royalties as a significant source of money for them. Jamaicans have developed other creative ways to capitalize on economies of reputation that are built through events like street dances. For singers, the challenge is how to extract value for a song one has performed on, if copyright is not working to do this. The tradition of "dubplates" and "jingles" (or "specials") has arisen to address this: once a particular song is famous, a sound system or DJ can commission an artist to make a customized version of that song, inserting the name of the DJ or the sound system into it. This enhances the named commissioner's reputation, demonstrating their proximity to a famous artist. At the same time, the artist gets paid a one-time fee for a creative act that usually takes only a few minutes to complete. This doesn't mean it is without skill: many artists develop considerable skills devising clever ways to incorporate a new name into an old song. It is common for respected artists to spend a profitable hour or two at a studio recording dozens of these commissioned jingles.

One day I was in the studio with a very famous singer whose main hits were from the 1990s but still being played twenty years later: in the space of two hours, various foreign DJs and sound systems came through the studio, from Spain, Japan, and Germany. I watched him retool one of his main hits over and over again, receiving a few hundred U.S. dollars for each one. At one point, he paused for a break and a bottle of water and announced to the room in his booming voice: "A this mi royalties!" (These are my royalties!). He knew that royalties are a way people make money from music; in this announcement, he identified his earnings by right (if not by law). He had likely not been paid much (if at all) for the original version of the song—a combination of a beloved riddim and his instantly recognizable vocals—now globally famous. In fact, he may not have been the legal copyright owner, given Jamaican law's tendency to assign copyright to who "caused the recording to happen," likely a producer or studio owner. But he could capitalize on his connection to the song through the aspect of it he had control over: his distinctive voice and personal association with the song. As with royalties, he profited more as the song circulated more. Unlike royalties, his payment did not depend on preventing people from having the recording but from the creation of a new recording reusing elements of the original (and also unlike royalties, he received significant cash in hand at the moment of creation).

Jamaican musical practitioners also developed creative traditions to make the most of this circulation. For a vocal artist, the lack of written information on a cassette, CD, or MP3 can be offset by an ability to be vocally distinctive—many artists developed idiosyncratic vocal styles, catchphrases, or sounds that enabled listeners to easily identify them. Studios and producers have innovated in this way as well, embedding the name of the producer into the riddim. These innovations mean that, despite lacking the written information, songs can still promote artists and producers. It is also important to recognize that since copyright law does not always recognize the artist as the owner, these practices allow for more people involved in the creation of the song to build reputation than would the formalities of written and registered copyright. By sonically linking identity with creative output, these practices claim one valence of power—the power to be recognized as a creator—on terms that copyright law does not in itself guarantee.

Dancers and mogglers, like vocalists, producers, and instrumentalists, also rely more on circulation and attribution than exclusive control over their moves and recordings. In fact, as recordings proliferate and technology makes them easier to make, performers who have created a professional brand could theoretically negotiate ownership for recordings of their performances.[60] Some dancers have publicly asserted this goal,[61] but this is practically unlikely due to social dance's poor fit with the law.

Unfortunately, these circulating recordings cannot necessarily increase royalties for Jamaican musicians either. Jamaican musical practice incorporates music from Jamaica's current and historical musical context, not limited by region, nationality, or ownership but instead shaped by cultural relevance or sonic interest. Moreover, Jamaica's musical creators' diasporic and resistant interests inspires them to continually insert their own voices and narratives into the foreign music still dominating Jamaican airwaves and official music venues. Increased visibility may increase the risk of lawsuits from international copyright holders, who until recently have been able to ignore local Jamaican practices.

Large commercial copyright owners do take advantage of changing technology to extend their reach: we have seen attempts to monitor music use on various new technologies, such as cell phones and ringtones.[62] Dancehall's increasing circulation in new technologies can lead to clashes over musical traditions, although the outcomes are not set in stone. In 2007, the record label EMI issued a stop order against the Jamaican vocalist Vybz Kartel, demanding that he cease production of recordings of a song that reused elements from a pop song they owned.[63] The decentralized circulation of music through riddims and digital copies makes it impossible for this stop order to be effective: not only were there numerous other vocalists using the same sonic elements, but the elements and his version, as well as many others, were circulated and copied by entities well outside of Kartel's control. To some extent, local practices still ruled on the ground. However, while these threats might not stop local circulation, they could limit Jamaicans' ability to use online platforms for music circulation and disadvantage those seeking international audiences.

These disadvantages are already embedded, although imperfectly, in U.S. media platforms like YouTube, which are subject to the U.S. Digital Millennium Copyright Act (DMCA).[64] The DMCA requires sites that host uploaded media to have a system in place for removing content a copyright owner alleges to be infringing. Many sites now use scanning software that compares the waveform of a sound to a database of waveforms submitted by copyright owners and automatically removes a file if the software detects a match.[65] Such filters could limit Jamaicans' global reach, if Jamaican music is disproportionately flagged. Technologically embedded copyright enforcement could interfere with local production techniques if copyright-specific filters were embedded in studio computers or mixing boards, as many copyright maximalists (those who argue that the more copyright enforcement, the better) have advocated: some U.S. corporations have already attempted to install such software on personal computers,[66] as well as mandate its installation on networks and studio production platforms.[67] Automated restrictions on music reuse in the process of composition would chill creative practices that rely on repetition and reuse even in the composition process.[68] Since the Jamaican musical tradition involves an incorporation of existing musical, sonic, and lyrical elements, limiting phonographic orality could shift the trajectory of Jamaican music and alter its ability to serve the urban poor, both through limiting reuse and through privileging nonsyncretic music.[69] Since ownership of copyrights even within Jamaica tends to gravitate to those most closely aligned with power, enforcing exclusive rights would limit far more creators than it would support.

While some acknowledge the difficulty of claiming essentially social practices like dancing in a group, an attorney and former dancehall queen recently made a suggestion that attempted to split the difference, crafting a legal argument that "would not stop those who love and want to share the culture from doing so. It will just prohibit those who make money from it from doing so without giving the creators their fair share."[70] This argument is interesting because it diverges from typical copyright law that requires a license for any use, not just profitable use: instead it attempts to differentiate between community practices and profit-minded practices. Such a distinction is difficult to make using copyright law (although the Creative Commons license does differentiate between commercial and noncommercial use), but it does reflect an understanding that cultural ownership in practice is more complex than a simple license. Jamaicans affiliated with exilic spaces have made claims outside of or beyond what the law typically recognizes, reflecting a desire to assert those values originating outside of the law within the law itself.

Phonographic Orality: The Street Dance as Collective Author

Phonographic orality is the central dynamic complicating Jamaican popular music's relationship to copyright law—it is a defining aspect of Jamaican creativity that best flourishes in exilic spaces. The practice is a dynamic interplay between recorded musical element and live performance; it includes DJs playing, manipulating, or combining recordings, adding vocal performances or interjections to the audio experience. At the street dance, phonographic orality also involves the creative decisions of audience members, collectively and individually. One night at Passa Passa, I observed this in action.

Field notes excerpt #5

My companion told me "this is a smaller crowd" as we walked up, but still I estimated four hundred people or more gathered between the looming, vibrating speakers (popular nights have reportedly attained attendance of over one thousand). As the crowd energy picked up, people began to talk more animatedly and dance more expressively. More people coupled up, dancing together with increasing vigor, and a few dance crews began to make short bursts of synchronized dance moves before breaking apart into individuals in the crowd. The DJ began playing tunes of increasing "hotness"— which means tunes that have a certain buzz or popularity about them—familiar already to the crowd.[71] A DJ's skill is partly in the selection of the vocals, as well as knowing when it is time to switch to a new instrumental riddim. One riddim had been especially popular this season—for the past two months I had heard "Hold Yuh," by Gyptian, at dances, on the radio, in shops and restaurants, as a ringtone. The instrumental version provided a backing track for at least fifteen other singers I was aware of. It wasn't until later in the night (or morning) that Hold Yuh's instrumental came over the sound system. When it did, there was a rush of excitement in the crowd, but also curiosity: what is the DJ going to do with this? Introducing the riddim with a less-known singer, it was immediately evident when the DJ got around to playing Gyptian's vocal because people screamed as the vocals came in. Couples broke apart and people rushed toward the center of the street and the thickest part of the crowd. Others were literally jumping up and down, and in a few places I saw young men lean back and use a can of hairspray and a lighter to improvise a homemade flamethrower that they shot into the air to symbolize that the tune is "fire!" Next, the DJ dropped a new vocal from another of the season's most popular vocalists, also on the "Hold Yuh" instrumental. Hearing him combine the familiar riddim and the new vocal from a famous vocalist brought people to a fever pitch—they responded so energetically that the DJ pulled up the tune, rewinding it to the beginning to start it over again.[72]

I recalled another occasion, when a DJ did not pull up the tune as the crowd demanded a rewind from the selector. A crowd member ran up and physically rewound the record for him, pulling back the song to the beginning again, so the crowd could experience the buildup and release again. A DJ's relationship with the audience could be marked by the audience literally taking control of his performance. This loss of control is a success, not a failure, signaling how his goals and the audience's merge in that moment.

It was striking to see how the audience physically embodied musical moments, mobilizing into clusters of bodies moving in synchrony. A DJ's skill includes attending to those moments in his selection of music, noting what seemed to hit with the audience and selecting accordingly. This information is also important for producers, who rely on audience response as part of their creative input. One seasoned producer I spoke with described it this way: "We have to observe these tings, observe it and say how these people react when we play certain songs. They would bawl 'forward!' [call for the song to be rewound] for certain songs, certain songs they would be relax[ed], not moving to this. So we would say OK this one not really grabbing same to the others."

Attending to the party's energy is a dynamic and reflexive process. While not every moment of audience interaction is as dramatic as that described above, audiences at street dances contributed more often and more energetically to the night's experience than they did at more elite nightclubs or spaces where homemade flamethrowers might endanger the venue as well as other patrons. I witnessed another pull up at an event called Bembe,[73] around five in the morning.

Field notes excerpt #6

The DJ, Tony Matterhorn (who took his name from his favorite brand of cigarettes), was building up suspense by delaying the sonic entrance of a particularly popular song. Baseball cap askew on his head, massive silver chain glinting at his neck, he smirked and watched the crowd. Matterhorn played version after version of other songs on the same instrumental, building expectation and tension in the crowd. When the most acclaimed version finally "dropped," it was like the whole place exploded. The audience erupted with vast enthusiasm, screaming wordlessly or exhorting Matterhorn to "pull up" at top volume, banging on the zinc walls lining the streetside edge of the dance floor, jumping on the stage, beating and stomping on the ground, and setting off homemade flame-throwers into the air. The uproar continued, overwhelming even the massive amplified sound system, until Matterhorn rewound the track to play it again.

The crowd at a street dance has tremendous influence over the night's atmosphere, as well as encouraging or discouraging DJs, performers, producers, or anyone else seeking validation. Its authority is reflexive in relation to its own membership: other attendees may wait to see whether an event is truly "hot" before they contribute their own energy, but it is everyone's energy that helps make it hot. As the above discussion illustrates, the DJ's authority is equally reflexive: he is not controlling the audience, but collaborating with them and sometimes is subject to their will. A DJ's reputation usually depends on his or her skill at negotiating this dynamic.

Producers and vocalists are also dependent on audience input. The studio producer quoted above also described how he and his sound system crew would test their recordings in the crowd and learn from audience feedback: "[When] we have new songs, we play them and watch the response of the people and know which songs would be the songs to hit."

Phonographic orality displaces the composer's and musician's authority onto the producer, the soundman, and the DJ, as well as onto the audience as they engage, respond, judge, and shape music at the dance. As Henriques points out, this collapses many of the dualities often assumed in music (and usually presumed and reinforced by copyright law): sound making versus listening, production versus consumption, transmission versus reception, and performance versus reperformance.[74] Sometimes DJs educate audiences through exposing them to new sounds. One interviewee described how it can take time for audiences to get into it (when they are not actively hostile): "Sometimes people will grow on a song you know, probably it's the first they are hearing it so they have to take their time."[75] This is one of the most important, delicate, and intuitive DJ skills: introducing unfamiliar sounds to an audience. Often the trick is to sandwich it between more familiar sounds or build up to it (as Tony Matterhorn did), but a DJ can sometimes boldly intrude into the flow of the music with a wholly new sound and it can hit the audience just right. This skill can only be developed in relation to a specific audience, since each audience has its own histories and expectations that a DJ must be in touch with to produce a positive (inter)reaction.

The audience affirms when the DJ has played the hot tune at the proper time in relation to the energy around them. Simply playing a tune might not trigger the crowd response. I have heard audience members and other DJs criticize a DJ for playing a hot tune too early in the night, and I have seen the same tune that drove a dance to explosive excitement fall mildly flat when the conditions were not right for it. This does not mean a DJ cannot positively surprise a crowd, but the interaction must be carefully gauged; otherwise, the DJ may "flop"—that is, fail at his task—by misjudging what an audience will enjoy.

An unimpressed audience at a street dance is serious business: one might face a stone-faced crowd of unmoving people, sucking their teeth and rolling their eyes—a daunting prospect. I have observed unhappy or hostile audiences shouting insults or throwing bottles at DJs. I have heard stories of DJs receiving physical beatings from displeased audience members.[76] Even the simple humiliation of a flop, where the audience turns away in disgust, can follow a DJ or other performer for some time, affecting his or her future work prospects.

Many moments of positive audience interaction are immortalized and reincorporated in the production process—the sound of the rewind (or pull up, or, as in chapter 1, lick back)—of a record being pulled back to the beginning to be played again—can now be heard on occasion in a particular song, a reference to the moment at which an audience goes wild. To properly understand the incentives and dynamics of creativity, the audience must not be discounted as a creative force. Attending to the collective aspect of phonographic orality also reveals gendered dynamics in the creative process: while sound systems are staffed almost entirely by men, audiences often reflect a more equal mix of men and women. This illustrates how important it is to attend to the dance floor, as it is an important site of female presence and authority, which women can sometimes use as a way to resist and redraw cultural values that attempt to limit their power, especially over their own bodies (about which see more below).[77]

The energy in the music and the way that it provides value to Jamaicans derives from multiple needs, none of which are well met by copyright law. Most saliently for those concerned with creativity, Jamaicans engage with music for the purpose of cultural survival in the face of colonial hostility that denies them agency on their own terms. To address the shared aspects of Jamaican culture and the creative interactions that cement the bonds between poor Black Jamaicans *requires* musical interactions that contradict copyright (alongside other laws). When Jamaican composers and performers incorporate music from outside Jamaica—especially popular music from media empires that dominate the legal media channels—that allows them to reclaim space, in a public forum, and speak their own reality back to American and other foreign pop narratives. Every major pop and hip-hop tune in the United States gets a Jamaican version—often with witty or subversive subtext. For example, Lorde's 2013 song "Royals" captures a particular slouchy indie-tinged critique of the trappings of nobility and monarchy: "And we'll never be royals. It don't run in our blood. That kind of luxe just ain't for us, we crave a different kind of buzz."[78] It also embodies a disdain for the visible displays of wealth. When the song arrived in Jamaica, it was a big enough hit to be incorporated into the popular music tradition—Demarco reused the instrumental and the melody to transform "Royal" into "Loyal," a song decrying friends who snitch. Another artist, Busy Signal, released a version that recentered local values on terms that challenge Lorde's lyrics: "A wi a run the whole town, Hustler make the money plenty!"[79] In the Jamaican context, where elites tend to emphasize physical restraint and modesty, excessive or exuberant display is celebrated among the poor. The distinctly local aspect of these values is heightened by the contrast with the original tune; they are in conversation with it. The Jamaican versions did not mask their relationship with the Lorde song but instead inserted distinctly Jamaican attitudes into it for contrast. Such sonic creative expressions require room to breathe, less restricted by regulations, costs, or permission.[80]

Decolonizing Creative Practices

Phonographic orality allows Jamaicans to assert local cultural values against and in dialogue with music made outside Jamaica, as well as engage with social and political issues in a way that centers the voices of the poor. In this way, street dances' transgressions against intellectual property law, as well as physical property law, make them sites of autonomous cultural formation at least partly independent from colonial concepts of personhood. Because the street dance is less dependent on material and cultural resources that flow from the historic centers of colonial power like British culture and white supremacist social mores, the dance is able to foster creativity and healing in the urban poor. The collective authority rooted in audience and the markers of poor urban life allow those with the least access to mainstream cultural authority to claim membership on their own terms. These are practices that can occur in the recording studio as well but must cycle through musical engagement in the dance to be affirmed.

The street dance illustrates one way that, as Denise Noble puts it, "Black music has deployed orality, sound and the body to challenge the hegemony of the scribal."[81] As a creative practice that is not based in the technologies of recording and writing, the street dance sonically occupies space, disregards copyright's definition of appropriate musical engagement, and requires bodily interjections and interactions. These practices center a simultaneous refusal and a demand: refusing the stratified social relationships and identities demanded by a colonized authority and demanding recognition nonetheless.

Asserting Local Cultural Values

To understand how local cultural values are nurtured in the street dance, it's worth focusing on transgressions and excesses of propriety in relation to the body. One could (and many do) critique the physical performance of dance moves that men and women enact that appear to be highly sexual. However, the context in which they are performed—a poor neighborhood dominated by poor people of African descent, framed by music that valorizes them at the center of the musical world—means that such acts take on different meanings than if they were carried out by other bodies or even by similar bodies in different contexts. To center women's bodies and sexuality in the dance can be to radically reenvision the meaning of dignity and authority, especially in contrast to colonially restricted and disempowering attitudes.[82]

Many women attendees at street dances of all ages, sizes, and skin tones were easily found wearing clothing that is usually advertised only for the slim and young. While plenty of others wear more subdued styles, the women who dress and dance in ways that accentuate their body quite often look considerably different from colonialist standards of beauty usually found on Jamaican and even more so on international fashion sites and magazines. Men's fashion, while not quite as body conscious, did often include extremely tight pants slung low about the hips, and styling with colors and accessories was also complicated and bright. Although I saw fewer older men wearing the neon colors, there were plenty with hats, rings, and other dandyish attire. These styles and women's large and glittering jewelry styles, multicolored eye lashes, and hair differentiated them from more subdued upper-class fashion and asserted a different definition of propriety. Anthropologist Gina Ulysse suggests that this fashion developed especially in 1980s-era dancehall and "signaled that the middle and upper classes no longer dictated standards of decency and respect."[83] It is notable that Jamaican men in street dances also diverge somewhat from colonial gender norms in their performance of masculinity. Elaborate brightly colored clothing and hairstyles, numerous accessories, and even makeup are not confined to women attendees but also adorn many male bodies in the street dance space. Men also dance in groups with other men and coordinate outfits to present a dramatic and pleasing whole. These practices do not fit with masculine gender roles valorized in upper-class realms but have echoes in older traditions of masculine identity rooted in colonial and precolonial traditions.[84] Ellis goes so far as to suggest these could be read as queer identities and sexualities in their challenging of heteronormative interactions and colonial masculinity.[85]

Women's dance moves in particular featured intense control over especially the lower body, from dropping to the ground in a split in time with music, to turning upside down, balanced on the forearms, and flexing legs and buttocks individually in time to the music. Centering sexuality and celebrating the body does not necessarily remove them from commodified social relations. However, at the dance, these women assert social relationships with their own bodies that go beyond commodification for male and/or capitalist consumption. Their movements are assertive and impressive, even intimidating. In the immediate space, a man approaching such a dancer needed a level of fortitude, as I saw women literally bounce a man away from her using her body or simply render him irrelevant through movements that were impossible for him to keep up with. This highlights the intimacy of their performance in the dance. These assertions of physical power were possible because of the physical proximity of those involved.

Cooper reads these bodily practices as acts of "erotic marronage," an "embodied politics of disengagement from the Eurocentric discourses of colonial Jamaica and their pernicious legacies in the contemporary moment."[86] While there is a debate among scholars about the extent to which they are truly liberatory, both women's and men's dancing and bodily performance and styling would mark them as disreputable in elite spaces. For many audience members, the street dance has provided an exilic space to celebrate a range of opposition to the coloniality of embodiment. This has served to defend participants against being fully engulfed in a white supremacist society that ultimately seeks to erase them or render them subservient. This is one method by which Jamaican popular music can aid in what Gray has called "the repair of cultural injuries."[87] However, changing technological and social dynamics can alter the exilic capacity of the dance.[88]

Challenging and Rechallenging the Hegemony of the Scribal

One night at Boasy Tuesday in 2009, I was struck by the proliferation of cameras and their varied and global reach. I saw a German film crew, made up of short-haired white men in dark T-shirts and jeans, brandishing expensive video and audio gear. They spent some time filming several Japanese women, in outfits fully as extreme in color and style as the most daring Jamaican dancehall queen, who were profiling for the cameras. A photographer from the local music website Yardflex.com (run by a middle-class Jamaican) was snapping shots with a large, expensive camera. My companions pointed out two other people with notably expensive cameras, who were local newspaper reporters. We also had to dodge two video men who circled the space, requiring that we dodge the cables connecting their cameras to the sound system. Their cameras illuminated the crowd in sections, with bright lights beaming forward, and dancers scrambled to be in the center. Alongside this, various other attendees brought their camera phones up to shoot pictures of themselves and others, at random intervals. It seemed apropos when, at around two thirty in the morning, the DJ played the tune "Video Light," one of many songs that acknowledges the video camera (behind the "light") presence and power in the dance.

> fi di videolight girls, aight then [for the video light girls, all right then]
> Walk up inna di video fah yuh cute gal
> Talu up [stand up tall] inna di video fah yuh cute gal[89]

Although these lyrics encourage women to show off, I observed men fighting as hard or harder for the video light. The circling, ubiquitous cameras and cables dramatize how the street dance has become a nexus of globally networked technologies. Visual recording of street dances has become ubiquitous, especially as mobile phones increasingly include cameras and are somewhat more affordable.[90]

Tracy Skelton's work on Black women and dancehall in London, as well as Carolyn Cooper's and Bibi Bakare-Yusuf's work in Jamaica, suggest that when dancehall is centered in Black communities, it still serves a celebratory purpose for Black women.[91] But the "when" is important: the ability to control context is necessary for maintaining that purpose. The material reality of street dances has historically provided protection, which can nurture a kind of cultural intimacy (one that does not valorize light skin, for example). That protection can be ruptured. The hegemony of the scribal continually threatens to reassert itself in new technologies of writing and recording.

Krista Thompson, in her work on the politics of visibility, suggests that women have increasingly sexualized their movements in response to videographers' presence and an increasing awareness of reputation beyond the dance and evoke a gendered gaze on the dancefloor and even more in the videos themselves.[92] Racism and colorism have also shaped this visibility, as for women and men both increasing visibility on a global stage has coincided with an increase in the practice of skin bleaching. Many suggest that participants have become more attuned to global preferences for performers with whiter skin.[93] New media technologies can strip away the local context and circulate images from the street dance far beyond the networks of popular music discourse that have traditionally answered to it.

Alongside the effect on women in particular, the global visibility and popularity of scenes associated with the poor are not necessarily liberating. Such images can be a voyeuristic way to reinforce racist assumptions about sexuality and propriety that fetishize Black people as hypersexual and aggressive. Street dances in their local context have had the ability to inscribe bodily performance with meaning beyond these exploitative terms, but that ability is contingent on their ability to be exilic.

The reach of visual media has also extended across the globe as digital images have become easier to upload and share online, while digital video uploading and streaming is not far behind. Videos have already entered the circulation of street-dance related media,[94] and their reach now extends beyond local news and television. Although the event organizers and soundmen are not the only people in charge of video recording, I regularly observed official videographers who plugged their cameras into the central power line and were generally given pride of place and attention by DJs and organizers.

This online presence makes street dances transcend the local, even if they still maintain some orientation toward Jamaica. While literally focusing on the bodies of people in a specific locale, the images and sounds circulate among a national and international audience joined by common culture even without a direct physical connection.[95] On social media sites, participants upload images; music blogs and portals also report on the musical events and gossip, and music websites advertise the street dances or the DVDs associated with them.[96] DVDs released for sale weekly (at record shops in Jamaica and beyond) catalog the most outrageous dances, fashions, and moments. These DVDs circulate all over the world—especially among Jamaican immigrant communities—wherever Jamaican music has found a foothold. I have found them in every neighborhood with a Jamaican presence in the United States or Europe—across the United States, in London and Toronto, as well as in record shops that stock current Jamaican music in Berlin, Brussels, and Amsterdam.[97] Increasingly, street dances are present on Jamaican-centric websites, as well as social media sites and YouTube.

This new kind of visibility transcends some of the borders that have defined the street dance. A positive aspect of this visibility is the increased interest from foreign music fans, who do bring themselves and their money to street dances. This more directly benefits poor Jamaicans than does the officially sanctioned tourism in resorts, which are mainly foreign-owned and walled-off affairs where money circulates without much spillover into local communities. However, so far, the international popularity of Jamaican popular music has not encouraged hearty investment or support from the mainstream tourist industry or the Jamaican government.[98] Street dances still do not fit state and elite narratives of respectability.

Non-Jamaicans, even white elite ones, do not suffer from the same crisis of legitimacy as do the Jamaican upper classes, whose domination is based partly on the denial of a relationship to poor Jamaicans. Thus, foreigners are more interested than many locals in participating in these events. This clash of interests was recently dramatized when Estonian dancehall fans visiting Jamaica were moved to complain publicly about police shutting down a street dance. In an open letter published in the *Daily Gleaner* and sent to the minister of culture, the Estonian dancer Riina Asamoa emphasized her potential economic value for Jamaicans outside of elite locations: "What differentiates us from the average tourist is that we spend our money with the locals. . . . Our money stays in Jamaica unlike the money the tourists spend in all-inclusive American owned resorts. We stay in smaller local hotels, use taxis, eat, drink and party in restaurants and shop at local stores. Also to be taken into consideration is the promotional value we have on the export of Jamaican dancehall culture, many of us are influential promoters, radio selektors [sic] and entertainers promoting and booking Jamaican dancehall artists and dancers internationally."[99]

International interest in Jamaican popular music includes foreign audience members but also the aforementioned foreign sound-system organizers commissioning dubplates and jingles. Both groups are taking Jamaican sounds and practices back to their home countries for fans there to enjoy. We might call the Jamaican music scene translocal, consisting of linked networks of Jamaican-music aficionados. Some scholars have described translocal scenes as producing "affective communities that transcend the need for face-to-face interaction as a requirement for scene membership."[100] But this does not fully fit the Jamaican experience.

It is true that many Jamaican musical practitioners do assert that increased visibility online is a powerful force, and maybe one for good. One male singer I spoke with said, "Definitely right now the internet ting . . . it tends to slope a lotta tings, promote a lotta tings more faster. Carry your voice more faster throughout di world." But at the same time, when I asked him how he made his money, he said, "I make most of my money from singing dubplates [another word for specials] [and] jingles. When I get more popular, bigger, have a hit song, probably I have more money from stage show." While acknowledging the general appeal of promotion on the global level, he saw his ability to make money as tied to more local institutions. These generate one-time fees that depend on people being embedded in sound-system culture that circulates and reuses musical recordings without paying royalties and still require markers of, to some extent, Jamaican-defined authenticity or that involves being physically present at Jamaican musical events.

Commissioning a dubplate might not require face-to-face interaction in the era of computers and mobile phones, but it does require some communication with the artist whose services are needed. Even in the 2000s, reaching individual artists was not always easy, and this relative inaccessibility by digital devices served to encourage many people to come to Jamaica to track them down—something that also enhances foreigners' reputation at home, as they have pursued an "authentic" Jamaican experience. So while Jamaican music may be translocal, the value of the Jamaican locale is still higher, and the less stable technological communication context increases its value. This difference in value also reflects unequal power dynamics. Jamaican popular music's economic and social value developed because Jamaicans could maintain some control over the social context in which music got made and money changed hands. In that context, Jamaican popular music's increasing accessibility is not simply an expansion of audience, but also a space for increased vulnerability, misunderstanding, and predation. Audibly illegal acts like copyright infringement could become risky as well, if greater integration with global media networks challenges the exilic capacity of street dance spaces. Since global media platforms increasingly embed various attempts at copyright law enforcement, this is not a hypothetical or remote concern.

Even within Jamaica, one's nighttime behavior might bring about social or legal repercussions in one's daily life. I was asked by a friend to edit the photograph I had taken of us at a dance because I wanted to post it online, as it would have revealed a participant in a way they did not want their employers to see. Visible presence at street dances can be seen as risky in other contexts.

Musical interest from abroad also affects the ability of Jamaicans to define and control the social meaning of their music. The terms of respectability defined at the dance are to some extent made effective by the local community's authority when one is physically present in the street dance. This social power can be ignored by remote viewers, who can safely observe and judge from afar—without a chance to become affected by closer relationships with the people at the dance. This can lead to predatory or fetishistic engagement. The means by which Jamaican popular music has resisted this are grounded in the locality and exilic nature, possibly under threat, of the street dance.

A Site of Cultural Authority and the Basis for Rude Citizenship

The local cultural authority generated in street dances can still spill over into other realms of performance and judgment. The 2009 Dancehall Queen competition is a notable example of this. A young woman named Kristal Anderson won the public competition with a dynamic dance performance onstage—but her physical presence was a stark contradiction to dominant Jamaican (and even more so international) media standards that tend to focus on slenderness and light skin. As a dark-skinned woman who weighed over two hundred pounds, she diverged notably from, for example, Jamaica's beauty pageant participants, newscasters, and other women in more middle- and upper-class media platforms, who were much more likely to have light skin and slender physiques. Her dance moves emphasized power and control, especially over the lower half of her body, including considerable work balancing upside down on her head and vibrating her backside to the music. But just as notable was a total commitment to performance and a cocky attitude of exuberantly taking up space. Neither the moves nor the attitudes are consonant with propriety as defined by and for upper-class Jamaican women, but they are aesthetic and skill-based values established in the dance. Anderson's triumph was not eternal, but it was indicative of the kind of cultural authority the street dance can have.

The street dance's location is still a key factor of its cultural authority within Jamaica and beyond.[101] The dances' exilic nature contributes to poor urban people's dominance in matters of fashion and flamboyance, keeping all eyes downtown. In these downtown locations, Jamaican musical engagement also reinforces a less colonial sense of self and social relationships. Even when Jamaicans use the language of legal rights, they translate the meaning of legal rights into local discourses of power, respect, identity, and mutual obligation, sometimes along exilic lines. In other cases, participants make claims within the terminology of the state and attempt to leverage state concepts of citizenship into greater recognition. These moments when the state has attempted to recognize local community practices have not been particularly successful.

Beyond the Shadow of the Law

Legal scholars have long discussed how people who do not litigate their disputes in court are still affected by the law. In this analysis, law was originally posited as a framework against which people define their negotiating positions and relationships.[102] Copyright scholars have asserted that for musicians, "legal restrictions and the potential for punishment influence [their] choices."[103] But relation to sample-based music in the United States, some artists deliberately flout the law to state their disregard for its authority. The California-based DJ Rob Fatal described how "some hip-hop or turntablist people see not securing rights as a 'fuck-you' to the industry. It's another way to rebel against the mainstream."[104] Fatal goes on to say that many others simply cannot afford to make the music they want legally, so while it may not be a conscious rebellion, they feel they have no choice. In the Jamaican context, flouting copyright appears the norm, to an extent that it is unclear to what extent the law is considered at all.

On several nights in 2009, I watched the DJs at Boasy Tuesday playing music on CDJs (CD players designed for DJs). They would draw from several piles of CD books stacked on top of each other, with other CDs slipping across the table. Many had hand-inked words on them or a scrap of paper taped to one side, suggesting they were home copied or noncommercially released, and none had anything resembling a commercial CD cover or printed artwork. This was the norm at most street dances I attended. Videographers recorded the DJs' actions every so often, especially when they interacted with the music by singing or talking over it and turned to the crowd. Both publicly performing by using copyrighted recordings and reproducing copyrighted recordings require a license. So any depiction of an artist publicly performing using a copied CD depicts two kinds of copyright infringement and may itself be a potentially infringing derivative work in that recording. However, if the musical recordings remain circulating within the Jamaican music scene, nobody seems inspired to sue. Most Jamaicans involved in music appear focused on gaining fame, and producers focus on popularity in the street dance rather than extracting royalties from the circulation of copyrighted material. This alternate orientation reflects a relationship to law that is not really in its shadow but instead seems to be in a space where copyright law casts very little shadow.

Despite its lack of force in daily life, people do still use the language of law and intellectual property rights in Jamaica. Especially in the past ten years, there are more examples of artists and organizations publicly stating they are suing or planning to sue others for copyright infringement. However, the reality seems to get in the way of these ambitions. In 2013, the *Jamaica Gleaner* headline "Dancers Want to Copyright Moves" was followed by the subheading "JIPO Not Ready to Facilitate Them Yet." There are many complexities regarding applying copyright law to dance and to other performative, iterative, improvisational creative practices. There is no shortage of artists or producers bemoaning others, especially foreigners, making money off of Jamaican music. However, these concerns have generally not led to legal cases. I searched a list provided by the recently revitalized JIPO of three years of cases regarding copyright infringement, which reveals that the only lawsuits filed were over unauthorized commercial sales of CDs and DVDs, not, for example, infringement by producers, artists, or other musical practitioners reusing recordings in creative practice.[105] This suggests that people may not feel their rights are violated in the creative process or that there are obstacles to using the law to redress their wrongs. Some of the obstacles I have described above: the law is poorly designed to redress the wrongs felt by most Jamaican musicians. However, those issues—especially producers and labels forcing unfair or unclear contracts—were rarely discussed in public discussions of copyright. When I spoke with people who described those problems, they asserted various reasons or simply remained vague about the lack of legal action on their behalf.

Legal scholars have pointed out that in situations of systematic, socially upheld inequality, the law is not a reference point for defining rights but is, in fact, a site of hostility and danger. When people see themselves as lacking power and see courts as places controlled by the powerful, those who see themselves as victims of injustice, as the legal scholar Kristin Bumiller put it, "the bonds of victimhood are reinforced rather than broken by the intervention of legal discourse." In fact, people "shun the role of victim [who is entitled to sue]" because they fear disrupting the balance of power in their daily lives.[106] This shunning was evident in silences and other practices by musicians I spoke with.

One striking pattern that arose from my conversations with artists and producers was the role of body language and tone of voice when discussing legal matters and the amount of talking past the examples being discussed. One artist, when I asked how copyright worked for him in relation to his songs appearing on mix CDs that circulated in Jamaica, said, "When you register the song [speaking softly, leaning forward] and when you register the song, if the artists who also produce the tune, put your name on the album, you can get your credit." In another case, I asked AC, a vocalist, when he joined JACAP, and he said, "Is a man come to me and say, 'DJ, you keep writing songs and singing songs why not get someone to um [leaning forward, speaking more quietly] do 'bout your copyright and your publishing and um . . . and direct . . . um in- instruct me and so . . . so me just take mi personal belongings and go register. Passport, birth certificate, national ID, get sorted out." The ellipses here reflect pauses and hesitations in his speech. In these and many other conversations, discussion of copyright and legal forms coincided with artists lowering their voices, leaning forward or hunching their bodies, and often speaking more hesitantly. This cumulatively gave me the impression that copyright law was not a site of clarity or ease for many people involved in music—even people who had been involved for a long time. I am sure my position as an outsider shaped this response—I do not know how people talked about copyright when I was not present. But even if they spoke about it a bit differently elsewhere that would reinforce my sense that copyright was seen by many Jamaican musicians as a place where foreigners, white people, might have more authority or at least more power to do harm, even when it is asserted at the same time as a right. The second quotation also links copyright with formalities akin to getting a foreign visa—joining an artists' rights agency was described as an onerous process that requires validation by many state-affirmed documents.

Quite often in my interviews, people discussing copyright asserted contradictory things. (This is not at all surprising or unique to Jamaica.) The producer I asked about mix CDs described above how promotion could work *if* one was registered and *if* one was credited on the CD. But neither of these things is usually the case—in another part of that interview, the same producer told me he had a lot of songs he had not registered, while most mix CDs tended to be nearly blank of artist or producer information, usually just providing the name of the DJ who mixed the CD. The gap between the practice of musical circulation and the language of the law remains wide. Given that copyright law as defined could not well serve a lot of the people in Jamaican popular music, it makes sense that it operates instead as a kind of rhetoric, and an uneasy rhetoric at that. On the local level, many were more assertive about what was valued in ways that often challenged how the law is currently written. AC also said about mix CDs: "The mixtape [mix CD] on di street—it a form of promotion, you know. It a form of promotion because, as a ghetto youth you can't really fight against the idea going around with music. There is a law against that, in terms of getting the songs out on the street mixing. . . . [But] as an artist you want to promote your CD locally and internationally—it on a mixtape it promote dem!"

Understanding the value of exilic spaces helps us see why simply legalizing practices or rendering them visible to the state is not necessarily going to be liberatory for the communities centered in the music. The law as written does not support many creative practices central to the music; nor does it recognize the decentralized and shifting centers of cultural authority.

In relation to copyright, even if the law does not totally enforce it, the law can limit musical practitioners' autonomy through its normalizing logic.[107] So long as it is able to normalize particular behavior against deviant or marginalized behavior, copyright law perpetuates a tiered system of participation. If copyright raises rewards for normalized behavior and raises the costs of deviating from formal law, musical practitioners must weigh their connection with their community against their ability to participate. Not only is this an unfair choice, but it is potentially harmful. Since poor Jamaicans' communities are places where they can valorize aspects of self (including Blackness itself) that are still not welcomed elsewhere, moving away from community can be psychologically, culturally, and even physically damaging. Since the music's vibrancy is tied to the energy of survival and resistance at the margins of the system, moving away from its very popularity and creative heart may alter the music itself in ways that limit its energy and global appeal. And on an economic level, many people find it hard to negotiate a strong economic position in relation to a formal institution. Musical practitioners would need to learn legal language and the skills of negotiating within the legal system to make informed decisions.

An individual solution to such systematic hostility will always place an undue burden on people already disadvantaged. However, individualism is the main frame for the advice I heard offered to Jamaican musicians: lawyers, policy makers, and businesspeople I spoke with, as well as official communications from the Jamaican Copyright Office, recommend that artists who currently fail to benefit from copyright enforcement embark on a project of personal self-improvement. While such projects may benefit some, they come with the obligation to meet the law in its own domain: courtrooms, paperwork, and legal terminology. The burden of negotiating within this domain becomes more and more costly the farther people are from it in their own lives. It is common among lawyers and businesspeople to speak of legal formalities as reducing uncertainty: advice to musicians quite often starts with "get it in writing."[108] However, cash up front is more certain than a contract for royalties that depend on future sales. Uncertainty is especially high for artists who do not already have a large following and significant money to outlay up front for costs of promotion. As well, contract negotiation is always easier for repeat players (more likely to be labels and distributors) or those comfortable in the realm of lawyers and paperwork.[109] Getting it in writing presumes that one will have the power to enforce the contract one has signed, which many poor people do not. Legal formalities are much more likely to be defined by the more powerful figure in the negotiation.[110] In contrast, capitalizing on one's community networks and local economies for support may be easier and more familiar, as the practices of support are collectively derived and familiar.

These problems, poor fit with local practice and unequal bargaining power, also exist at the level of international copyright disputes. New media technologies provide new avenues for foreign copyright owners to intervene in local creative practices or demand state intervention.[111] Technologies that take the structure and function of copyright for granted may harm or reshape rather than foster creativity. The colonial context for copyright makes equality an urgent concern: colonially informed disdain for poor people's creative practices have meant that their persons and creativity have already been discounted. Attending more to the different positions of participants can also foster creativity associated with communities that have previously been undersupported.

Legal scholars who focus on ownership and cultural practice, and cognitive researchers as well, have emphasized the importance of flexibility, experimentation, serendipity, and play for a healthy creative environment.[112] Concepts such as "breathing space"[113] or "degrees of freedom" and "contextual play"[114] emphasize that law that "freezes the play of signification"[115] in the creative process works against music's creative and democratic values to society. In places directly affected by colonial power, it is important to recognize the specific histories and traditions by which people disadvantaged in the global system have gained the levels of success they have been able to achieve and to consider the possibility that these strategies continue to serve the interests of the disadvantaged in ways that dominant practices may not. Any policy that seeks to shape local practices ought to weigh the advantages of inclusion against the advantages of exclusion.[116] Integration into an unequal legal and social system is not automatically liberating to people without power in that system. Jamaican practices of phonographic orality, so central to the development of its music, could end up entangling Jamaican musical practitioners in a thicket of legal wrangling. The increased technological integration into global media systems with embedded copyright law enforcement technologies could render that playing field hostile or further unequal for people who draw on Jamaican traditions.

The Jamaican street dance embodies the intricate dynamics between communities, material and social resources, state power, and international markets. Both the input and the output of economic activity are diverse and diffuse and, in both cases, center the urban poor, due to the location of street dances in poor neighborhoods. The inputs and outputs of musical creativity are similarly diffuse and diverse but centered on the urban poor. Beyond inputs and outputs is the attention to a shared community life, knit together through knowledge, negotiation, and celebration. This shared life requires exilic space—not dependent on state- or upper-class-defined social norms—in which to flourish. Such space can be supported, be vulnerable to interference, or ignored or allowed to fly under the radar of formal law. These possible responses depend on the kinds of surveillance and restrictions embedded into networked technology or enacted in policy. In addition, street dances' translocal nature, with foreign participants and global visibility, suggests that surveillance and restriction could serve interests outside Jamaica, including interests that already limit Jamaican economic and social autonomy. An important lens by which we should examine any system, whether legal or technological, ought to be how that system affects the ability of music to continue to "challenge the oppressive limits of a colonial and neocolonial sociopolitical structure."[117]

3 Counteractions

Musical Conversation against Commodification

. . . .

"Let Me Go, Girl," Slim Smith and the Uniques (1967)

"Me Never Hold You," Dawn Penn (1967)

"What the Hell the Police Can Do?," Echo Minott (1986)

"Tell You What the Police Can Do," Lady Junie (1986)

"(In Love with a Man Who Is) Twice My Age,"
   Kristal and Shabba Ranks (1988)

"Half My Age," Sanchez and Lady G (1988)

"Exactly My Age," Max Romeo (1990)

The above Jamaican song titles depict works in conversation with each other. In each example, drawn from the extensive catalog of Jamaican music dating back to the 1960s, after a song has been met with a response, Jamaicans call these subsequent songs "answer tunes," or sometimes "counteractions."[1] In the above examples, each title is an element in a larger conversation. Representative (although not exhaustive) of Jamaican popular music preoccupations, the songs' lyrics also engage in conversations within and between songs. These conversations address issues ranging from romantic disputes to the police's appropriate role and power to the appropriate age differences in a relationship. The Patwa grammar ("What the Hell the Police Can Do" or "Me Never Hold You") and the sonic references arise primarily from the world of Jamaica's poor majority and signal the existence of a communal discourse in which recorded songs are a crucial element.

In this chapter, I analyze recordings created in line with common Jamaican musical traditions. This analysis is informed by ethnomusicology but primarily used to ground in Jamaican musical practitioners' attitudes and practices an alternate mapping of claims to citizenship and ownership than that assumed by copyright. The previous chapters articulated this alternate mapping of ownership and citizenship grounded in the ethnographic experience of street dances and in a history of Jamaican popular music: here I turn to the musical recordings themselves to see how they embody many of those same dynamics. As recordings that initially existed in physical form on vinyl records, the songs discussed below are the presumed target and appropriate site of copyright law (protecting only works "in fixed form"). We might expect that an exclusive right would be easy to attach to something that appears by nature to be exclusive; that is, a vinyl record is a physical object that can only be held by one person at a time. But this presumption of physical recordings' supposed limitations contradicts the reality of how they were used in practice. People's use of vinyl recordings was shaped by the cultural needs they had, especially for a platform more accessible to the poor majority than upper-class or government-controlled media channels.

Through these songs people publicly engage in ongoing and timely debates about politics, morals, taste, and desire. Notably, the engagement centers in style and content on things the Jamaican poor majority considers important. This is reflected both in practices of musical engagement, such as the sound system itself (as addressed in chapter 2), and within the structure of song making. Answer tunes and other forms of musical conversations embody cultural dynamics that redefine both property and propriety. The ability to participate is dictated by quite different gatekeepers than in formal media platforms. Beyond challenging social and technical restrictions on public discourse, these practices also embody a decolonized relationship to time and space: conversations can happen within and across months, years, or decades and across distance and discourses, including vigorous engagement with geopolitical issues of the day. These participatory practices are a particular aspect of phonographic orality that tie the concept to the specific needs of colonized people. Answer tunes are but one way phonographic orality[2] is embedded in Jamaican musical traditions, which makes them a rich site of analysis for understanding how Jamaican musical engagement continually challenges and subverts a colonial social order.

As a reminder, the social order of Jamaica, although participated in by Black and white Jamaicans (as well as Chinese, Lebanese, and Indian Jamaicans), is shaped by Jamaica's colonial past. In this context, markers of Blackness are not only physical but also cultural and expressive, tied to definitions of respectability that link Blackness with poor people and exclude people based not as much (or not only) on appearance but on deportment, language, style, and the ways one takes up space. Scholars of popular music have well addressed the ongoing dynamic of hostility to Blackness in musical content in upper-class-dominated media, such as state-run radio and television and the highbrow newspapers,[3] but this hostility also happens at the level of form: the rules of copyright and property law cannot welcome Jamaican popular music practices, which do not respect the official property, linear time, or cultural authority associated with the upper classes.

When scholars and industry professionals outside Jamaica discuss practices of musical reuse, they often presume musical reuse became significant only with the rise of digital media technology, with its increased capability to record, copy, segment, and layer audio. However, hip-hop and dance music practitioners, and the Jamaicans who have influenced them, had already developed whole cultures from these practices well before the digital era.[4] Julian Henriques identifies a chain of scholarly arguments situating "cutting" and "mixing" as integral to cultural practices that define a particular era, but each group of scholars identifies a different time. For Dick Hebdige, the practices of "cut 'n' mix" are the defining characteristic of 1980s music, while for Christoph Cox and Daniel Warner these are quintessential practices of 1990s DJ culture. Henriques situates cutting and mixing in his observation of sound system "sessions" in the 2000s, although the practice is, as we have seen, several decades old.[5] The physical ability to cut and mix audio recordings goes back at least a couple of decades before the 1980s: we can trace the ability to separate vocals from the instrumental, which was happening in Jamaican DJ culture as early as the 1950s. By the 1960s, Jamaican music studios often released the instrumental version of a song as the B-side on a single, which materially embodies phonographic orality: sound recordings understood as potentially incomplete vocabulary elements in a musical conversation.

Cutting and mixing reveals Jamaican music makers' particular orientation toward the institutions that fix music in a recording—a challenging and subversive approach both to the industry that produces recordings and to the legal institutions that recognize recordings as the prime repository of authorship and ownership. The logic behind reuse is a participatory logic, bounded not so much by law or formal authority as it is by community-generated norms. These norms arise from poor Jamaicans' experience, which is where these practices originate. Katherine McKittrick describes how musical elements—"the beats, rhythms, acoustics, notational moods, frequencies that undergird black music—affirm, through cognitive schemas, modes of being human that refuse antiblackness just as they restructure our existing system of knowledge."[6] It is worth examining musical elements in detail, to see how participatory practices restructure systems of knowledge based in a commodified and fixed relationship between people and musical recordings.

Saying Some Things: Monson, Manuel, Marshall, and Wynter

Participatory creative practices are important survival tactics. The foundation of this ability to be participatory is the existence of moments of shared knowledge and familiarity. Their shared nature is what maintains a connection between player and listener, which is true whether that listener is another player or an audience member. This baseline of shared knowledge is especially important for improvisatory or spontaneous interactions. As Ingrid Monson, a scholar of jazz improvisation, has described, the essence of musical meaning arises from collaborative aspects of interaction within improvisatory moments and not from the individualistic solo performance. The act of incorporating known pieces of music or references to them is integral to the ability to be properly heard.[7] Although Monson mainly addresses music through observing instrument players (not dancers or other audience members), the musical examples are replete with references to shared cultural experiences that go beyond professional musicians: whether they reuse another artist's riff or make reference to a commercial jingle, movie, TV theme song, or a nursery rhyme, there is an implied presence of other listeners who also hold and recognize those references.[8] For jazz musicians, this reuse occurs in improvisatory moments where musicians replay the references. The Jamaican popular music tradition functions similarly but incorporates references through the replaying of recordings.

Practitioners of phonographic orality, or more playfully (per Peter Manuel and Wayne Marshall) of "the riddim method," recognize this kind of musical reuse as a virtue rather than a transgression against individual rights.[9] Such participatory musical practices in jazz, as in Jamaican popular music, are "anchored to associative sounds, lyrics, myths, rituals, songs, and experiences—associative because they are familiar waveforms, stories, and tunes that the musician, the listener, the dancer, the audience, come to know jointly."[10]

Such shared cultural knowledge is not homogenously shared across all communities. People whose cultural expression has historically been suppressed or erased have a particular need to make culture out of fragments of culture both passed down and borrowed. This is what makes sharing capable of a "subversive politics" in which "shared stories, communal activities, and collaborative possibilities" require that "one must participate in knowing," as Sylvia Wynter reminds us.[11] If you cannot participate without already knowing the terms of participation, the practice tends to reinforce community relationships—for to really "know" Jamaican popular, music you must get familiar with the musical sounds and Jamaican practices of musical engagement. In the Jamaican context, where colonial legacies have meant that the upper classes regularly look down on those practices (and the lives that inform them), sharing in them can be a kind of collective, cultural intimacy.

Such practices are strategically powerful methods of regeneration and support for people surviving colonial erasure. In addition, many scholars identify them as rooted in ways of engaging with culture that predate colonialism. The Jamaican scholar Annie Paul identifies these practices as vernacular creativity. Much like Patwa itself (the language spoken by most poor Jamaicans and sung by them too), these practices are "native grammars" that are "capable of creating and exploiting entry points into the world economic system."[12] Paul's phrasing could suggest that native grammars facilitate people working within the system rather than against it; however, in the Jamaican context, the system is not so totalizing as to absorb and defang these native grammars; nor are the grammars themselves without an existential challenge to the system's foundational assumptions.

Both the relationship to recorded cultural works and the participatory logic of Jamaican musical authorship reveal how the practices of musical interactivity can, in fact, be resistance to coloniality: working against a system rooted in the erasure, the fragmentation, and the repressive inclusion of Black people and Black communities. In Jamaica, answer tunes subvert and transcend this coloniality.

Answer Tunes: Subverting Commodification with Living Culture

An answer tune's essential characteristic is that it is a response to a previous musical work. Answering is not confined to lyrical content but can happen on the level of a musical reference: a particular song responds to another by reusing musical vocabulary instead of or alongside lyrics. for example, Artist A records a song, consisting of a bass line, drums, guitar, or keyboard parts, the sung melody, and other sounds; the song can be divided into sections, such as verse, chorus, and bridge. The song also consists of lyrics that put forth an opinion or embody a perspective. When Artist B makes an answer tune, the way in which she signals to listeners and Artist A that her song is related to Artist A's song usually involves tying it sonically and textually to Artist A's song. She may reuse the bass line or the entire backing track (the riddim), she may sing her own lyrics on the same melody, she might reuse the chorus's lyrics or melody or repeat/recontextualize fragments of lyrics, but a response requires reusing elements from the previous song to create a dialogue.

The term "answer" suggests a conversation, an interaction between multiple speakers.[13] As a practice, it also implies the presence of listeners beyond the performers, listeners who at least partly share vocabulary with performers—in order that the audience understand a tune as an answer. An answer tune also faces the public and is not directed solely at the tune or performer to which it responds (which could be done by private communication). Producing and performing an answer tune signals the presence of a wider discursive community engaging in the conversation. A true answer tune has to be recognized as an element in a community conversation.

Because music pervades Jamaican daily life in a way that invites participation from the schoolyard to the recording studio,[14] shared cultural references from all aspects of daily life in Jamaican music heighten the flow of interaction and commentary. Shared experiences provide a framework of musical and narrative references that serves to attract an audience's attention. A shared musical vocabulary also develops from these interactive practices—one that artists and audiences use. This vocabulary is not a static resource—it is a way of understanding and interacting with the symbolic world: if a song plays on the radio, it can enter the musical vocabulary of all who hear it, the more so if it circulates widely and repeatedly. Jamaican music making involves contributing to and creating a shared vocabulary of musical elements. This means the music and the elements that make it up (lyrics, bass lines, musical phrases, and figures) circulate independent of the bounds of the recording that copyright recognizes as a protected, fixed work. These elements do not circulate as mini commodities: they are not primarily bought and sold as commodities in their own right but instead are fragmented away from other songs when people recognize their usefulness as communicative elements.

Categories of Answer Tunes

This chapter categorizes several kinds of answer tunes that in practice are not separable; nor do musical practitioners in Jamaica use these categories. I impose this rough taxonomy only strategically to tell a few different kinds of stories about how answer tunes work and how deeply they are embedded in Jamaican popular culture. They reveal different aspects of social relationships—between people, between cultural referents, and between people and cultural referents. This taxonomy is a rough way to categorize the different kinds of conversations, with different political and social implications, that are happening simultaneously in music. However, across these categories, the incentive for artists and audiences to become invested in the conversation contradicts copyright law. The logic of conversation does not require formal permission.

I name two main categories of conversation "textual conversation" and "sonic conversation," with two subcategories in each. In textual conversation, the text and lyrics of different songs are dialogue at the level of words. For example, in a song called "Ring the Alarm," the singer Tenor Saw asserts that one should ring an alarm because his sound system was so powerful it would "kill" a rival sound system: "Ring the alarm, another sound is dying."[15] In response, another singer, Nitty Gritty, recorded a song entitled "False Alarm," warning potential competitors that it is dangerous to overstate one's power when one's sound system is not powerful enough to win a battle. "False alarm, [to] talk about the sound dying"[16] Nitty Gritty's response to Tenor Saw conceptually ties his statement to Tenor Saw's by reusing words and phrasing: this encompasses a textual conversation.

As will be discussed below, some conversations reflect actual relationships or differences of opinion that exist in the world beyond that of rival DJs, sound systems, or producers. These songs engage with the court of public opinion to mobilize audiences in supporting one side or the other in ways that reach beyond the musical moment. Other songs are part of conversations between fictional or archetypal characters, such as a mistress, a landlord, or a judge, and explore questions about love, relationships, politics, law, or economics. The diversity of textual conversations reveals how embedded they are in Jamaican popular culture, especially among the poor, who use popular music engagement to discuss, take sides on, or simply air out social problems, as well as to engage as listeners and dancers celebrating their own experiences and identities through songs that reflect them.

Another layer of conversation is sonic conversation, which occurs at the level of sound itself—when musical elements of different songs (such as a bass line or melody) are shared in such a way as to suggest a relationship between the two songs. One example is the Jamaican artist Elephant Man's recording of "Bless We More" (2009), which reused the melody and music of a U.S. pop tune by Beyoncé, substituting his own lyrics. Elephant Man, by evoking the Beyoncé tune, which most of his listeners would have heard, made his tune a kind of response to Beyoncé's tune through the contrast between his lyrics and hers.

Sonic conversation actually encompasses several musical practices. Riddims (discussed in detail in chapter 1) are musical elements drawn from the instrumental track of a song. They sonically tie together many, sometimes hundreds, of songs in a symbolic relationship. Vocalists also reuse the melodies of other songs, including those from other venues familiar to the audience, such as TV commercials, radio jingles, nursery rhymes, or folk tunes. In addition, sampling, or reusing shorter segments of a song or other audio element, can also evoke a relationship between the sampled work and the work incorporating it.

In general, textual conversation alone would contradict copyright less than sonic conversation. Copyright doesn't restrict the reuse of short words and phrases. But copyright does sometimes restrict the reuse of audio recordings, in whole or in part. In practice, sonic and textual conversations often occur simultaneously: "False Alarm," for example, also reused the melody and riddim of "Ring the Alarm." Quite often the reuse of sounds is what signals to the listening public that a song is an answer, because it makes an audible connection to the song being responded to.[17] Below I examine these different practices in more detail, drawing out their significance in the context of Jamaican musical practice.

Textual Conversation Type 1:
Reflecting a Lived Personal Relationship

In 1962, the year of Jamaican independence, Prince Buster cowrote a song with the teenaged singer Derrick Morgan, called "They Got to Go." This song criticized the corruption he saw in the nascent music industry in Jamaica. Catching the spirit of a rising nationalist consciousness that contrasted "authentic" Jamaicans' moral purity against the corruption of powerful people and institutions in the country, this tune became a hit and made Derrick Morgan a rising star in the Jamaican music scene.

Shortly afterward, Morgan left Buster to work with a rival producer, the Chinese Jamaican Leslie Kong.[18] Buster took umbrage when Morgan and Kong recorded "Housewife's Choice," which allegedly reused part of a tune associated with Prince Buster. (As we will see below, the sense of ownership Buster asserts reflects a local understanding but not necessarily a legal one.) The story has it that Morgan and Kong's reuse was the tipping point for Buster, who then came out with a tune called "Blackhead Chinaman":

You stole my belongings and give to your chiney man
God in heaven knows, he knows that you are wrong
Are you a chinaman, or are you a black man?
It don't need no eyeglass to see that your skin is black
Do you prefer your chineyman to your fellow black man
Speak up friend, it's plain to understan'
It won't be very long, they'll have a change of plan
To use you to use you and use you, then refuse you
Cause you are the first blackhead chineyman
I did not know your foreparents were from Hong Kong
Every man has a right to where he belong
So declare yourself and tell me where you are from.[19]

Buster claims ownership by referring to his "belongings," which he says Derrick Morgan has stolen. No historical account or interview mentions any material theft, so Buster is likely talking about a different kind of property. One account suggests that the theft was actually a solo performed by the saxophonist Headley Bennett on an earlier song, "They Got to Go," which Bennett also performed on a track produced by Kong called "Forward March."[20] If this is the case, Buster is claiming ownership in another person's musical work, which Buster chose to reuse or asked Bennett to reperform. But Buster declares himself the owner and addresses Morgan as the thief. Buster's concept of ownership of musical elements appears to be at the very least confusing—and a copyright-centric analysis, could it be ascertained, would not clarify much. The confusion is compounded by the fact that the reuse of musical elements was extremely common among all the recording studios and among many musicians and did not always trigger such a response. It is unlikely that infringement as defined by law is the reason for Buster's vehement response: the language of theft may be best understood as a metaphor for several kinds of disrespect that Buster felt he was facing.

One source of Buster's outrage arises from the context in which Morgan reuses the element. In 1962, the year of Jamaican independence, Buster had a Jamaican nationalist sensibility—his Voice of the People sound system, including Derrick Morgan, was the first self-consciously Jamaican sound system, playing predominantly Jamaican music rather than covers or tunes brought in from overseas. Buster may have seen Morgan allying himself with the Chinese Jamaican Kong as an insult to Buster's vision of Jamaican nationalism and to a narrower, ethnically based claim to ownership of Jamaica music. Alternatively, Buster may have made use of racist language to dramatize his anger over a more personal situation, or it is possible that rivalry between the studios led to various claims of misuse.

Although he talked of thievery and stealing, Prince Buster did not mobilize the force of law but instead mobilized the force of public opinion. His claims to ownership are complicated by the way that those claims are in themselves a symbolic assertion in the context of a larger conversation. Claiming ownership is a rhetorical device an artist—or anyone—uses to assert his or her position vis-à-vis another person or group. This is not to say that artists expect those claims to be backed up absolutely by law—this is not even the case for real property in Jamaica, where squatting is relatively common (a 2008 estimate was 25 to 33 percent of the population).[21] Ownership is important, but it is a matter of community-defined social claims rather than law.

The dense network of social relationships in music making, made visible through their breach in the "Blackhead Chinaman" affair, functions to constrain behavior, enforce obligations, and otherwise act in the way that the law might, although not necessarily along the same contours. Certain kinds of loyalty are portrayed as expected between artists and studios, and there are also points at which either side would consider separation.

Kong and Morgan answered "Blackhead Chinaman" by recording "Blazing Fire" (which reuses the melody of another Buster-released tune, "Madness," and references "They Got to Go," Buster's first big hit). In "Blazing Fire," Morgan sings,

You say I am a blackhead chiney
but when I go with you I was like a bull in a pen. . . .
Live and let others live, and your days will be much longer![22]

Morgan asserts that working for Buster infringed on his freedom, and he advises Buster not to interfere with his professional and creative choices. In his response, he ignores the race-baiting and reaches for the moral high ground, including biblical-sounding language, a common practice in Jamaica. Saying "when I was with you, I was like a bull in a pen," Morgan suggests that his own sense of freedom, or perhaps his career interests, required that he switch professional allegiances. In a later version of a chorus, also reuses another Prince Buster lyric, saying "time is longer than rope." Both tunes also reuse or refer to musical elements in Prince Buster songs.

The dispute did not end with this interchange but was continued through other songs. Over the ensuing months, each side traded songs and responses back and forth.[23] Each side rallied their own supporters who condemned the other side and defended their own, in conflicts that were enthusiastic enough that the state got involved. In 1960s Jamaica, competition between sound systems was intertwined with political and neighborhood-based violence among the newly armed Jamaican poor, often called "rude boys." Derrick Morgan described how the fans were so heated that the government had to step in: "Prime Minister Shearer had to come in and we had to take pictures in the paper, showing that we are the best of friends, just to cut down on the consequences."[24]

That the outcome of this dispute involved the public, and eventually the state, reveals how the significance of popular music to Jamaicans as a social force goes beyond the strictly artistic; to this day, it is headline news when artists and producers feud. In 2009, Vybez Kartel and Mavado, two luminaries of dancehall, were at the center of an ongoing rivalry that (as in the past) became fodder for violent confrontation between fans. The *Jamaica Gleaner* reported on their public attempt to stand down in their article titled "DJs Mavado, Vybz Kartel Pledge to End Lyrical Feud." The dancehall stars used a meeting with three government ministers at the prime minister's office to announce an end to hostilities, while calling on their supporters to end their hostilities as well.[25] Lived personal relationships in these songs are not only metaphors for social forces; they reveal and embody them. Jamaican popular music is able to affect social order as well as reflect it. This makes it a site of interest for many powerful entities that use musical practices to assert or create a relationship with the public through participatory interchanges within and across musical works.

Jamaican popular music involves different kinds of competitive interactions, one of which has developed into an influential musical institution: the sound clash. At a soundclash, rival sound systems set up near each other and compete for audience attention, both through the selection of songs they play and also the quality and quantity of sound their system is able to produce. DJs play prerecorded tunes, speak into a microphone to introduce the tune, explain its significance, and wittily insult the opposing sound system. Soundclashes have been a key impetus for the production of answer tunes that articulate and heighten this competition. Tunes have often been written and recorded for particular sound systems or soundclashes: these may be either customized versions of already popular tunes or wholly new tunes created for a one-time special event. Any tune that becomes popular in the soundclash is incorporated into the common vocabulary of tunes used in future soundclashes. In soundclashes, as in other interactions, clever reference or reuse of an earlier tune's lyrics or music remains a respected rhetorical move against one's opponent.

The conversation between Tenor Saw and Nitty Gritty quoted above is an archetypal example. The lyrics to Tenor Saw's "Ring the Alarm" begin,

Ring the alarm: another sound is dying, Whoa, hey
Ring the alarm: another sound is dying
Some sound sounds like a big drum pan
Listen: the sound like a champion
Ram the dance in any session
Rock up the woman, rock up the man.[26]

When Tenor Saw talks about "a sound" he is referring to a sound system. The second paragraph's first line uses the word "sound" in two ways: the first to mean sound system, the second as in the verb "to sound like." The first line expresses the theatrical concern for a rival sound system's symbolic death—losing a competition for audience attention with the Tenor Saw–endorsed sound system. The last two lines describe the evidence for his sound's dominance: it makes people crowd tightly into the event ("ram the dance") and makes both women and men dance. A competing sound system could decide how to respond to a rival playing this tune in a soundclash. The well-known answer to "Ring the Alarm" comes from the most direct, rival sound system singer, Nitty Gritty (mentioned above): "False alarm, talk about the sound dying."[27]

Nitty Gritty's reuse of language is all the more powerful because it directly engages Tenor Saw's lyrics. This reuse relies on audiences being familiar with the previous song—while not free riding on the earlier song's popularity, the answer tune uses it as fodder for commentary or interaction. In this case, the reuse goes beyond the lyrics. The identical instrumental track of "Ring the Alarm" also plays underneath Nitty Gritty's vocals, and he sings a nearly identical melody to Tenor Saw. The music provides an added level of interaction and intensity of engagement. Using the same instrumental track demonstrates an artist's attempt to build on or outshine the work of another artist using the same materials. Nitty Gritty recorded this song for a rival studio, on the label run by that studio's owner, Lloyd "King Jammy" James. Neither was the first to use the instrumental track, which had been produced ten years before and was circulating as a semiautonomous musical element—the riddim, an element that will be discussed further below.

Textual Conversation Type 2: Expressing Theoretical, Archetypal, or Fictional Relationships

Other answer tunes engage in more fictionalized disagreements that call on archetypal experiences or issues for the audience. One long-standing musical tradition is for a singer to narrate one side of a romantic relationship and another singer to record a response speaking for another side. Closely read a series of tunes from the 1980s in Jamaica, and you can see how such a musical interaction provides a platform for performers and listeners to raise issues of social importance, including physical violence, the role of police, and the legal system.

Sugar Minott, a popular singer since the 1970s, achieved further fame in 1986 with "What the Hell the Police Can Do?" The song was considered on the cutting edge because a synthesizer produced the backing track; it was an early song to use this new technology rather than recording amplified musical instruments. At the time, the synthesizer gave the song a feeling of currency. However, the song was also notable for expressing a vision of life in the ghetto, with ambivalent relationships to both violence and the police:

Me an my girl was fighting
It happens to be a misunderstanding
I accidentally tump har in she face   [I accidentally thump her in her face]

She run go di police station   [She ran to the police station]
To tell the police fi true.   [To tell the police, it's true]
Gal after me feed an clothe you
Give yu everyting yu have to
    comfort you
Leave the house gone look money fi
    me an' you
When mi come back   [When I come back]
yu gone wid Bwoy Blue   [You've gone with Boy Blue]
Tump yu in yu eye   [I thump you in your eye]
an' it black an' blue   [and it's black and blue]

Run go to di police go tell dem fi true
But what the hell the police can do?[28]

Although the song was a big hit, the Jamaica Broadcasting Corporation declared it "not fit for airplay."[29] The state radio station's censorious response was due to its depiction of casual violence, the word "hell" in its title and chorus, and the protagonist's attitude toward the police. This vision of life was very different from the music being promoted through official channels like Jamaican radio (which at that point still refused to play most Jamaican music if it was associated with the poor). Although songs about romantic disputes were common enough, this song caused controversy among upper-class Jamaicans and those who sought acceptance from them.

Upper-class tastes and a top-down, "civilizing" mission have dominated radio for much of Jamaican musical history. In such an environment, the lives and experiences of poor people were generally not considered fit for airplay, especially if they involved conflict or disrespect for authority.[30] Their exclusion from dominant media has meant that songs on these themes are doubly popular among the poor majority. Even in recent years, when a much broader set of perspectives representing the poor have been evident in Jamaican radio, upper-class Jamaican cultural gatekeepers still strongly critique the baseness of popular culture, and there are regular backlashes and restricting to sort out the "good" from the "bad" popular music. With this critique, upper-class Jamaicans in charge of cultural policy justify restricting poor people's presence on mainstream media platforms while simultaneously giving artists rebellious cachet as voices of the ghetto.

Despite its popularity, not everyone found Sugar's narrator to be sympathetic. Some apparently thought the story needed another side. Another talent, Lady Junie, followed up with a response, "Tell You What the Police Can Do," released on the same label in the same year.

Man, after me wash an cook for you
me press out your shirt make it look bran' new
give you lots of loving that's romantic fi true
when me take a sec you gone with Mary Lou
me puff out mi face, get jealous and a screw[31]
me run go to the police an tell them fi true
but me a go tell you what police can do
me ago tell you what police can do

cuz them will: wine yu up [wind you up] and make you move
   like robot,
wine yu up and make you move like robot!
Box you in the face and kick you inna the gut
grab you in the collar an tear up your shirt
take out them weapon and give you gun-butt![32]

Lady Junie sings over the same riddim and uses the same melody as Sugar Minott to give the woman's side. She adds a new twist—the character of "Mary Lou," with whom she asserts Minott's character is having an affair—and she emphasizes her own efforts to be a good partner who takes care of her man's domestic life. This contrast highlights the beater's unjust behavior. Junie asserts the police's right to intervene in their dispute, including a gleefully violent catalog of acts that she wants the police to visit on her boyfriend. Any listener might have suspected another side to Sugar Minott's story; Lady Junie went a step further, asserting her right to publicly participate in it.

But the story didn't stop with Lady Junie. Another artist, Lovindeer, then already known as a comedy musical performer engaging, in song, with current events, made a smashing entrance from the police officer's point of view. Lovindeer announced himself as "Constable Brown," the illicit lover of the woman beaten by Sugar Minott, who is also the police invoked by both earlier songs:

I am constable Brown, them call me boy blue
I have here a warrant to arrest you
cause you beat up your girl till she black and blue
and ask what the hell the police can do
I come to show what police can do,
I going to show what the police can do
I have a baton—I going to introduce it to your jawbone
box out your teeth give you moan and groan
Make your ears dem ring like a government phone
broke up your nose and bust up your looks
cause you shouldn't call me Babylon boops![33]

"Boops" is a slang term for sugar daddy, and Babylon is Rastafari terminology for police (or other state agents). Lovindeer's character argued he should be taken seriously as an authority, on pain of extreme violence, and explicitly rejects the name "Babylon boops," which implies he is indeed the

woman's wealthy benefactor. Despite the character in the song rejectin
nickname, Lovindeer titled the song "Babylon Boops," applying the
name to himself. Lovindeer's interjection was wildly popular, for its
tion of a new voice to the popular and ongoing story, for the frisson caused
by someone publicly portraying a police officer caught up in this kind of
dispute, and for the publicly disrespectful nickname. Capitalizing on the
buzz, Lovindeer eventually released an entire album called *Government
Boops*, in which he played the comic figure of a corrupt official abusing his
power for the sake of love. Lovindeer's musical interjections wittily convey
the idea that law enforcement is not outside the disputes that they may be
called on to settle.

These songs and their interactions reveal a great deal about poor urban
Jamaicans' attitudes and experiences, and they also reveal the democratic
value of interacting musically in this way. Taken together, the songs form a
much richer conversation, in which more participants claim a public hearing than might be possible if interactivity were limited—for example, if artists were forced to comply with copyright's requirements and get permission
for reusing such musical elements as melodies and backing tracks.[34]

Reusing sounds and references also serves an emotional purpose for artists who want to connect to audiences. For a listener, the unexpected reap-
pearance of a familiar memory creates a shock of recognition or delight.
Both emotions are of paramount importance in building positive interactions between audiences and artists as well as the DJs who play songs that
trigger these emotions. As the above examples suggest, Jamaican music is
full of such moments that delight, surprise, and entertain. In Jamaica, these
moments occur most often through the song's performance on the radio and
at dances.[35] In these moments a vocalist (prerecorded or live) rallies a living audience with words and references and calls on cultural resources
the audience is already familiar with. Reusing musical elements plays an
important role in tying various musical pieces together. Lady Junie reused
Minott's exact words, in several places of his song, to place herself in immediate conceptual proximity to him, inhabiting the story of his earlier
song. An added layer of significance comes from the fact that she is contradicting him using his own words. Repetition here is criticism and resistance, a way of throwing his words back in his face (and the faces of those
who would subscribe to his point of view). In Lovindeer's case, repetition
of words is an explicit parody for comedic effect.

Conversation doesn't have to be oppositional; it can also be celebratory.
It can be a compliment to a vocalist's lyrical skill when someone reuses

lyrics in a new song. The up-and-coming Jamaican vocalist SN described to me how a catchphrase she created for a song became so popular that other vocalists incorporated it into their lyrics: "That song did really really well. In fact, [my song] became an anthem in dancehall; up to this day people are still using that line!" SN expressed happiness for the enhancement to her reputation that comes from people seeing her lyrics as good enough to be incorporated into a living musical tradition. This inviting and collaborative social structure relies on shared knowledge acquired and generated especially among the Jamaican poor. Thus, it allows much more space for poor people's authority and knowledge as interlocutors in this shared conversation and places them as the arbiters of inclusion.

Non-text-based musical elements are also elements in this shared tradition: they create an audible proximity or linkage between songs. This put songs into sonic conversation, within or instead of conversation based in lyrics.

Sonic Conversation Type 1: Riddims

In chapter 1, I discussed riddims' origins in the beginning of Jamaican recording studios and pressing plants. Some of those first riddims remain popular today, incorporated into a living Jamaican tradition.[36] Riddims, in the predigital era, were encoded onto vinyl records to be circulated. This makes it possible to continue practices of oral culture while using written recorded media. Oral cultures solve the problem of retaining and retrieving complicated ideas or creations by framing them in memorable patterns that can be repeated. Ideas "come into being in heavily rhythmic, balanced patterns, in repetitions or antitheses, in alliterations and assonances, in epithetic and other formulary expressions."[37] This description applies well to linguistic and sonic practices that dominate Jamaican popular music, especially to the riddim. While not sung, it is a repeated musical pattern that facilitates learning and memory for the purposes of interaction by singers, DJs, and dancers. The musical changes within a particular riddim cycle pass, in an order that quickly becomes familiar, and the whole riddim is repeated across multiple songs, which means they become engrained in the memory as one hears or dances to a song. It is this practice of phonographic orality[38] in Jamaica that makes musical recordings not only products to be consumed or collected but also "raw material in a complex process of creative improvisation in which new texts are continually being produced and reproduced, and new meanings wrung from them."[39] As well, riddims gain in value through reuse. The sheer familiarity of a popular riddim (which can have hundreds of versions) can be a source of meaning. The Stalag riddim, originally recorded in 1974 as an instrumental piece of music, has at least 279 different versions, including the aforementioned "False Alarm" and "Ring the Alarm."[40] When a singer decides to sing over the Stalag riddim, they are asserting their importance to a widely known musical tradition. Many foreign artists attempting to break into dancehall or assert their importance to their own dancehall scenes will "jump on" classic riddims to assert themselves as part of that tradition.

Engaging musically with long-standing riddims can also be a way of collapsing and complicating the linear time marked out by a song's performance. A riddim can reach back a generation or more, evoking cultural associations that have accrued over time, based in its moment of origin or in its most salient use. In performance, DJs "run the riddim"—play a series of vocals on the same riddim, one after the other, sometimes including an instrumental for vocalists to sing over in live performance. When DJs relied on vinyl, this practice was extended to anyone who had access to a record player and record that had an instrumental. By the 1970s, Jamaicans were releasing records with just the riddim on one side, enabling anyone with the record to sing over it and increase the options for running a riddim. Running the riddim was not seen as lack of creativity but a way of threading a musical narrative together—still exercising track selection through the order of which version to play next and engaging with the shared memory of riddims reaching across time and within a community of knowledge.

The opening anecdote of this book describes a 2009 dancehall competition judge criticizing a singer's choice of riddim, saying he wished the singer had used "a more original riddim, one that has been tested in the marketplace already." This definition reflects how even people embedded in the industry can discuss originality as a quality that is conferred by the public, and it is conferred through familiarity rather than unfamiliarity. Riddim traditions emphasize the way Jamaican popular music relies on shared knowledge as a foundation for creativity.

Riddims reinforce shared cultural competency through the repeated experience of hearing, identifying, and anticipating musical elements. Repeating these references contributes to a shared sense of identity, helping to build a sense of common culture.[41] Alongside the symbolic or lyrical references to shared experience, riddims permit and embody coordinated but flexible interactive moments among participants in the dance. For marginalized social groups who are denied access to other kinds of public representation, these shared physical and social experiences are vital to building a sense of community. Denied access to other kinds of representation, they nevertheless build cultural authority on other terms. In the Jamaican context, the state's political and economic authority is incomplete, unable to incorporate or support everyone, and its orientation is fundamentally hostile to the presence of poor people in any but subservient roles. The way Jamaican music has asserted cultural authority has allowed the poor not only to define themselves but also to connect with a global audience.

Riddims are also an early example of how recording techniques made it possible to separate a single song into parts and to reuse particular parts. While initially a riddim was pressed onto the B-side of a record (often called a "version"), where the song with lyrics would be the A-side, that record made the riddim in its entirety available to anyone else who wished to use it. Vocalists would often treat lyrics the same way—selecting or quoting lyrics (and melodies) from each other's songs (or from jingles, folk songs, and the like). In later years, the ability to reuse recordings got more granular as recording technology developed. Producers especially had access to more than a single instrumental track and could select or engage with individual tracks or could select sections of songs to reuse. This practice of sampling— the ability to incorporate selections of prerecorded sound into a new song— has been increasingly discussed in the past twenty years. But to a great extent, the practice can be traced to the use of riddims and musical conversation. Producers use samples (as we will see below) as elements of conversation between songs and sonic elements.

Sonic Conversation Type 2: Remixes and Cover Songs

A producer makes a remix by altering an existing song, adding or subtracting such elements as bass lines, vocals, instruments, or drum patterns. In contrast, in a cover song, an artist and instrumentalist replay an already existing song (using their own instruments to replay the instrumental parts) and sing the original lyrics without adding or diverging from the song's structure or content (although there are often divergences in style of singing and playing). Cover songs are not understood as reusing recordings, while remixes usually do use recordings from the song to be remixed. This fact is at the basis of copyright law's distinction between their legality—a cover song does not require permission to be performed and, if recorded, only requires a fixed payment (rather than a negotiation with a copyright owner). Reusing the recording itself requires copyright owners' permission. In Jamaican practice, many people sing cover songs over the riddim used by song they are covering, because these instrumental tracks are readily available. Especially with the advent of electronically generated music, it is not always possible to sonically distinguish a reused riddim from a synthesized replay. Although U.S. and Jamaican copyright law distinguish starkly between cover songs' and remixes' legality, creative practices in Jamaican popular music do not draw such a clear line. Both remixes and covers are interactive musical practices: interactive not only for the singer and the remixer but for the audience, for whom hearing the remix or cover engages their intellectual and physical knowledge of the previous song. A musical interactions' social and cultural meanings shape the audience response.

In the following discussion of a relatively popular example of musical interplay from the late 2000s, we see the multilayered interactivity of musical conversation that involves remixing, covering, riddims, and sampling.

The original tune, by a U.S. artist named Mims, is called "This Is Why I'm Hot." It was a hit in the United States (reaching the *Billboard* charts) and popular in Jamaica, ubiquitous when I was there in 2007. The Jamaican remix, called the "Blackout Remix," incorporates multiple new singers and samples of Jamaican music into the Mims tune while still retaining much of its original structure. Most of Mims's lyrics except for the chorus were removed, and the Jamaican singers Junior Reid and Baby Cham sing instead.

In table 1, I have divided the song into "parts," where each represents a musical moment in the song, in order of its appearance; each part is a different length of time. The division is conceptual, more than temporal; each part has a different set of meanings associated with it as a new musical element is introduced. For reasons of space, I do not transcribe all lyrics in parts 5 and 6, only identifying them as Jamaican vocalists. The terms "JA" and "US" in the Musical and Lyrical Significance columns signify that the sound is evoking a reference to Jamaica or to the United States. For example, Mims's vocals evoke the United States through his identifiable voice and accent and known identity as a U.S. pop rapper while Junior Reid's vocals evoke Jamaica due to his voice and use of Patwa, as well as his known identity as a Jamaican reggae star. Following the table is an extended discussion of each part and its significance.

The song begins with the musical introduction and Mims's opening line. This is interrupted, in part 2, by the sound of an airhorn, a common sonic

TABLE 1 "This Is Why I'm Hot (Blackout Remix)," the first 1:65, Featuring Lyrics from Mims

	Music	Musical Significance	Lyrics	Lyrical Significance
Part 1: 0:00–0:25	Minimal synthesized melodic line in minor key	US: signifying US content to most listeners Intro to hip-hop track, already famous	Mims: "This is why I'm hot"	US: hip-hop vocalist, boasting about his fame
Part 2: 0:25–0:44	Introduced by siren, continuing the same as the Mims tune, same melody with drums and bass	JA: signifying Jamaican content to most listeners Siren is a common soundclash tool, evoking live performance in a Jamaican setting US: signifying US content to most listeners	Junior Reid: "Tu-tu-tweng!" Resings Mims's lyrics with a slight change: "This is why we hot"	JA: Reid himself, artist signature phrase; "we" suggests a collective answer, contrasting Mims's individualism
Part 3: 0:45–0:49	Instrumental intro for "You Don't Love Me"	JA: signifying Jamaican content to most listeners A 1974 Jamaican hit still popular today, likely a cover of a U.S. tune from the 1960s (which most listeners wouldn't know)	No lyrics	n/a

Part 4: 0:50–1:02	Return of Mims's backing music (synthesizers, drums, and bass)	US: signifying US content to most listeners	Junior Reid: "This is why we hot, this is why we ho-o-ot"	JA: translating U.S. lyrics into Patwa, showcasing vocal virtuosity, building suspense
Part 5: 1:03–1:06	One bar switches to horn playing a simple solo line	JA: signifying Jamaican content to most listeners Stalag riddim, popular in Jamaica from 1974 to the present	Junior Reid continues	JA: singing
Part 6: 1:06–1:65	Mims backing music continues	US: signifying US content to most listeners	Junior Reid 1:26 Mims and Junior Reid, 1:51 Baby Cham (JA), another Jamaican vocalist	JA, US/JA, then JA: Reid including the line "the whole America know this is why we hot"; Reid and Mims overlapping, "This is why I'm/we hot"; Baby Cham reuses lyrics from one of his big radio hits, non-Patwa but Jamaican accent; combining a reference familiar to Jamaican music fans with a U.S. pop hit

Source: Mims, "This Is Why I'm Hot" (Los Angeles: Capitol Records, 2007), and Mims, Cham, and Junior Reid, "This Is Why I'm Hot (Blackout Remix)" (Los Angeles, CA: Capitol Records, 2007).

punctuation in Jamaican music, familiar from any live experience in a street dance. Junior Reid then marks his vocal entrance by interjecting the phrase "tu-tu-tweng," which is a catchphrase he has sung in many previous songs. This catchphrase identifies him to the knowledgeable Jamaican listener, without him saying his name. Then Reid recasts Mims's main line into a simultaneously individual and collective statement of Jamaican greatness, by saying, "This is why we hot." The use of Patwa grammar ("we hot" instead of "we are hot") also evokes a Jamaican speaker. Many of Reid's turns of phrase explicitly reference both local and international stardom and demonstrate his vocal ability as a singer, which contrasts with Mims's American hip-hop vocal style.

Part 3 is introduced with a sample—a few seconds taken from the musical introduction to a popular and historic song in Jamaica and abroad: "You Don't Love Me (No No No)." Even as the song's actual origins are likely American (although this is contested), Jamaicans have such respect and long-term familiarity for this popular and famous tune that it constitutes Jamaican musical history and is likely to be understood by most listeners as a Jamaican reference.[42] The musical sample does not include lyrics: the reference is purely musical but instantly identifiable to anyone familiar with the tune. Contemporary listeners can identify the "Blackout Remix" as having inserted a classic Jamaican reference into a current pop song.

In part 4, Reid's vocals return, continuing to layer Jamaicanized Mims lyrics in his own vocal style, followed by part 5, when another classic Jamaican instrumental is inserted into the song, the Stalag riddim, discussed above. The overall blending of Jamaican with foreign materials, in both cases familiar tunes, cannot be understood only as piggybacking onto an already famous song—although that is one dynamic in play. Symbolically, both "No No No" and the Stalag riddim have been wildly popular in Jamaica and in the reggae and pop music scene internationally. Especially because the samples are musical rather than involving lyrics, they become stand-ins for a particular type of song—the Jamaican hit that went worldwide and influenced the pop world. They assert local history and the prowess and popularity of Jamaican music as a globally popular force that has withstood the test of time. The 2009 dance floor experience of the "Blackout Remix" demonstrates the positive excitement Jamaican audiences experienced when hearing Jamaican sounds interjected into a U.S. pop hit.

In part 6 a new vocalist enters: Baby Cham, who raps lyrics from another song of his, which was currently popular at the time the remix was released and familiar to a Jamaican audience. His vocal style has a Jamaican accent but is not Patwa, and his style here is closer to that of American-style rapping, with phrases like "ballin' in the VIP booth" that use U.S.-style cultural references. This brings the song into the current era and demonstrates his prowess at American-style rapping.

The audience response suggests multiple readings, ranging from anti-imperialist to simply celebratory. To see how people understand this as a Jamaican intervention into a narrative of Jamaican-U.S. cultural relations, the anti-imperialist reading starts with the common knowledge that the United States towers economically and culturally over Jamaica. Jamaicans are intensely aware of their position as a small nation with a history of economic and cultural domination by neighboring powers like the United States. Many Jamaicans migrate temporarily or permanently to the United States to work, sending money back to their families.[43] Jamaicans circulate through the United States while American music inundates Jamaica on all major media channels (partly as an aspect of American global media dominance). Jamaicans have expressed concerns over cultural imperialism and the survival of Jamaican culture in venues from government studies to the popular press—as early as Prince Buster's desire to "push out that American thing" and concerns from Jamaican pundits that, for example, "we have replaced British colonialist mentality with American cultural imperialism. . . . Our young people . . . know more about American culture than their own—and they are proud of that."[44] Within the community of Jamaican musical practitioners among the urban poor, this concern is exacerbated by Jamaican elites' continuing hostility to local music. In that context, reworking U.S. pop tunes provides the chance to insert distinctly Jamaican voices into a global conversation. As well, people may simply be excited to hear their favorite local star alongside a U.S. one. But in either case, the delight in asserting Jamaican culture's importance on local and global stages goes beyond a quest for market dominance.

Market forces do matter, especially because the U.S. music market (including Jamaican expatriates and their descendants) dwarfs Jamaica's. Interactions with U.S. music bring Jamaican voices closer to U.S. ears, in ways that might translate into overseas fame. However, rather than connecting with a U.S. or global pop audience by erasing intensely local markers of Jamaican culture, such as Patwa (even though Patwa is not comprehensible to mainstream non-Jamaican audiences), the remix layers and intertwines Patwa with American-centric pop and hip-hop references. This both highlights the dramatic audible difference in vocal styles and shows points of sonic connection for a listener. In this way, these kinds of musical engagements are a negotiation between different audiences, over the terms by which a Jamaican artist can be comprehended. Unlike other crossover successes (like Shaggy) who eschewed Patwa completely, these artists present both languages interacting.

The use of historic riddims emphasizes both the long history of Jamaican music and its continuing influence. Both riddims were hits in Jamaica and permeate global pop music. Stalag, with at least 279 versions recorded to date, is one of the most commonly used riddims. "No No No" (or "You Don't Love Me") reflects how Jamaican phonographic orality redraws musical origins, through the Jamaican methods of musical engagement. As mentioned above, the tune released in Jamaica by Dawn Penn as "No No No (You Don't Love Me)" was likely a reinterpretation of a 1960s tune by U.S.-based Willie Cobb. Penn's song was a massive hit inside Jamaica and a riddim that has circulated globally since then, completely eclipsing Cobb's song (which many say is drawing on an earlier Bo Diddley number). The riddim and samples of it have appeared as far away as Poland, in the Polish rapper DonGURALesko's song "Pamiętaj," and have also recirculated through U.S. and Caribbean pop, more recently covered by the Barbadian/ U.S. pop star Rihanna in conjunction with the Jamaican dancehall vocalist Vybez Kartel. The circulation of this riddim, continually updating into new genres and styles, from rhythm and blues to reggae to dancehall, reflects the "routes and roots" identified by Paul Gilroy as part of a Black Atlantic tradition with "histories of borrowing, displacement, transformation and continual reinscription."[45] Russell Potter describes how the music of the Black Atlantic "reach[es] back to draw from African melodic and rhythmic roots, even as it is shaped by its own transatlantic routes of transmission," and in the development of genres: "American R&B travelled to Jamaica and was reborn as Ska, which in turn gave rise to rock steady, reggae, dancehall."[46] Repetition, imitation, fragmentation, and reconstitution are all important aspects of maintaining these routes and roots.

Circulating Decolonial Music Practices

The rise of new media and social media and the spread of digital technology have both revealed and intensified the practices that serve diasporic communities like that of Jamaicans. In the comments section of a Caribbean music group, Jamaican music fans discussed the Lovindeer tune and, twenty-five years after its appearance, revealed their enjoyment in interaction and reenactment. One commenter shared: "I used to have Babylon

Boops on vinyl. Ah used to perform dat tune in meh living room all de time when ah was small."[47] And on a Caribbean music Facebook discussion a fan reminisced: "I remember dem Lovindeer vibes in class boy, we used to be reenacting the intro to Babylon boops and all!"[48] These quotes online echo the statements of many artists in which reenactment and imitation of popular tunes and current events play an important role in how people enjoy and make meaning from music. Some reenactments expand or spill over into new recorded works, as with Lady Junie and Lovindeer, while others simply enter public consciousness and debate and become part of shared memories and stories.

Participation in the shared memories is structured but not by legal requirements of permission and license. Instead, social forces shape the global circulation of Jamaican popular music and popular culture. For example, note the Patwa-inflected spellings in the above commentary. In my online searches for discussions of "Babylon Boops" and Lovindeer, Patwa was extremely common, as in Lovindeer's lyrics across his discography and performance. His popularity as a comedian and singer is centered on audiences who share in his interests and understand his language. In contrast to Jamaican mass media platforms, where the poor majority continually struggle for self-expression and representation, Jamaican popular music has continually centered those who could play by the cultural rules established among the poor, relying on shared knowledge to recognize the riddims and speak the same language.

These cultural boundaries for musical reuse and reinterpretation still cross time and space but not randomly or indiscriminately. These crossings assert diasporic cultural boundaries and flows. Gilroy has said that the music of the Black Atlantic offers (among other things) "an analogy for comprehending the lines of affiliation and association which take the idea of the diaspora beyond its symbolic status as the fragmentary opposite of some imputed racial essence."[49] In fact, this musical circulation goes beyond an analogy; it embodies, reflects, and animates diaspora. In some cases, it even permeates linguistic boundaries: "Babylon Boops," in fact, cycled out of Jamaican Patwa and into the Spanish language via the Panamanian reggaeton scene, where the song itself and Spanish interpretations of it flourished. Here, too, the song circulated in scenes and genres, such as reggaeton, that were not seen as respectable by the upper classes in Panama and were associated with a poor and Black underclass, with the participation and influence of Jamaicans, Jamaican Panamanians, and Afro-Panamanians. The song's content and style also appealed to a similar dynamic of poor people at odds with dominant authority; "Babylon Boops" inspired a song ("D.E.N.I.") on the same theme: poking fun at police as supposed authority figures caught up in the same domestic dramas as everyone else.[50]

Jamaican popular music practices, at home and abroad, continually work to center poor people's voices. Foreign artists attempting to break into Jamaican audiences, or at least seeking validation from them, must properly engage with musical elements that are already circulating. For example, foreign artists may sing over riddims that are recognized as classics, which can get them included in the pantheon of participation in those riddims— or simply capitalize on their familiarity. It is less common for foreign vocalists' versions to become popular within Jamaica and usually requires close replication of Jamaican musical and vocal styles and often closeness to Jamaica; for example, Gentleman, a German reggae singer, is a white European but is nearly indistinguishable in voice and demeanor from a Jamaican reggae vocalist. Vocal and to some extent bodily performances are the most difficult avenues for non-Jamaicans demonstrating commitment or connection to Jamaican musical tradition. In contrast, Jamaican riddims circulate as building blocks for many musical practitioners outside Jamaica: vocalists, DJs, and producers.[51] As well, producers outside Jamaica also create riddims to enter into the flow of Jamaican-centric and Jamaican diasporic music. In fact, Jamaicans outside of Jamaica can have trouble getting their music respected in Jamaica, even as they may be central to expatriate and multigenerational diasporic musical scenes abroad.

In contrast, Jamaican artists often answer or otherwise engage with pop tunes that originate overseas. This was true for the "Blackout Remix" or more recently when the Jamaican artist Busy Signal reused the melody and instrumental of "Royals" from the New Zealand pop singer Lorde, playfully flipping its antibling anthem to a celebration of hustlers making money.[52] Even while affirming a distinctly (petty) capitalist approach, Busy Signal's practice of engagement also subverts an easy understanding of property rights that institutions like copyright law seek to pin down. The pleasure of hearing the cover both relies on and subverts the original song's authority.

This playful and pleasurably subversive method of violating copyright is increasingly vulnerable to technological and legal interference. This has implications for Jamaican cultural intimacy and autonomy—since daily life, from living rooms to classrooms, is increasingly intertwined with networked technology. In fact, YouTube, mobile phones that record and broadcast video and audio, and other networked devices play an important part in Jamaicans' interactions with each other and with the world, incorporating practices of remixing, covering, reinterpretation, and sampling in a wide range of media artifacts. Searching for a popular Jamaican song online brings up hundreds of homemade videos using it as part of a broader conversation, as background music for an animated skit or meme. Such reuse plays an important role in Jamaica's widespread transnational community, whose members socialize and reaffirm a diasporic Jamaican identity online. Although reenactments and interactions occur in a context many have assumed to be outside the music industry (such as living rooms), nowadays people might find their social practices restricted, or even their access to digital media platforms restricted, if copyright law were strictly enforced on these platforms. And increasingly the platforms attempt to include that enforcement capability.

Jamaican musical practitioners' rerooting of originality outside of the Western intellectual property tradition, itself rooted in modern Western art music traditions,[53] illustrates how the underlying assumptions about the best way to make music are different in Jamaica, even when Jamaicans use the same language as American or English artists. I also observed the concept used in other ways—among some reggae musicians, I heard Rastafarians say "original" in a way that seemed to refer to a connection to a primary, (pan)African source of creativity, one that was tied to pan-African belief in shared knowledge and traditions. The term "original" is unchanged, but its meaning is used to reframe our relationship to the past and present.[54] Claiming originality can be part of a broader goal, to connect with a shared identity.

These Jamaican modes of engagement with such a foundational concept of seemingly sovereign ownership—originality—suggest that Jamaican practices facilitate what Wynter calls the "development and legitimation of new modes of social kinship relations, reciprocal exchanges that do not replicate colonial family figurations or individualist models."[55] The widespread appeal and prevalence of answer tunes, riddims, and other kinds of phonographic orality demonstrate Jamaican popular music's internal logics and affirm rights to participate, to respond, and to critique cultural works and cultural forces within and outside Jamaica.

The Value(s) of Conversation

The elements of interactivity that foster creativity in Jamaican musical practice arise out of a playful approach with deep roots: a flexible, contingent, often spontaneous creativity that also draws on and reinforces a shared history. In the U.S. context, scholars of popular culture have argued for popular culture's value "both [as] a resource and a playing field for the exercise of democratic culture and civic association."[56] In this light, "the process of bonding and community building, and reflection on that bonding, that is implied in partaking of the text-related practices of reading, consuming, celebrating, and criticizing"[57] is foundational to a sense of community. In contrast to that, copyright law has tended to privatize culture. The legal scholar Shubha Ghosh characterizes privatizing in this context as deorienting social interaction away "from the centrality of the political and civic spheres to the centrality of the market and individual experience."[58] Ghosh is concerned about the harm done to communities when they are not welcomed as part of civic and political engagement, but in Jamaica, the civic and political spheres have never been especially open to poor Jamaicans. When poor Jamaicans do participate in a public sphere, that participation has been as much along lines of conscious rudeness or disruption as it has been through claiming citizenship on compromised, colonial terms.

This regular exclusion is why it matters that Jamaican popular music centers on those excluded from the centers of power. Rather than being foundational to a supposedly democratic state, Jamaican musical practices destabilize the state's ongoing colonial orientations and reinforce associations that, like oral traditions themselves, are rooted in precolonial or anticolonial social relations, including those based in lingering or rejuvenated African traditions. In this light, rather than citizenship in the legal sense, Jamaican popular music is a struggle to claim a kind of sovereignty that goes beyond the definitions of legal statehood or citizenship.

In Jamaica, the collective social experience of a song marks a kind of ownership. Similar to how a jazz musician is sometimes said to own a song they did not write through playing a vibrant and creative cover version of it, Jamaican musical practitioners appear to feel ownership of music at least partly through the depth and skill of their engagement with it, whether or not they actually penned the lyrics or composed the melody.

Answer tunes on first glance may not appear to challenge assumptions about authorship and creativity, since many appear to be a unitary work with a single voice as the author.[59] But in many cases, the closer one gets to identifying an author, the more the story of creativity becomes contested. It is not clear that artists mean by ownership exactly what the law means by ownership, which can lead to claims over tunes that copyright law might not recognize their rights to. The song "You Don't Love Me" performed by the Jamaican singer Penn is one example. In a recent interview, Penn tells a creation story of when she was invited by "Sir Coxsone" Dodd to sing for him at Studio One in 1967:

> You Don't Love Me (No No No) was our first recording and I remember standing next to Jackie Mittoo, the keyboard player from the Skatalites, following his chords as I sang about lost love. In church, we used to sing this old gospel thing, "Yes, yes, yes, Jesus loves me", so I sang, "No, no, no." People said: "It's too negative. It'll never sell." But it was a big hit in Jamaica. I made more records, but never saw any money for them, and in 1970 left Jamaica. . . . After 17 years, I came back to Jamaica and found the island alive with dancehall. I was asked to rerecord the song for Studio One's 35th anniversary. They made it a bit more dancehall, then Atlantic picked it up and it became a global smash. The moment that happened, eight different people claimed they wrote it. Eventually, it was decided that some of my lyrics were similar to Willie Cobbs' 1961 blues song You Don't Love Me, which itself was similar to Bo Diddley's 1955 track She's Fine, She's Mine.[60]

Penn situates herself as the creator, in a way that is fairly compatible with individualistic narratives of creativity; for example, she describes consciously crafting her lyrics to be different from another song. She describes the familiar situation whereby the song's circulation within Jamaica does not appear to generate much money for her, and it is not until a foreign record label picks it up that it becomes a global smash. However, one thing missing from the story is the riddim tradition: the instrumental for the song had been circulating within Jamaica and beyond during those seventeen years, building up reputation and familiarity among audiences. This was the popular energy Penn could capitalize on when she jumped back on the riddim in 1987. Without that energy, generated by DJs, other producers, and vocalists reusing the riddim, and audience response, the song would not have been valuable. So who is entitled to profit? When listening to Willie Cobb's 1961 song, it is hard not to hear Penn's version as a cover or reinterpretation—they are extremely similar. Although it is possible for people to independently create nearly identical works, it is also possible that Penn heard the song without taking note of it, in the six years before she stepped into Studio One. Cobb or the copyright owner of that recording could potentially sue her for this if that were the case, as it is possible to unconsciously infringe a copyrighted work.[61]

The problem is, claiming authorship is important in multiple ways, and the presence of royalties overdetermines authorship's importance. Unlike songs that have not yet been released to the public, there is no uncertainty about the value of "You Don't Love Me," which raises the stakes for identifying an authors. Dynamics like this make questions of authorship and ownership extremely difficult to settle, and multiple origin stories abound for many highly valuable musical recordings. It is common in Jamaican music for many Jamaican artists to claim ownership of some works and regularly reuse the work of others. It is unlikely they would apply the criteria of copyright equally to others' practices and to their own. It also unlikely they would apply the same rules of ownership and permission to different kinds of people, local and foreign, poor and rich. When Jamaican popular music practitioners differentiate between various rights of ownership and authorship, they ground that in a set of values articulated in the street dance, centering the urban poor as actors and creators on their own terms.

Jamaican audiences tend to see "You Don't Love Me" as a Jamaican song. This is to some extent independent of its specific origins. Jamaicans feel a song is truly Jamaican because of its importance to Jamaican musical history, regardless of whether it is legally owned or authored by Jamaicans. Vernacularizing the basis of ownership contradicts the formal legal definition.

Answer tunes have a function that confounds an individualistic notion of creativity. Their interrelationship undermines assumed boundaries that focus on a particular recording as a fixed object whose meaning resides primarily within its own borders. In answer tunes, an interactive dynamic between creative voices is foregrounded. Entry into the conversation is possible at many points, but the popularity and circulation of each engagement is dependent on a community's vetting of the new interlocutor, on grounds that are defined by that community.

Critical copyright law scholars (a growing movement) also make the case for recognizing the value of alternative social practices in relation to creative works in supposedly fixed form: some suggest that interactive practices like those involved in answer tunes can spur creativity (the constitutional justification of U.S. copyright law) by preventing "established ways of seeing, hearing, and thinking the world from becoming calcified."[62] The Jamaican experience highlights how calcification in this context is not simply an unwanted rigidity where there should be movement but also a freezing of social relationships defined by colonial power. These relationships are rooted in a system where Black people, as well as their cultural expressions, were defined as things. In that context, the incompleteness and flexibility of music and the social interactions that structure its existence reflect life in the face of objectification. For Jamaicans, like all descendants of enslaved Africans, the market has been the site of dehumanization and suffering, and even now is a place many are only conditionally present in, or for whom presence is contingent on redefinition to fit the terms of inclusion. In light of repressive inclusion, marginality is not always a disadvantage—by participating in marginal or gray markets, Jamaicans, especially poor Jamaicans, are not required to make themselves legible to the state or respectable according to the upper classes' terms.

Phanuel Antwi has suggested that a key value in another Jamaican form of cultural expression, dub poetry, is that "dub poetry does not commodify our modes of listening, in the sense that dub sounds and their textual-visual connotations are not separated; what we see when we hear is profoundly shaped by not just personal but also incomplete collective histories."[63] Answers and riddims embody this characteristic in a uniquely material way through their continual reincorporation of fragments and references of familiar and historic audio recordings. While decommodifying musical recordings does not mean they are taken out of market circulation entirely or that money and capitalism play no role, the dynamics of phonographic orality reveal how material objects like recordings can be deobjectified and reincorporated into a living cultural tradition.

If musical practice can be an exercise of sovereignty, it is not clear that all musical practices function in this way. We ought to think carefully about the preconditions for that exercise. Not only do musical practitioners require physical spaces in which to associate themselves and their performances; they need the freedom to associate lyrics and sonic references with each other and with different peoples. The legal scholar Julie Cohen uses a metaphor from physics, "degrees of freedom," through which we can evaluate institutions in light of "the extent to which they permit purposive creative experimentation, but also the extent to which they enable serendipitous access to cultural resources and facilitate unexpected juxtapositions of those resources."[64] Cohen suggests that too much regulation or regularization can stifle important components of creativity that are not necessarily planned. This is certainly true, but the Jamaican context also reminds us that the absence of the legal regularization of creative practices does not mean that everything not legalized is spontaneous; it also means that there can be another order, developed by *community, not law.* "Serendipity and unexpectedness" does not describe the practices by which cultural resources are incorporated into a tradition—the practice of including, as a riddim, sample, or reference, relies on traditions rooted in the survival of colonized

people. Degrees of freedom takes on a new meaning in the history of en-
slavement and erasure that Jamaica's urban poor have experienced. Rather
than simply being leeway written into law, colonized people need protection from the law or being outside its view. Exilic spaces for creativity, where
state actors and upper classes are not in authority, are necessary to maintain these cultural traditions. To have sufficient degrees of freedom, marginalized people need the ability to control physical space and discursive
space outside of law, in which to play.

Why outside of law?
Why not refocus the law to support/foster
community-driven creativity?

Conclusion

New Visions from Old Traditions: Autonomy from the Commons

The imprint of colonialism on the world, especially on nations founded within and after the colonial project, continues to shape human activities. In Western law, the person, understood as an individual, is the fundamental actor in the ability to make claims recognized by the legal system. But the category of person itself is structured by race. As the anthropologist Deborah Thomas reminds us, the categories of personhood available as a basis for making claims from law are rooted in "a sovereign violence—grounded in the plantation—which works through racialized categories of personhood."[1] The historical fact of colonial violence challenges any assumptions we might have about the value of being recognized as a member of a system still shaped by that initial violence. For people whose bodies and cultural practices are still recognized by a colonial system as objects of control and exploitation, legal recognition holds ambiguous appeal. In this context, it makes sense for people to avoid using legal systems, claims, or terminology because they recognize the dangers of participating in a "hegemony of juridical resolution, itself grounded in the violence of law."[2]

At the same time, the plantation-economy history of Jamaica left space for a set of claims not available, for example, in the colonial metropole of England or the settler colony of Canada. Black Jamaicans' numerical dominance with respect to white colonizers gave them certain claims on everyday life based on the extent to which they could live a little out of sight from the colonial structure. The relative weakness of Jamaica's postindependence state, still largely organized on colonial lines but without material support from England, left more room for alternative social structures. This is one reason why the Jamaican state has at times recognized rights on the basis of custom and tradition absent or even in contradiction to the letter of the law. In fact, this is true in relation to land as well as creative works. When I was in Jamaica in 2011, I observed a new highway being built and noticed that when the government added paved driveways to homes along that highway, they did not discriminate against homes occupied (or in some cases hand built) by squatters on land they did not legally own. Long-standing use of resources has, in Jamaica, sometimes enabled people to claim a degree of membership in society.[3] Such customary rights are not defined by the state but instead are validated by community recognition. Recall how, at the beginning of this book, Skatta reclaimed the concept of original when he told a singer, "I wish you'd used a more original riddim, one already popular." As this famous producer publicly judged a performer's skill and choice of music, he did not see the descriptor "original" as rooted in the Western legal tradition of individual, independent creation. Instead, he negatively evaluated the performer's choice to write his own music—"I can tell he wrote that himself," he said in a critical tone, shaking his head—rather than to reuse something Jamaican audiences had already enjoyed.

When value comes from community validation, communities have some leverage to claim a different kind of sovereignty, over their culture and, in some cases, their bodies. In Jamaican popular music, the street dance has ensured that the ears and bodies of poor, Black Jamaicans validate songs rather than upper-class program directors, state-run radio stations, or international media gatekeepers. Jamaican popular music practices reassert cultural ownership on their own terms, even when Jamaicans use the same words as the law. These assertions echo beyond the realm of cultural production, shoring up communities' self-conceptions in ways that can circumvent colonial social hierarchies. When people assert themselves based in those community values, they make claims to belonging but on terms that are not strictly "proper" according to the expectations of those in power.

Music is a cultural form that is intrinsically embodied; it must be heard, felt, and played to exist. This is one reason why it has been such a powerful force in Jamaica among communities who do not have easy access to or control over the mechanisms of many other kinds of cultural expression. Filmmaking requires enormous capital (and few within Jamaica have done it successfully). Access to television production and broadcast has been structured by state interest within Jamaica and by non-Jamaican global media conglomerates outside. Jamaican terms of musical engagement to a great extent have filled the gap left by other media platforms' structural hostility to poor and Black Jamaican bodies, voices, and modes of creativity. This helps to explain why Jamaican musical practices tend to center social relations on different terms than those of the colonizer.

Vernacularization, Negotiation, Negation

Jamaican musical practitioners are not isolated. They actively engage with the wider legal and economic landscape. Sometimes they use the same terms, phrases, or even arguments for their rights that others would use. Legal scholars use the term "vernacularization" to describe the process by which local people retool foreign- or state-generated terms and concepts to suit the practices of everyday life. For example, although the legal concept of human rights is defined officially in international law, for that concept to become meaningful in specific local settings, it must be reinterpreted into vernacular local meanings.[4] One could describe Jamaicans' retooling of such words as "original" or "royalties" as vernacularization. However, there is a spectrum of vernacularization: on the one end are terms and practices originating outside the colonizer's worldview; on the other is simply translating or tweaking colonizer concepts into more palatable forms. It is hard to tell what kind of vernacularization has occurred, because there is convergence in language, if not in interests, between the Jamaican state (and its agents, such as the Jamaica Intellectual Property Office [JIPO]) and the Jamaican poor. But the devil is in the details: How much does the language reflect an actual practice, and how much is it simply lip service? The Jamaican government has attempted to leverage this vernacularization to bridge conceptual gaps between legal conceptions of correctness and those found on the street: at one point, JIPO launched an anti-infringement campaign entitled "All T'ief Is T'ief." This campaign attempted to simultaneously mobilize the moral language of theft ("t'ief" being Patwa for "thieve" or "steal") and the vernacular language of Jamaica (Patwa) to reach Jamaicans. However, the aim was to reduce the complex and context-driven issue of copyright infringement to one of syllogistic simplicity. This campaign was not in itself particularly successful, addressing neither the complexities of permission and exclusion embodied in phonographic orality nor the power imbalances that enable powerful actors to legally end up with copyright ownership of artists' songs. However, despite these gaps between language and practice, for most concerned people who discuss Jamaican music's economic and legal situation, the language of copyright still dominates.

This helps explain why Jamaican musical practitioners do on occasion assert their support for copyright enforcement, despite copyright's ill service of their needs up to this point.[5] Jamaicans within and outside the music industry use the language of copyright to make claims for Jamaica's position in relation to the global music industry. Many Jamaicans have expressed pride and a sense of ownership in Jamaican music. They take pride in its global popularity and are dissatisfied at the relative lack of reward reaching the island. Most involved in Jamaican popular music believe (correctly) that foreigners and upper-class Jamaicans have profited disproportionately from Jamaican music. In this context, Jamaicans use copyright terminology to assert ownership over their culture, collectively, and proclaim that copyright enforcement will ensure that foreigners' money reaches Jamaica and gets poor artists paid.[6] However, local definitions of ownership, authorship, and originality inform their expectations of how enforcement should actually work. One artist I spoke with complained mildly about hearing his music on CDs sold by men in the streets of Jamaica who had not paid royalties. When I asked him if he thought police should arrest the seller and take the CDs (as occasionally happened in raids), the artist emphatically said no. He pointed out "man has to make a living" and mused perhaps the seller would "pick up a gun" and turn to a life of (presumably worse) crime, if denied this livelihood. And at the same time, he observed that CDs were "good promotion to get my name on the road," which perhaps deserved some measure of allowance. The musician's priorities and vision of law were that it should not act in isolation, defining people's rights and responsibilities only in relation to the letter of the law under consideration. Instead, he addressed the social relations that brought the CD seller to his place in life, as part of the same social relations that brought himself, the artist, to his own place in life, recognizing their shared interest as poor Black Jamaicans. The musician used the language of copyright law, but through his broader discussion, it was evident he believed that copyright law should be informed by broader social concerns. This is one reason why asking people about their attitudes toward copyright law does not reveal as much as one might think: people tended to leave exceptions and complications out unless specifically asked, and people tended to think of rights as the language of moral obligation and of dignity of the rights owner rather than of something defined by the letter of the law.

Absent systematic copyright reform, people could seek to use courts to clarify the confusing aspects of copyright. In the United States, this has not been much of a success, even though—or perhaps because—there are powerful organized entities on various sides (if a bit less on behalf of audiences). But even in the United States, the vast majority of people with disputes simply do not litigate—and generally do not appear to see litigation as a reasonable avenue for settling disputes. This is even truer in Jamaica, where courts and the law are far removed from daily life and identified as sites of colonial corruption (Babylon) by some. This has not stopped Jamaicans from making public claims of ownership or demands for enforcement through the media. In some cases, it may be advantageous to make claims verbally and publicly because one can define rights in a more contextual way than the letter of the law allows: people can use legal language as a kind of moral suasion. This persuasion, however, depends a lot on authority that comes from the government, an entity that most people experience as unreliable.

If we think of vernaculars, per Annie Paul, as "subaltern practices of expressive engagement,"[7] that brings power relations to the fore. One of Jamaican popular music's ongoing triumphs has been its ability to speak its literal vernacular. Patwa doesn't just signify "local"; it can also represent a negative intrusion into so-called civilized society. Using Patwa in places of power can sometimes have negative repercussions for the speakers. It is striking that Jamaican popular music has kept its vernacular—in the sense of Patwa and in the sense of vernacular creative practices—across the world and even required others to speak it too, in order to engage. In a context of structural inequality at the level of resources as well as cultural and institutional norms that mark outsiders as inappropriate, these practices remain resistant and risky. This has also meant that quite often Jamaicans simply remain silent about practices that do not fit well enough with the dominant language. In my discussions with Jamaican musician practitioners I noticed that when discussing copyright, very few of them addressed the contradictions of riddims, sampling, and other traditions of reuse while claiming ownership in the recordings made from them. Similarly, in a recent presentation to the Jamaican government on the Jamaican music industry in which all accounts recognized sound systems as the driving force, and even though the researcher had spent extensive time communicating with sound system operators, in the end sound system operators were not named; nor were their concerns discussed in the formal report.[8] Such striking gaps and silences exist across many formal venues that attempt to address, integrate, or build on Jamaican popular music.

Silence may be better than being included on the wrong terms. It is doubtful that the current legal or state system is capable of incorporating practices and people nourished in exilic spaces. This is one example where technology's connective power can be dangerous: it draws copyright enforcement mechanisms closer to Jamaican musical practice and renders visible people and relationships who cannot define their terms of visibility.

Music promotion and listening platforms from Spotify to YouTube all embed automated copyright enforcement software in their upload process, while in some cases copyright enforcement is even embedded in music-production software, introducing enforcement into the experimentation and learning process and before any work is finished, published, or sold. These technologies do not recognize or respond to local contexts. If copyright law were more heavily and intimately enforced, the many factors outlined previously would further prevent copyright from redistributing wealth from the Global North to the Global South or from rich to poor within Jamaica.

Practices associated with subaltern, or colonized, people need space in which to play out their rich engagement with the changing realities of life. These engagements are necessarily read as excessive and inappropriate when viewed through the lens of the upper classes. This "rude behavior" with respect to cultural works and cultural practices has flourished in exilic spaces. Exilic spaces provide a place that is not always visible or, when visible, not quite legible to local or international authorities. However, their legibility is also structured by the colonial assumptions held by local and global elites, who can see these spaces and practices as negatively influencing Jamaican life and Jamaica's global position.[9] Anyone concerned with equality and the flourishing of culture ought to recognize that these spaces and strategies are important, even given their limitations. In fact, there are pushes from within Jamaica, in recent years, to do just that—for example, many sound system operators in Kingston have organized themselves into a sound system association, while the organizers of Passa Passa (carefully not calling themselves "community leaders" but at the same time acting something like leaders of a community) have sought its protection as cultural heritage site. These movements are important and interesting but also pose certain risks. What this book argues is that without significant alteration in the terms of inclusion, state recognition will require redrawing the lines of community participation or will simply exclude the most dynamic actors, because the law requires people who invoke it to rewrite themselves into the kind of actors the law can recognize.[10] In Jamaica, progressives and even Marxists have historically tended to assign "civility, manners and conduct as sole possession of the Brown middle class"[11] and not the urban and Black poor and to look to traditional modes of political expression rather than to culture. While poor Jamaicans asserted, through music especially, their own modes of deportment and respect, there has not been enough success at translating those into terms that can be recognized by the power structure. Many of the trade-offs faced by Jamaicans within and outside Jamaica still reflect this dilemma: the law and those in power read their practices as unruly, disorganized, *uncivilized*.

To improve poor Black Jamaicans' lives across the board, or at least within Jamaican popular music, we must understand how or if Jamaican musical practitioners themselves can make claims on their own terms rather than on the terms handed to them by a colonial system. This requires we recognize how Jamaicans redefine not only property but also propriety. Further, we must recognize the link between notions of civility and conformity to colonial ways of being. It is necessary to redefine terms of engagement so that practitioners are less dependent on colonially allocated resources, including respectability. The way many Jamaicans in music have done this is through rude citizenship: making claims on Jamaica rooted in community-based cultural norms of social engagement, centering Blackness and practices associated with Blackness that directs authority and resources to those most exploited by colonial power.

To examine the conditions that enable people to define and claim rude citizenship, I have mapped the contours of exilic spaces. This is to assess how Jamaicans and those sympathetic to them can recognize or help such a project. On the theoretical side, one possible framework for analyzing how exilic spaces function is scholarship on "the commons." In fact, there are two strains of this scholarship that provide different insights: critical copyright studies originating especially in the fields of law and technology and historical examinations of actual commons that have occurred in communities at particular moments in time (such as the Russian mir, the Indian panchayat, or the English commons).

Critical copyright scholarship has tended to enthusiastically but ahistorically assert the value of sharing, openness, reuse, and collective authorship. However, many of these assertions poorly account for the inequalities that ultimately structure the outcomes of sharing-based systems and do not care to identify if there are any patterns in who is best able to profit (or flourish) through sharing and openness. It is true that within the street dance's exilic space, people do share, repeat, and reuse certain cultural forms relatively freely. However, the ability to do so is structured by a series of physical, geographic, and cultural borders that allow local people to limit participation by outsiders to the particular community of dancehall. Thus it would not make sense to call dancehall an unbounded commons or a shared resource in a general way, as many law and technology scholars do when valorizing the commons. Such a claim would also echo uncomfortably with the colonial practice of declaring some people's resources open to exploitation for others.[12] Copyright scholars who look at race and intellectual property have sometimes raised the useful point that the liberal-individualist framework of rights enshrined in dominant legal frameworks in the West tends to be unsuited to addressing structural inequality, which also explains why either openness or closedness across the board is unlikely to solve the problem of historically unequal access to resources. Facially neutral laws, including copyright, are poorly suited to addressing racial inequality.[13] However, a more historical approach to commons scholarship provides further clarification on the contexts that could support more liberatory conditions.

Exilic spaces in which shared cultural practices occur, as in Jamaican popular music, are in some ways more similar to the historical commons or peasant land commune (not the ahistorical caricature of Garrett Hardin's "Tragedy of the Commons").[14] Access and use are grounded in specific relationships that are historical, geographic, and cultural.[15] These existing material and temporally grounded relationships define who can use a commons and in what way.[16] Certainly, claims to enclose these cultural practices in current copyright law should raise concerns similar to those raised by people fighting the enclosure of land (better understood as a forced restructuring of existing cultural practices of land use).[17] While commons users or communal owners did not necessarily focus on the right of refusal to outsiders who might wish to free ride, the majority of communal land systems were long-lasting communities of people who lived alongside one another for generations and for whom outsiders were relatively rare. A historical understanding of commons reveals they have always required maintenance and management, often achieved not through formal law but through social relationships of mutual self-interest, shared culture, and the realities of being linked together by geography over time.[18] The "moral economy" is not an economy that is uniquely moral but is rather one that is structured by particular local morals that develop out of specific communities whose members understand each other and whose interests are bound together.[19] Moral economies exist within capitalism, but also predate that system and require specific conditions to serve the needs of the people involved in it. The bounded nature of land communes is fundamental to their ability to function, a dynamic that we can also see in the ways that geography, reputation, language, and culture shape how outsiders enter into exilic spaces. Communal land owning, for Indigenous people and peasants both reflects and shores up communities' social bonds. One way the post-

colonial experience differs from Indigenous commons practices is in extending this function in the face of colonial hostility to those social bonds and
precolonial identities: exilic spaces must also function as sites of refuge,
imagination, and the birthplace of new identities, through which people's
practices allow them to slip beyond the state's view and to survive without
being wholly dependent on state-controlled infrastructure.[20]

The inconsistencies of the Jamaican state, the law's poor fit with local
practices, and the value of practices like creative reuse, circulation, and collective forging of identity all demonstrate that inclusion in state institutions like copyright is not the only way to power and autonomy. Recognizing
exilic space's social function for marginalized people requires understanding its position outside law, one that cannot necessarily be secured or ad-
vanced by legalization. Naming the space and validating its exilic nature
reshapes the analytical framework by which we understand social value.

It is important to name practices affirmatively as well as to identify how
they don't fit with hegemonic structures. Terms like "exilic space" and "phonographic orality" highlight central aspects of Jamaican musical practice
that deserve more respect and accommodation. If legal and economic institutions account for policies' effects on phonographic orality or exilic spaces
and the specific values that they affirm, such policies may be more supportive of local needs. Even more broadly, the term "DJ culture" can evoke
crucial aspects of phonographic orality: the focus on using recordings as
elements in a live performance or creative conversation and the fact that it
is a living, community practice. DJ culture easily evokes vocalists, DJs,
sound systems, and dancers and could be a rallying cry for asserting value
in musical practices.

Negotiating with Colonial Copyright and the (Parasitic) State

While acknowledging the history of law as an expression of power used to
dominate the weak, some also suggest the law can be used by the weak to
limit the depredations of the powerful. E. P. Thompson famously argued
that despite the rule of law being "a mask for the rule of class," it was also
true that "the rule of law itself, the imposing of effective inhibitions upon
power and the defense of the citizen from power's all-intrusive claims, seems
to me to be an unqualified human good."[21] But how likely is law to limit
power, when the system that enacts it is weak, unreliable, or bound up in
structures of power that predate and transcend it?[22] As we saw with the inconsistent police presence at Boasy Tuesday and Passa Passa, some aspects

of Jamaican musical practice are disciplined as much by street dynamics as by legal ones. A parasitic state (a term highlighting how Jamaica's governmental bodies lack resources to rule from above)[23] makes reliance on the rule of law a chancy proposition. It is unclear whether Jamaica has experienced the rule of law in the way that even the most trenchant sociolegal critics admit it to have value.

Jamaican musical practice, then, is not just an interesting case study for copyright law. It provides evidence of how people oppressed by racial and class inequality, in a country disadvantaged in the global system, develop strategies for relating to the state without giving up their autonomy. This enables them to be enormously creative without being wholly dependent on structures of power that have served to disadvantage them. Jamaican popular music also provides important insights into ongoing debates in relation to copyright law—especially while some scholars and musical practitioners suggest that copyright law is crumbling in the digital era.[24] While copyright is not evaporating just yet, its presence or absence is variously argued to better serve society. Unfortunately, in practice it has not reliably served those marginalized in relation to power. The same can be said for the state itself—it has failed to serve marginalized people and failed most violently when it has come to defining property law, whether to dispossess Indigenous people of land or to dispossess Africans of their rights over their bodies and lives.[25]

However, outside, alongside, and in the shadow of law, Jamaicans have created and maintained a global network of traditions and products under their own creative authority and contributed significantly to the cultural economic life of Jamaica and the world. Not enough attention has been given to the affirmative value of practices that occur outside of the law's reach. To simply redraw the boundaries of the law so as to encompass them is not a solution. At its best, a street dance is a triumphant assertion of cultural power by the poor but not as a place of peace, equality, and harmony—rather as a place where people struggle and experiment with the resources available to them.

In terms of their engagement with the national and global system, poor Jamaicans at a street dance are not more disadvantaged than a poor Jamaican in the U.S. immigration system, the dairy farmer rendered destitute by IMF structural adjustment policies that led to the destruction of the domestic dairy industry,[26] or indeed more than the forty residents of Tivoli Gardens alleged by Amnesty International to have been "extra-judicially executed" by Jamaican security forces in 2010.[27] The example of the Jamaican dancehall artist Vybz Kartel, also known as Adidja Palmer, embodied the complexity of relationships between the state, the poor, morality, and propriety both through his verbal engagement and his embodied interactions. Many of his enormously popular songs have been banned from the radio by the government for their explicit sexual content. In response to one ban, he published a letter in the national newspaper pointing out that sexual or even violent lyrics are less harmful to the nation than poverty, lack of opportunity, and government corruption (including its fostering of gun violence). As he put it, "The devastating impact on the psyche of Jamaican children is not caused by daggerin' [violent/sexually explicit] songs but rather by socio-economic conditions which leave children without free education, with single-parent homes (or shacks), lack of social infrastructure in ghetto communities, unemployed and disfranchised young men with no basic skills who are caught up in the 'gun culture' cultivated by our politicians in the 1960s/'70s."[28] At the same time, Palmer wrote that from jail while awaiting trial for complicity in a murder case. While he may well have been involved in an act of terrible violence, that does not set him apart from many state agents: not much can be said about the presence or absence of his respect for life that could not also be said about the Jamaican police force. The 2010 incursion into Tivoli Gardens was not an anomaly. Faced with terrible violence from the state, with little recourse (although Jamaican and international human rights organizations did mobilize), poor Black Jamaicans especially need the power of refusal.

A key aspect of exilic space is how it enables and depends on the power of refusal. Refusing the totality of legalization is of increasing importance in a global system where many states are raising the price of exclusion while narrowing the avenues toward inclusion. Similar to how squatters and pirate radio broadcasters in England could break some laws but not always face extreme penalty or to how the United States has (on occasion) granted people who immigrate without legal documentation the chance to remain, work, get an education, and attain citizenship, states have sometimes recognized social values beyond compliance with the letter of the law. These choices of exemption or decriminalization rather than legalization may provide more degrees of freedom for people whose presence in the system is always going to be policed.

Even if exilic spaces are protected from intervention, it is also necessary to analyze the divisions and inequalities within them and how they relate to broader concerns with equality. Just as commons were not utopias but were rife with social inequality, so too the street dance is not a site of internal equality. Many activities at the dance are competitions that create winners and losers, and in the future, the stakes of those competitions and the ways they affect participants' ability to flourish ought to be further explored. Some terms of competition remain aligned with values not shaped by colonial power, but in other ways, the hierarchies of competition may reflect social inequalities. Gender, most notably, is clearly a vector that shapes who is able to participate in different ways in Jamaican popular music: women are notably not present as DJs, selectors, sound system operators, or engineers (while they are more present as dancers and monopolizing the role of mogglers). This might lead us to investigate whether exilic spaces serve women as well as men (placed in context with the different terms of inclusion for women in nonexilic spaces). Challenging respectability is often riskier for women (and non-gender-conforming people) than for men, so how or when do women make rude claims to citizenship? These questions are yet to be answered. I hope by more carefully delineating the contours of an exilic space, this work provides groundwork for pursing them productively to better understand the conditions under which people can claim power on their own terms.

Sovereignty, (Rude) Citizenship, Autonomy

Jamaican popular music practitioners assert both citizenship and sovereignty in their music. Citizenship implies membership and belonging in something, typically a state. Some Jamaicans' asserting of rights and relationships fits a claim of citizenship if we see them as redefining the term away from simply being a subject of the state, on the state's terms. But this form of citizenship is then disruptive to the smooth functioning of the state. Sovereignty is perhaps more outward looking, addressing the right to refuse, the power to grant permission, and the ability to act autonomously. Although sovereignty can include violence and exploitation, that is not necessarily a defining characteristic. For example, Indigenous people claim sovereignty over life, land, and culture on quite different terms from the kind of sovereignty claimed by colonizers. The ability to act autonomously is perhaps the most important: the term "autonomous" captures both the condition of being self-governing and of being able to assert oneself against others. Each term creates possibilities for making claims against or demands from other powerful actors. When Jamaican dancers complain about Jamaican dance moves "going viral" on the internet without anyone giving credit or other compensation to Jamaicans, they are claiming a kind of sovereign interest in culture (although not necessarily exclusive or bound to geographic borders). When Jamaican musicians suggest that poor people selling bootleg CDs on the street should not be criminalized, they are asserting these practices are necessary for life within a community. Musicians make a claim for protection and understanding by the Jamaican state, as people who expect the state to respect them. At the same time, many aspects of Jamaican popular music complicate this desire for protection by the state. Since poor Jamaicans often see (and experience) the state and elites as hostile, it may be that sovereignty is necessary against them as well. That same sovereignty also has been a basis for musical practitioners to build relationships beyond Jamaica's borders (including with non-Jamaicans), which in turn can give them more power to negotiate and be respected at home.

Approaches to Policy in Jamaica

These complexities of sovereignties and citizenship suggest different kinds of policy approaches. One advantage of claims of citizenship is that it is more easily tucked into policy arguments grounded in Jamaican law. The Jamaican Constitution of 1962 asserts a right to freedom of expression (although it can be limited to protect the rights of others).[29] Demanding a deeper recognition of the democratic value of popular culture in Jamaica could lead to a broader interpretation of this right. As Jamaicans become increasingly active on the internet, it appears that some policy makers at the regional level are taking seriously the question of censorship and freedom of expression online.[30] However, as far as I have been able to learn, the case made for limiting copyright in the interest of freedom of speech in Jamaica has not yet been made in relation to music online.

The language of sovereignty might be more useful when addressing the international context. As a country with a history of disadvantage on the global scene, Jamaica might make use of a more protectionist attitude in relation to its cultural practices. Common property theory and history provide one model that supports this, that of a "limited commons," in which access is based on membership in a limited community, and beyond the community's boundaries access is restricted.[31] This model is supported by historical studies of common property systems at the center of peasant life in many places in the world, in which members lived close enough to each other to negotiate social norms and social enforcement. Local systems of sharing resources in all these places were governed by local rules that, in the modern era, looked quite different from those who wished to rule them from afar. Jamaican musical practices have always followed a different set of rules than those beyond Jamaica's borders, especially those in the Global North, based on local cultural and institutional capacities. It is possible that formalizing distinctive rules of community-based exclusion or limitation might provide some security for creative practices within Jamaica. Within these limited commons, inequality would still have to be addressed; for example, the class-based inequality arising from the wealth disparity between middle-class soundmen and poor attendees (for example) might take on a new significance. As well, the notion of sovereignty can all too easily collapse into reinforcing state power without addressing how different people have access to that power. Who can define membership in the community for the purposes of inclusion or refusal? In Jamaica, the urban poor claim their own kind of sovereignty separate from the state, and their ability to flourish would require that they have the power to define it on their own terms. Recent developments along these lines suggest possibilities: for example, sound system operators have begun to self-organize, especially in response to what they see as unfair treatment in relation to the Noise Abatement Act and other state interventions. If they also addressed the role of riddims in sound system culture, they could perhaps argue for an exception or limitation to copyright based on their cultural or professional association— they could require a mandatory license (such as that granted for cover songs), for example, or a tax on recording and copying equipment paid into a fund for riddim copyright owners based on tracked circulation or reuse. Tailoring copyright in this way could account for the specific function that recorded music plays in sound system culture and also account for the differential economic situation of studios compared to individuals.

Such alterations in law and legal claims would contradict a strong tradition of international intellectual property that suffers from presuming false equality based on neutral policy. The trend in international intellectual property law has been to heighten pressure to enforce copyright, increase minimum standards of copyright enforcement, and increase surveillance, without attending to local needs or definitions. These trends are embedded in technologies intimately connected with Jamaican popular music so that copyright's reach expands via the digital environment in which standardization privileges particular kinds of musical properties and practices over others. Some scholars have pointed out that copyright currently "constitute[s] a dead weight loss on already fragile economies."[32] As copyright law increasingly crosses Jamaican borders, its impact must be carefully weighed, more so than has yet been done.[33]

The practices and sites of Jamaican popular music also hold lessons for the rest of the world regarding new ways of obtaining financial returns on creative works. However, because Jamaica faces significant disadvantages in the global economy, it requires (along with other nations similarly disadvantaged) particular consideration in international copyright policy.[34] Such a protectionist argument may be uncomfortable for policy makers who favor facially neutral policies, and at the international level, there has been a focus on formal equality in the context of substantive inequality.[35] The philosophers Amartya Sen and Martha Nussbaum suggest true freedom requires a "capabilities approach"; closer to my example, the legal scholar Margaret Chon's critical copyright approach argues we must be outcomes centered (rather than procedural) to properly address this situation,[36] while Anjali Vats and Diedre Keller have begun articulating how race in particular structures intellectual property law outcomes.[37] But what produces the capabilities that increase the likelihood of better outcomes?

Beyond Copyright Policy

Copyright, as a regulation of cultural practices, does reach surprisingly far into the intimate interpersonal realities that shape cultural expression. But the forces that motivate cultural expression and give it meaning originate outside of law. At its root, cultural expression is fundamental to what it means to be human. Humanity is a category of existence that coloniality has sought to limit. This raises an urgent question, which is well framed by Thomas: "How, then, do we address the question of what it means to be a human capable of acting in and on a world that hides the ontological entanglements of the violences that have been foundational to its formation?"[38] I can answer no better than M. Jacqui Alexander, who has said, "There is no other work but the work of creating and re-creating ourselves within the context of community."[39] In her discussion of Black women's friendships, the necessity of this work arises from living in a system that placed Black women at the center of intersecting forces of racial and gender oppression that also originate in colonialism. Without erasing the specificity of Black women's need for community, this recommendation holds promise for all people seeking to flourish against or beyond colonial structures.[40] Similarly, the most salient power hindering Jamaican musical practice is the force that hinders poor Jamaicans' flourishing more generally: poverty and a legacy of colonial inequality. Many of my interlocutors made clear demands for government interventions that addressed both problems, going far beyond the expected scope of copyright. My interlocutors asserted that the government should invest in the poor areas that have fostered Jamaican musical practices, such as the (still!) desperately poor Trenchtown, the neighborhood of Bob Marley's musical awakening, or the Alpha Boys' school that has had little formal recognition as a wellspring of music most Jamaicans and thousands of foreigners know and love.[41] Recognizing such places could revitalize and foster respect for the poor communities that support such musical talents.

This is not only a plea for government investment and support in local communities, although that is an important site at which interventions can be made. Reparations from England and all countries that profited from the trade in enslaved Africans would go a long way toward making that support effective. Alongside this (and in the struggle to achieve what is clearly owed) local communities can also organize in what Boaventura De Sousa Santos calls "counter-hegemonic globalization." In this model, communities work to coordinate on the global stage, not leaving this organizing to multinational corporations and governments. Given the diasporic reach of Jamaicans across the world and the even farther reach of their music—music that in some cases takes on an exilic nature in new locales—there is some groundwork for counterhegemonic global organizing. Government (or international regulation) is not irrelevant to this project. Governments still influence the infrastructure that allows global organizing to occur—from material borders, passports, and transportation to the building, funding, and regulating of communications infrastructure in ways that allow non-elites to use them in confidence and relative privacy. Wherever this use happens, supporting it requires "articulating struggles and resistances, as well as promoting ever more comprehensive and consistent alternatives."[42]

The struggles and resistances of Jamaican musical practitioners, in the face of ongoing colonial inequality reinforced by laws written through the lens of Western cultural practices, may suggest the contours for better claims of citizenship for other communities as well. Jamaican popular music's ability, at different moments and different locations, to recenter the most exploited and the most vulnerable to colonial capitalism, highlight several aspects of participation in cultural life that current legal and economic frameworks do not well account for. Between legalization and criminality, these exilic spaces and practices flourish best in partial invisibility—or at least with local control over the terms of visibility and participation. This twilight freedom facilitates ongoing negotiations over the meaning of sovereignty, ownership, and collectivity within and across different communities. Such struggles are evident in many places across the world with respect to intellectual property. For example, pharmaceutical companies have mined Indigenous communities' knowledge of local plants, interested only in that knowledge's potential economic value. Indigenous communities have been left to grapple with how to put their claims over shared cultural knowledge into terms that intellectual property law will recognize. In the past twenty years, this has led to the development of newer categories of intellectual property: traditional knowledge and traditional cultural expressions, which are defined and protected differently from a patent or a copyright. Such interventions are hopeful but also raise risks of visibility—especially to the extent that categories of creative expression can be designated as "resources" to be exploited.[43] While this is an interesting step, it also creates a new set of within-community negotiations at the level of ownership. Ascribing ownership to traditions also raises political questions akin to those raised by the definition of authorship in copyright: these traditional knowledge holders must also develop a process and rationale for assigning collective ownership so that there is an entity capable of granting or refusing access. This can also shatter or reconstitute notions of identity and belonging.[44] Thankfully, critical scholarship on race and intellectual property is developing, including the important work of scholars like Vats, who are pushing to reframe intellectual property, as I do, as a way of thinking about citizenship, power and narratives of belonging.[45] More local, grounded studies of creative communities are needed to inform these powerful critiques.

The Jamaican example does not offer easy solutions but highlights issues that ought to be at the front whenever a community that predates a legal system (or is defined against it) is facing inclusion and visibility. I am making not just a plea for particularism but an argument for attention to the material resources that make legal engagements meaningful—for without the right to refuse, one cannot negotiate fairly. One lesson of the Jamaican experience is that inclusion or legalization in a global system cannot be the only alternative available to marginalized people: Jamaican music has shown us there are other alternatives. In recent years, increasing communities and activists inside and outside the realm of technology design and policy have begun to argue for increased power to refuse to be included, seen, or surveilled by technology.[46] Jamaican popular music provides an interesting example of a community that has historically managed entrance and participation in ways that new technologies may restrict: prefiguring some of the struggles now evident in other locations and communities. Of course, Jamaica is not the first; unequal inclusion has always been a central aspect of exploitation, and oppressed communities almost always develop ways to protect spaces of cultural intimacy. Still, it is worth asking how various kinds of technologies that "see" us, especially those of us who are already oppressed in one form or another, might compromise exilic spaces, harm cultural intimacy, or limit degrees of freedom. Given ongoing and historic oppressive systems, sites outside the system or under the radar remain extremely important. Another lesson from the Jamaican context is that people make use of whatever existing centers of power or counterpower (like dons and garrisons) are available. If resources were more widely available to all, including the poorest and including women, their ability to negotiate the terms of participation would be greatly increased in relation to their own internal hierarchies as well as those outside.

In that context, a significant action for supporting the communities at the center of Jamaican popular music would be simply to provide more security in the material conditions of life. No matter how creative Jamaicans are, royalties are not a guarantee of steady income; nor will they necessarily even minimally reward the urban poor communities that foster musical creativity. Investing in roads, water, and other infrastructure, as well as education and health care, while sounding rather far afield from copyright, could center the whole being whose denial of personhood lies beneath the lingering coloniality of life. A piecemeal recognition of a human being as a property owner, passport holder, or other legalistic identity will not provide the conditions for flourishing nor for liberation. That kind of recognition can provide new excuses for intervention and influence from the top down. I hope it is not mundane to return to an argument that the basics of life, such as education, clean water, housing, health, and food, are an important baseline for negotiation over all other terms and could be addressed especially by reparations and reallocations of resources away from colonial systems that send resources upward (within Jamaica) and outward (to those outside its borders). Exilic practices reveal the limits of institutionalized, colonial social relations and reflect how people play outside, within, and through them. By naming and identifying these current practices' contours and limits (including further exploration in relation to gender and sexuality), it is possible to identify how we can improve their effects and support those who need it most. It is my hope that this book has demonstrated some ways that Jamaican popular music can help us do that.

Notes

Introduction

1. Jamaican television features many musical competition shows. The Magnum Kings and Queens of Dancehall competition, sponsored by a local energy and male potency drink, hosted the interchange described above. Like similar shows in other countries, the competition is between vocalists, who sing songs over prerecorded music played by a DJ (who is provided by the competition and does not have a creative or performance element during the vocalist's performance). None of the participants are signed or recorded before this event. "Magnum Kings and Queens of Dancehall off to a Good Start," *Jamaica Observer*, December 16, 2009, sec. Entertainment, http://www.jamaicaobserver.com/entertainment/Magnum -king-and-queen.

2. Cordel "Skatta" Burrell. Producer and writer at Downsound Records, Kingston, Jamaica.

3. "Riddim" is the term for the instrumental part of a song—the music minus the contributions of the vocalist.

4. In earlier traditions of artistic creation, this might not have been the case. Mark Rose, *Authors and Owners: The Invention of Copyright* (Cambridge, MA: Harvard University Press, 1993).

5. George Lipsitz, "Midnight at the Barrelhouse: Why Ethnomusicology Matters Now," *Ethnomusicology* 55, no. 2 (May 27, 2011): 197. "The object of our studies should be the creative act, not just the created object, [and] our interpretation and analysis become part of that act. This explanation enables us to write about musical texts in relation to their full social and historical contexts, but it also requires us to view those texts as inseparable from their performance."

6. Deborah A. Thomas, "The Violence of Diaspora: Governmentality, Class Cultures, and Circulations," *Radical History Review* 2009, no. 103 (December 21, 2009): 83–104, https://doi.org/10.1215/01636545-2008-032.

7. Lloyd Bradley, *Bass Culture: When Reggae Was King* (London: Penguin Books, 2001); Dennis Howard, "Punching for Recognition: The Juke Box as a Key Instrument in the Development of Popular Jamaican Music," *Caribbean Quarterly* 53, no. 4 (2007): 32–46; David Katz, *Solid Foundation: An Oral History of Reggae* (London: Bloomsbury, 2003); Sonjah Stanley-Niaah, *DanceHall: From Slave Ship to Ghetto* (Ottawa: University of Ottawa Press, 2010).

8. Aaron Kamugisha, "The Coloniality of Citizenship in the Contemporary Anglophone Caribbean," *Race and Class* 49, no. 2 (2007): 20, 25, 49.

9. Dennis Howard, "Setting the Record Straight on Slackness," Music Journalism and History, *Kingston Outpost,* March 2009, http://dennishoward.blogspot.com/2009/03/setting-record-straight-on-slackness.html.

10. Norman Stolzoff, *Wake the Town and Tell the People: Dancehall Culture in Jamaica* (New York: Routledge, Taylor & Francis, 2000), 233; P. C. Hintzen, "Reproducing Domination: Identity and Legitimacy Constructs in the West Indies," *Social Identities* 3, no. 1 (1997): 70; Stanley-Niaah, *DanceHall,* 114.

11. Carolyn Cooper, *Noises in the Blood: Orality, Gender, and the "Vulgar" Body of Jamaican Popular Culture* (Durham, NC: Duke University Press, 1995), 41.

12. Katherine McKittrick, "Rebellion/Invention/Groove," *Small Axe* 20, no. 1 (2016): 81.

13. "Whatever influence the materially deprived and socially marginal urban lower class exercised in the society . . . came largely from the group's historical occupancy and creative use of what may be termed exilic social space . . . a social site for dissidence and the repair of cultural injuries." Obika Gray, *Demeaned but Empowered: The Social Power of the Urban Poor in Jamaica* (Kingston: University of West Indies Press, 2004), 92.

14. Jason Toynbee, "Copyright, the Work and Phonographic Orality in Music," *Social and Legal Studies* 15, no. 1 (2006): 77–99; Gray, *Demeaned but Empowered,* 92.

15. See Anibal Quijano, "Coloniality of Power, Eurocentrism, and Latin America," *Nepantla: Views from South* 1, no. 3 (2000): 533–80; Walter Mignolo, "Introduction: Coloniality of Power and De-colonial Thinking," *Cultural Studies* 21, no. 2/3 (May 2007): 155–67; Kamugisha, "Coloniality of Citizenship"; Obika Gray, "The Coloniality of Power and the Limits of Dissent in Jamaica," *Small Axe* 21, no. 3 (November 1, 2017): 98–110, https://doi.org/10.1215/07990537-4272022.

16. Hintzen, "Reproducing Domination."

17. Stuart Hall, "Minimal Selves," in *Black British Cultural Studies: A Reader,* ed. H. A. Baker, M. Diawara, and R. H. Lindeborg (Chicago: University of Chicago Press, 1996), 115.

18. Paul Gilroy, *The Black Atlantic: Modernity and Double Consciousness* (London: Verso, 1993), 101.

19. Toynbee, "Copyright, the Work and Phonographic Orality in Music."

20. Gray, *Demeaned but Empowered,* 93.

21. Gray, 94.

22. Quijano, "Coloniality of Power," 233.

23. Mignolo, "Introduction"; Kamugisha, "Coloniality of Citizenship," 23. "The concepts of 'the modern' and of modernisation were fused in a calculus which regarded a Euro-American 'modern' and modernisation as the only future for the region. . . . In the terms of a Caribbean elite that sought to define itself on the standards of a global bourgeois class, this meant adopting the consumption patterns of the West and acquiring its cultural capital. That the consumption patterns of the middle classes of the Anglophone Caribbean are incompatible with the economies of the Caribbean is a point that has been made incessantly by Caribbean scholars like George Beckford and Rex Nettleford. Moreover, to critique the desire for those tastes from a cultural nationalist position quickly risks being fruitless, as such tastes

are no longer understood as 'foreign', 'white' or 'colonial'. They are the 'styles' and 'tastes' of development, and modernity's prerequisites for equality."

24. Kamugisha, 109.

25. Kamugisha, 21.

26. This also affects social norms relating to sexuality. See M. Jacqui Alexander, "Not Just (Any) Body Can Be a Citizen: The Politics of Law, Sexuality and Postcoloniality in Trinidad and Tobago and the Bahamas," *Feminist Review* 48 (Autumn 1994): 5–23.

27. Deborah A. Thomas, "Caribbean Studies, Archive Building, and the Problem of Violence," *Small Axe* 17, no. 2 (2013): 40.

28. James Holston describes this dynamic in Brazil as "a historical norm of citizenship [that] fosters exclusion, inequality, illegality, violence and the social logics of privilege and deference as the grounds of belonging." James Holston, *Insurgent Citizenship: Disjunctions of Democracy and Modernity in Brazil* (Princeton, NJ: Princeton University Press, 2008), 6; Harris describes this done explicitly in the era of slavery in the United States, as well as done implicitly afterward. Cheryl Harris, "Whiteness as Property," *Harvard Law Review* 106 (1993): 1744.

29. Thomas, "Caribbean Studies, Archive Building," 42.

30. James C. Scott, *Seeing Like a State: How Certain Schemes to Improve the Human Condition Have Failed* (New Haven, CT: Yale University Press, 1999).

31. Camille Nelson, "Lyrical Assault: Dancehall versus the Cultural Imperialism of the North-West," *Southern California Interdisciplinary Law Journal* 17 (2008): 258. In the U.S. context, property law was of course similarly defined. Harris, "Whiteness as Property."

32. Harris, 1762.

33. Heather Royes and Tom Tavares-Finson, "Current Status of Copyright Legislation in Jamaica," *Jamaica Journal* 16, no. 1 (1983): 14.

34. Unlike the UK Copyright Act, the Jamaican act was not revised between 1962 and 1994.

35. Bradley, *Bass Culture*, 228; Royes and Tavares-Finson, "Current Status," 15; Stolzoff, *Wake the Town*, 59.

36. Zeljka Kozul-Wright and Lloyd Stanbury, *Becoming a Globally Competitive Player: The Case of the Music Industry in Jamaica* (Geneva: UN Commission on Trade and Development, 1998), 24.

37. Harris, "Whiteness as Property," 1766.

38. Copyright Act of 1976, 17 USC §12.1.1; Jamaica Copyright Act of 1993 § 2, part 6.

39. Copyright Act, 1911, Geo 5, c. 46, part 1, sec. 1(1), https://www.legislation.gov.uk/ukpga/Geo5/1-2/46/contents/enacted)

40. Copyright Act, 1911, Geo 5, c. 46, part 2, § 35(1), and part 1, sec. 5(1).

41. The UK Copyright Act was revised to include broadcasting in 1956, at which time the law also applied in Jamaica.

42. The Copyright Act of Jamaica, 1993, part 1, § 1(2)(a).

43. Anupam Chander and Madhavi Sunder, "The Romance of the Public Domain," *California Law Review* 92 (2004): 1153, 1161; Darrell Addison Posey and Graham Dutfield, *Beyond Intellectual Property: Toward Traditional Resource Rights for Indigenous*

Peoples and Local Communities (Ottawa: International Development Research Centre, 1996); V. Shiva, "The Need for Sui Generis Rights," *Seedling* 12, no. 1 (1994).

44. Daniel Fischlin and Ajay Heble, *The Other Side of Nowhere: Jazz, Improvisation, and Communities in Dialogue* (Middletown, CT: Wesleyan University Press, 2004), 29; also see Paul Gilroy, ". . . To Be Real: The Dissident Forms of Black Expressive Culture," in *Let's Get It On: The Politics of Black Performance*, ed. Catherine Ugwu (Seattle: Bay Press, 1995).

45. Gilroy, "To Be Real," 24.

46. Jason Toynbee argues that if copyright had been enforced, Jamaican music would never have developed as fully or spread as far as it has. Toynbee, "Reggae Open Source: How the Absence of Copyright Enabled the Emergence of Popular Music in Jamaica," in *Copyright and Piracy: An Interdisciplinary Critique*, ed. Lionel Bently, Jennifer Davis, and Jane C. Ginsburg, Cambridge Intellectual Property and Information Law, vol. 13 (Cambridge: Cambridge University Press, 2010), 358.

47. United Nations. "Towards E-Commerce Legal Harmonization in the Caribbean." UNCTAD, 2017.

48. Margaret Chon, "Intellectual Property and the Development Divide," *Cardozo Law Review* 27 (2005): 2840; Michael P. Ryan, *Knowledge Diplomacy: Global Competition and the Politics of Intellectual Property* (Washington, DC: Brookings Institute, 1998), 12–13.

49. WIPO, *Introduction to Intellectual Property Theory and Practice* (London: Kluwer Law, 1997), 59.

50. UNESCO and WIPO, *Proceedings of Regional Seminar on Copyright for English-Speaking Caribbean States* (Paris: UNESCO/WIPO/KCS, 1981), 7.

51. Chon, "Intellectual Property," 2832; Ruth L. Okediji, "TRIPS Dispute Settlement and the Sources of (International) Copyright Law," *Journal—Copyright Society of the USA* 49, no. 2 (2001): 611; Peter Drahos and John Braithwaite, *Information Feudalism: Who Owns the Knowledge Economy?* (London: Earthscan, 2002): 75.

52. Shiva, "Sui Generis Rights"; Posey and Dutfield, *Beyond Intellectual Property.*

53. Keith Aoki, "Distributive and Syncretic Motives in Intellectual Property Law (with Special Reference to Coercion, Agency, and Development)," *UC Davis Law Review* 40 (2006–2007): 717–801.

54. Boatema Boateng, *The Copyright Thing Doesn't Work Here: Adinkra and Kente Cloth and Intellectual Property in Ghana* (Minneapolis: University of Minnesota Press, 2011).

55. UNESCO. "Decision of the Intergovernmental Committee: 13.COM 10.B.18." Non-Government Organization, 2018. https://ich.unesco.org/en/decisions.

56. Towse examines data from collecting societies on money artists earned from copyright. Ruth Towse, "Copyright and Economic Incentives: An Application to Performers' Rights in the Music Industry," *Kyklos* 52, no. 3 (1999): 369–90. Other works draw on surveys or brief case studies. Marlene Cuthbert and Avonie Brown, "Local Musicians in Jamaica: A Case Study," in *Whose Master's Voice? The Development of Popular Music in Thirteen Cultures*, ed. Alison J. Ewbank and Fouli T. Papageorgiou (Westport, CT: Greenwood, 1997), 135–51; Amanda Lenhart and Susannah Fox,

Downloading Free Music: Internet Music Lovers Don't Think It's Stealing, Pew Internet and American Life Project (Washington, DC: Pew Research Center, 2000).

57. Julie E. Cohen, "Pervasively Distributed Copyright Enforcement," *Georgetown Law Journal* 95 (2006): 1–44; Aram Sinnreich, *Mashed Up: Music, Technology, and the Rise of Configurable Culture* (Amherst: University of Massachusetts Press, 2010).

58. Aram Sinnreich, *The Piracy Crusade: How the Music Industry's War on Sharing Destroys Markets and Erodes Civil Liberties* (Amherst: University of Massachusetts Press, 2013).

59. Peter Manuel and Wayne Marshall, "The Riddim Method: Aesthetics, Practice, and Ownership in Jamaican Dancehall," *Popular Music* 25, no. 3 (2006): 447–70; Toynbee, "Copyright, the Work"; Toynbee, "Reggae Open Source."

60. Alongside several ethnographic works cited here in depth, some useful approaches include Alpa Shah, "Ethnography? Participant Observation, a Potentially Revolutionary Praxis," *HAU: Journal of Ethnographic Theory* 7, no. 1 (June 11, 2017): 45–59, https://doi.org/10.14318/hau7.1.008; Linda Tuhiwai Smith, *Decolonizing Methodologies: Research and Indigenous Peoples* (London: Zed Books, 2013); Anna Lowenhaupt Tsing, *Friction: An Ethnography of Global Connection* (Princeton, NJ: Princeton University Press, 2005); Miguel Zavala, "What Do We Mean by Decolonizing Research Strategies? Lessons from Decolonizing, Indigenous Research Projects in New Zealand and Latin America," *Decolonization: Indigeneity, Education and Society* 2, no. 1 (2013): 55–71.

61. Andrew Spencer and Dalea Bean, "Female Sex Tourism in Jamaica: An Assessment of Perceptions," *Journal of Destination Marketing and Management* 6, no. 1 (2017): 13–21.

62. Gray, *Demeaned but Empowered*, 71.

63. In some cases, I did feel harassed, invaded, exhausted, or insulted, but the main injury was to my pride and to my perhaps-naive hope that I could demonstrate my good faith. I mostly did not feel I was at risk of physical harm as long as I took reasonable care. One factor at play was the likelihood of police intervention or retaliation, should anything happen to me, particularly given historic patterns of police power mobilized on behalf of white women.

64. Thomas, in *Exceptional Violence*, addresses her concerns with this conflation of "violence" with "Jamaica" or with poor Black people in Jamaica. Deborah A. Thomas, *Exceptional Violence: Embodied Citizenship in Transnational Jamaica* (Durham, NC: Duke University Press, 2011).

65. Winnifred Brown-Glaude, *Higglers in Kingston: Women's Informal Work in Jamaica* (Nashville: Vanderbilt University Press, 2011); Gina A. Ulysse, *Downtown Ladies: Informal Commercial Importers, a Haitian Anthropologist and Self-Making in Jamaica* (Chicago: University of Chicago Press, 2007); Anne M. Galvin, *Sharing the Wealth: Community Development and the Dancehall Music Industry in Contemporary Kingston, Jamaica* (New York: New School University, 2006).

66. Braun-Glaude describes it as legalized but not licensed or taxed. Brown-Glaude, *Higglers in Kingston*.

67. Thomas, *Exceptional Violence*.

68. Not "a culture of violence," but as Thomas argues, conditions that enact violence and only recognize violence. Thomas.

69. "Utech Guards Fired," *Jamaica Observer*, November 30, 2012, http://www.jamaicaobserver.com/news/UTech-guards-fired-_12902530; Annie Paul, "Literate Mobs: UWI's 2006 Brush with Gay Lynching," *Active Voice* (blog), November 5, 2012, https://anniepaul.net/2012/11/05/literate-mobs-uwis-2006-brush-with-gay-lynching/.

70. Cooper, *Noises in the Blood*; Lena Delgado de Torres, "Swagga: Fashion, Kinaesthetics and Gender in Dancehall and Hip-Hop," *Journal of Black Masculinity: The Philosophical Underpinnings of Gender Identity* 1, no. 2 (Summer, 2011); Donna P. Hope, *Man Vibes: Masculinities in Jamaican Dancehall* (Kingston: Ian Randle, 2010).

71. Nadia Ellis, "Out and Bad: Toward a Queer Performance Hermeneutic in Jamaican Dancehall," *Small Axe* 15, no. 2 (July 1, 2011): 7–23, https://doi.org/10.1215/07990537-1334212.

72. Alexander, "Not Just (Any) Body"; Cooper, *Noises in the Blood*; Ellis, "Out and Bad"; Hope, *Man Vibes*.

73. Moji Anderson and Erin MacLeod, eds., *Beyond Homophobia: Centering LGBTQ Experiences in the Anglophone Caribbean* (Kingston: University of the West Indies Press, 2020).

74. Charles V. Carnegie, "The Fate of Ethnography: Native Social Science in the English-Speaking Caribbean," *New West Indian Guide/Nieuwe West-Indische Gids* 66, no. 1–2 (January 1, 1992): 18, https://doi.org/10.1163/13822373-90002002; quoted in Thomas, "Caribbean Studies, Archive Building," 42.

Chapter 1

1. Kim-Marie Spence, "When Money Is Not Enough: Reggae, Dancehall, and Policy in Jamaica," *Journal of Arts Management, Law, and Society* 49, no. 1 (January 2, 2019): 45–60, https://doi.org/10.1080/10632921.2018.1528191.

2. The nearly heroic efforts of Keith Nurse, including *The Caribbean Music Industry: A Report Prepared for Caribbean Export Development Agency* (St. Michael, Barbados: 2001) from within Jamaica; and reports such as Vanus James, *The Caribbean Music Industry Database: A Report Prepared for the United Nations Conference on Trade and Development (UNCTAD) and the World Intellectual Property Organization (WIPO)*, ed. Vanus James (Geneva: UNCTAD, 2001) were all written in the last twenty years; and the repeated inclusion of Jamaica by scholars like Krister Malm and Roger Wallis, *Big Sounds from Small Peoples: The Music Industry in Small Countries* (New York: Routledge, 1984), are some of the few such accounts.

3. Jeff Todd Titon and Bob Carlin, *American Musical Traditions: African American Music* (New York: Schirmer Reference, 2002), 117.

4. Lloyd Bradley, *Bass Culture: When Reggae Was King* (London: Penguin Books, 2001).

5. Cecelia Conway, *African Banjo Echoes in Appalachia: A Study of Folk Traditions* (Knoxville: University of Tennessee Press, 1995).

6. Garth White, "The Evolution of Jamaican Music, Part 1: 'Proto-Ska' to Ska," *Social and Economic Studies* 47, no. 1 (1998): 9; Robert Witmer, "'Local' and 'Foreign': The Popular Music Culture of Kingston, Jamaica, before Ska, Rock Steady, and Reggae," *Latin American Music Review* 8, no. 1 (1987): 1–25.

7. Lord Creator, *Big Bamboo* (Dynamic Sounds, 1964).

8. Homiak, John P. "Dub History: Soundings on Rastafari Livity and Language," in *Rastafari and Other African-Caribbean Worldviews*, ed. Barry Chevannes (New Brunswick: Rutgers University Press, 1998), 128.

9. There are studies still to be done on the influence of specific religious groups in Jamaican popular music, as well as the influence of Christianity. A starting point might be Markus Coester and Wolfgang Bender, *A Reader in African-Jamaican Music, Dance and Religion* (Kingston, Jamaica: Ian Randle Publishers, 2015). For this book, Pocomania, Kumina, and Revival (for example) did not appear to add a distinctive aspect to Jamaican creative practices' engagement with copyright. In the interests of time, this chapter does not discuss church and religious influences except where they directly affect my analysis.

10. The classic work of scholarship on Rastafari's rich and complex history is Barry Chevannes, *Rastafari: Roots and Ideology* (Syracuse, NY: Syracuse University Press, 1994).

11. Obika Gray, "The Coloniality of Power and the Limits of Dissent in Jamaica," *Small Axe: A Caribbean Journal of Criticism* 21, no. 3 (November 1, 2017): 103, https://doi.org/10.1215/07990537-4272022.

12. Sonjah Stanley-Niaah, "Kingstons's Dancehall," *Space and Culture* 7, no. 1 (2004): 102; Norman Stolzoff, *Wake the Town and Tell the People: Dancehall Culture in Jamaica* (New York: Routledge, Taylor & Francis, 2000), 62, 147.

13. Bradley, *Bass Culture*, 122; David Katz, *Solid Foundation: An Oral History of Reggae* (London: Bloomsbury, 2003), 39–40, 61, 117, 156, 158; Martin Mordecai and Pamela Mordecai, *Culture and Customs of Jamaica* (Westport, CT: Greenwood, 2001), 140.

14. Stolzoff quotes the Jamaican musician Hedley Jones, "It was generally understood that boys who emerged from these institutions [made music] because . . . they had nothing better to do." Stolzoff, *Wake the Town*, 37.

15. Stolzoff, 233; Percy C. Hintzen, "Reproducing Domination: Identity and Legitimacy Constructs in the West Indies," *Social Identities* 3, no. 1 (1997): 70.

16. There are various spellings and names for this language, including a push to call it "Jamaican." This book uses Patwa, as it was what I most commonly heard it called by the people I observed and conversed with. Patrick also notes that this is what the language "is popularly called." Peter L. Patrick, "Jamaican Creole," in *Languages and Dialects in the US: Focus on Diversity and Linguistics*, ed. Marianna Di Paolo and Arthur K. Spears (New York: Routledge, Taylor & Francis, 2014), 126.

17. Patrick, "Jamaican Creole," 127.

18. Mervin Alleyne, "Communication and Politics in Jamaica," *Caribbean Studies* 3, no. 2 (1963): 22–61.

19. Witmer, "'Local' and 'Foreign,'" 15.

20. Katz, *Solid Foundation*, 99; Paul Kauppila, "'From Memphis to Kingston': An Investigation into the Origin of Jamaican Ska," *Social and Economic Studies* 55, no 1–2, 2006, 75–91; Stolzoff, *Wake the Town*, 42.

21. Garth White, "The Development of Jamaican Popular Music, Part 2: Urbanization of the Folk; The Merger of Traditional and Popular in Jamaican Music," *African-Caribbean Institute of Jamaica Research Review* 1 (1984): 50.

22. A helpful beginning to remedying this is Heather Augustyn, *Songbirds: Pioneering Women in Jamaican Music* (Chesterton, IN: Half Pint, 2014).

23. Katz, *Solid Foundation*, 3.

24. Bradley, *Bass Culture*, 61; Katz, *Solid Foundation*, 56.

25. Witmer, "'Local' and 'Foreign,'" 8.

26. Grant Fared, "Wailin' Soul: Reggae's Debt to Black American Music," in *Soul: Black Power, Politics, and Pleasure*, ed. Richard C. Green (New York: New York University Press, 1998), 68; Stolzoff, *Wake the Town*, 36, 38.

27. Simon Jones, *Black Culture, White Youth: The Reggae Tradition from JA to UK* (Oxford: Macmillan Education, 1988).

28. Gray, "Coloniality of Power," 108.

29. Zeljka Kozul-Wright and Lloyd Stanbury, *Becoming a Globally Competitive Player: The Case of the Music Industry in Jamaica* (Geneva: UN Commission on Trade and Development, 1998), 31; Krister Malm and Roger Wallis, *Media Policy and Music Activity* (London: Routledge, 1992), 57.

30. Jason Toynbee, "Reggae Open Source: How the Absence of Copyright Enabled the Emergence of Popular Music in Jamaica," in *Copyright and Piracy: An Interdisciplinary Critique*, ed. Lionel Bently, Jennifer Davis, and Jane C. Ginsburg, vol. 13, Cambridge Intellectual Property and Information Law (Cambridge: Cambridge University Press, 2010), 357–73.

31. Khouri partnered with future prime minister Edward Seaga. Marie-Claude Derné and Keith Nurse, *Caribbean Economies and Global Restructuring* (Kingston: Ian Randle, 2002), 17; Katz, *Solid Foundation*, 13; Seaga's understand of the importance of music to the Jamaican poor is relevant to his political success. See also Obika Gray, *Demeaned but Empowered: The Social Power of the Urban Poor in Jamaica* (Kingston: University of West Indies Press, 2004).

32. Katz, *Solid Foundation*.

33. Katz, 24.

34. Quoted in Hopeton S. Dunn, *Globalization, Communications, and Caribbean Identity*, 1st ed. (New York: St. Martin's, 1995), 201.

35. Alejandra Bronfman, *Isles of Noise: Sonic Media in the Caribbean* (Durham: University of North Carolina Press, 2016), 10.

36. Jamaican Language Unit, *Report for Language Attitude Survey of Jamaica*, (Kingston: University of the West Indies, November 2005), https://www.mona.uwi .edu/dllp/jlu/projects/Report%20for%20Language%20Attitude%20Survey%20 of%20Jamaica.pdf.

37. Heather Augustyn, *Ska: The Rhythm of Liberation* (Lanham, MD: Scarecrow, 2013), 51.

38. "While the island's inhabitants were struggling to free themselves of their colonial shackles, its musicians were striving to establish a popular music they could truly claim as their own." Katz, *Solid Foundation*, 37.

39. Bradley, *Bass Culture*, 57.

40. Sonjah Stanley-Niaah, *DanceHall: From Slave Ship to Ghetto* (Ottawa: University of Ottawa Press, 2010), 119; Carolyn Cooper, *Noises in the Blood: Orality, Gender, and the "Vulgar" Body of Jamaican Popular Culture* (Durham, NC: Duke University Press, 1995), 11, 123, 141.

41. Stolzoff calls this mixing of cultural references "creolization." Stolzoff, *Wake the Town*, 15; Kerry-Ann Morris, *Jamaica* (Milwaukee, WI: Gareth Stevens, 2003), 21.

42. Bradley, *Bass Culture*, xv.

43. Louis Chude-Sokei, "Post-Nationalist Geographies: Rasta, Ragga, and Reinventing Africa," *African Arts* 27, no. 4 (Autumn 1994): 80–96.

44. Jones, *Black Culture, White Youth*, 39.

45. Kevin O'Brien Chang and Wayne Chen, *Reggae Routes: The Story of Jamaican Music* (Philadelphia: Temple University Press, 1998), 26.

46. Dick Hebdige, *Cut'n' Mix: Culture, Identity and Caribbean Music* (London: Routledge, 2004), 45; Katz, *Solid Foundation*, 174; White, "Part 2."

47. Patrick Hylton, "The Politics of Caribbean Music," *Black Scholar* 7, no. 1 (1975): 27.

48. Quoted in Bradley, *Bass Culture*, 55.

49. Mordecai and Mordecai, *Culture and Customs*, 140.

50. Julian Henriques, "Sonic Diaspora, Vibrations, and Rhythm: Thinking Through the Sounding of the Jamaican Dancehall Session," *African and Black Diaspora: An International Journal* 1, no. 2 (2008): 455; Katz, *Solid Foundation*, 3, 116.

51. Bradley, *Bass Culture*, 203.

52. Bradley, 40.

53. "Soundsystems . . . are still the primary mode of musical dissemination." Chang and Chen, *Reggae Routes*, 175; Witmer, "'Local' and 'Foreign,'" 15.

54. Clinton Hutton, "Forging Identity and Community through Aestheticism and Entertainment: The Sound System and the Rise of the DJ," *Caribbean Quarterly* 53, no. 4 (2007): 18.

55. Peter Manuel and Wayne Marshall, "The Riddim Method: Aesthetics, Practice, and Ownership in Jamaican Dancehall," *Popular Music* 25, no. 3 (2006): 449; Katz, *Solid Foundation*, 28, 54.

56. Mark Slobin, *Subcultural Sounds: Micromusics of the West* (Middletown, CT: Wesleyan University Press, 1993), 64.

57. White, "Part 1."

58. Katz, *Solid Foundation*, 66.

59. Bradley, *Bass Culture*, 306; Chang and Chen, *Reggae Routes*, 74, 94; Katz, *Solid Foundation*, 31; Kozul-Wright and Stanbury, "Globally Competitive Player," 18.

60. An acetate is the first recording made of an audio performance in the era of vinyl records. Acetates were the first, or master, recording from which a "stamper," or metal plate, was made, which could be used to press more records.

61. Katz, *Solid Foundation*, 168.

62. Bradley, *Bass Culture*, 24.

63. Katz, *Solid Foundation*, 20.

64. Chang and Chen, *Reggae Routes*, 32

65. Gray, *Demeaned but Empowered*, 27; George. E. Eaton, *Alexander Bustamante and Modern Jamaica* (Kingston: Kingston Publishers, 1975), 123.

66. Bradley, *Bass Culture: When Reggae Was King*, 158, 165.

67. Morris, *Jamaica*, 21.

68. Bradley, *Bass Culture*, 160.

69. Joseph Heathcott, "Urban Spaces and Working-Class Expressions across the Black Atlantic: Tracing the Routes of Ska," *Radical History Review* 87, no. 1 (2003): 196.

70. Manuel and Marshall, "Riddim Method," 447; Jones, *Black Culture, White Youth*, 39.

71. Gray, *Demeaned but Empowered*, 44; Chude-Sokei, "Post-Nationalist Geographies."

72. George Lipsitz, "Immigration and Assimilation: Rai, Reggae, and Bhangramuffin," in *Dangerous Crossroads: Popular Music, Postmodernism and the Poetics of Place* (London: Verso, 1997), 127.

73. Fared, "Wailin' Soul." "My Boy Lollipop" was a cover song of a U.S. pop tune sung by Barbie Gaye in 1956.

74. Michael Veal, *Dub: Soundscapes and Shattered Songs in Jamaican Reggae* (Middletown, CT: Wesleyan University Press, 2007), 221; Jones, *Black Culture, White Youth*.

75. Jamaica Copyright Act, part 1, section 2(iii)(e).

76. Michael Witter, "Music and the Jamaican Economy" (Geneva: UNCTAD/WIPO, 2004), 51.

77. Bradley, *Bass Culture*, 41.

78. White, "Part 2," 50.

79. Heather Royes and Tom Tavares-Finson, "Current Status of Copyright Legislation in Jamaica," *Jamaica Journal* 16, no. 1 (1983): 14–18.

80. Tony Laing, interview, September 10, 2000.

81. Toynbee, "Reggae Open Source," 369; David Throsby, *The Music Industry in the New Millennium: Global and Local Perspectives* (Paris: UNESCO, 2002), 13.

82. Stolzoff, *Wake the Town*, 59.

83. Some historians suggest there was a transition from studios paying per song to paying wages. Bradley, *Bass Culture*. Bradley describes how Coxsone Dodd "took the unprecedented step of putting the nucleus of the island's best musicians on wages, rather than hiring them as'n'when and paying them per side cut [per side of a vinyl record that was recorded]." See also Johnson Okpaluba, "'Free-Riding on the Riddim'? Open Source, Copyright Law and Reggae Music in Jamaica," in *Copyright and Piracy: An Interdisciplinary Critique*, ed. Lionel Bently, Jennifer Davis, and Jane C. Ginsburg (Cambridge: Cambridge University Press, 2010), 376.

84. Katz, *Solid Foundation*, 167.

85. Adrian Boot and Michael Thomas, *Jamaica: Babylon on a Thin Wire* (New York: Schocken Books, 1976), 34.

86. Klive Walker, *Dubwise: Reasoning from the Reggae Underground* (London: Insomniac, 2005); Bradley, *Bass Culture*, 111; Jones, *Black Culture, White Youth*, 39.

87. This is common in the United States and beyond—despite a focus on royalties benefiting musicians, power relations often led to them not owning copyrights either and having to capitalize on other aspects of their roles in the industry. The ability to profit from royalties in the United States also tracks the United States' own colonial experience—the power to own copyrights accrued much more to the white and already wealthy. See Aram Sinnreich, *The Piracy Crusade: How the Music Industry's War on Sharing Destroys Markets and Erodes Civil Liberties* (Amherst: University of Massachusetts Press, 2013).

88. Katz, *Solid Foundation*, 105; Okpaluba, "'Free-Riding,'" 376–77.

89. Louis Chude-Sokei, "'Dr. Satan's Echo Chamber': Reggae, Technology, and the Diaspora Process," *Emergences: Journal for the Study of Media and Composite Cultures* 9, no. 1 (May 1999): 47–59.

90. Hebdige, *Cut'n' Mix*; Ajay Heble and Daniel Fischlin, *Rebel Musics: Human Rights, Resistant Sounds, and the Politics of Music Making* (Montreal: Black Rose Books, 2003); Malm and Wallis, *Big Sounds*.

91. J. M. Chernoff, *African Rhythm and African Sensibility: Aesthetics and Social Action in African Musical Idioms* (Chicago: University of Chicago Press, 1979), 111–12.

92. Ingrid T. Monson, "Riffs, Repetition, and Theories of Globalization," *Ethnomusicology* 43, no. 1 (Winter 1999): 46.

93. Peter Manuel and Wayne Marshall, "The Riddim Method: Aesthetics, Practice, and Ownership in Jamaican Dancehall," *Popular Music* 25, no. 3 (2006): 448.

94. Peter Tosh, *Equal Rights* (Dynamic Sounds, 1977).

95. Aldrie Henry-Lee, "The Nature of Poverty in the Garrison Constituencies in Jamaica," *Environment and Urbanization* 17, no. 2 (2005): 120.

96. Stolzoff, *Wake the Town*, 171–73; Deborah A. Thomas, *Exceptional Violence: Embodied Citizenship in Transnational Jamaica* (Durham, NC: Duke University Press, 2011), 3.

97. Stolzoff, *Wake the Town*, 28; Eaton, *Alexander Bustamante*, 139–49; Anthony P. Maingot and Wilfredo Lozano, *The United States and the Caribbean: Transforming Hegemony and Sovereignty* (New York: Routledge, 2005), 140.

98. Bradley, *Bass Culture*, 516; Stanley-Niaah, *DanceHall*, 43, 73.

99. Gray, *Demeaned but Empowered*.

100. Donna P. Hope, *Inna Di Dancehall: Popular Culture and the Politics of Identity in Jamaica* (Kingston: University of the West Indies Press, 2001), 98.

101. Gray, *Demeaned but Empowered*, 288.

102. Anita M. Waters, *Race, Class, and Political Symbols: Rastafari and Reggae in Jamaican Politics* (Piscataway, NJ: Transaction, 1989), 85, 129, 130.

103. Bradley, *Bass Culture*, 305.

104. Veal, *Dub*.

105. Chris Potash, ed., *Reggae, Rasta, Revolution: Jamaican Music from Ska to Dub* (New York: Schirmer Books, 1997), 145.

106. Kembrew McLeod, Peter DiCola, Jenny Tooney, and Kristin Thomson, *Creative License: The Law and Culture of Digital Sampling* (Durham, NC: Duke University Press, 2011), 78.

107. Veal, *Dub*; Phanuel Antwi, "Dub Poetry as a Black Atlantic Body-Archive," *Small Axe* 19, no. 3 (November 1, 2015): 65–83.

108. Chang and Chen, *Reggae Routes*, 55.

109. Jon Stratton, "Chris Blackwell and 'My Boy Lollipop': Ska, Race, and British Popular Music," *Journal of Popular Music Studies* 22, no. 4 (2010): 436.

110. David Vlado Moskowitz, *The Words and Music of Bob Marley* (Westport, CT: Greenwood, 2007), 131.

111. Malm and Wallis, *Big Sounds*, 179.

112. Witter, "Music," 52.

113. Royes and Tavares-Finson, "Current Status," 17.

114. Bradley, *Bass Culture*, 253.

115. Bradley, *Bass Culture*, 253.

116. Katz, *Solid Foundation*, 167.

117. Anne M. Galvin, *Sharing the Wealth: Community Development and the Dancehall Music Industry in Contemporary Kingston, Jamaica* (New York: New School University, 2006).

118. Toynbee, "Reggae Open Source."

119. Jeff Chang, *Can't Stop Won't Stop: A History of the Hip-Hop Generation* (New York: Picador, 2005), 21–22, 313.

120. Chude-Sokei, "Post-Nationalist Geographies."

121. Chude-Sokei; Grant Farred, "The Postcolonial Chickens Come Home to Roost: How Yardie Has Created a New Postcolonial Subaltern," *South Atlantic Quarterly* 100, no. 1 (January 1, 2001): 287–305.

122. George Lipsitz, "World Cities and World Beat: Low-Wage Labor and Transnational Culture," *Pacific Historical Review* 68, no. 2 (May 1, 1999): 213–31.

123. Chude-Sokei, "Post-Nationalist Geographies."

124. Louis Chude-Sokei, "The Sound of Culture: Dread Discourse and Jamaican Sound Systems," in *Language, Rhythm, and Sound: Black Popular Cultures into the Twenty-First Century*, ed. J. K. Adjaye (Pittsburgh: University of Pittsburgh Press, 1997), 185, 197.

125. Cutty Ranks, *The Stopper* (Fashion Records, 1990).

126. Chang and Chen, *Reggae Routes*, 375.

127. Marvin Sterling, *Babylon East: Performing Dancehall, Roots Reggae, and Rastafari in Japan* (Durham, NC: Duke University Press, 2010).

128. Chude-Sokei, "Sound of Culture," 187; Monson, "Riffs, Repetition," 43, 46.

129. Stolzoff, *Wake the Town*, 106.

130. Deanna C. Robinson, Elizabeth B. Buck, and Marlene Cuthbert, *Music at the Margins: Popular Music and Global Cultural Diversity* (New York: Sage, 1991), 193. Also see Marlene Cuthbert and Gladstone Wilson, "Recording Artists in Jamaica: Payola, Piracy and Copyright," in *Caribbean Popular Culture*, ed. John Lent (Bowling Green, Ohio: Bowling Green State University Popular Press, 1990), 64–78.

131. Joeri M. Mol and Nachoem M. Wijnberg, "Competition, Selection and Rock and Roll: The Economics of Payola and Authenticity," *Journal of Economic Issues* 41, no. 3 (2007): 10.

132. Malm and Wallis, *Big Sounds*, 178.

133. "More Heat on Howard," *Jamaica Observer*, April 11, 2018, http://www .jamaicaobserver.com/entertainment/more-heat-on-howard_130155?profile=1120.

134. Percy Hintzen describes this colonial politics of taste by pointing out that finding music of the poor distasteful is seen as part of "the 'styles' and 'tastes' of development." "The Caribbean: Race and Creole Ethnicity," in *A Companion to Racial and Ethnic Studies*, ed. David Theo Goldberg and John Solomos (Malden, MA: Blackwell, 2002), 475–94,

135. Daraine Luton, "On the Dancehall Bandwagon—Local Academics Being Blamed for Falling Standards," *Jamaica Gleaner*, December 27, 2009, http://jamaica -gleaner.com/gleaner/20091227/lead/lead4.html.

136. Erin Macleod and Joshua Chamberlain, "Soundsystem Culture in Jamaica: Still the Voice of the People?" (Pop Conference, Seattle, WA, April 14, 2016).

137. Robinson, Buck, and Cuthbert, *Music at the Margins*, 89; Witter, "Music," 34.

138. Baz Dreisinger, "Non-Jamaican Reggae: Who's Making It and Who's Buying It," *The Record*, November 12, 2011, http://www.npr.org/blogs/therecord/2011/11/17 /142254188/non-jamaican-reggae-whos-making-it-and-whos-buying-it.

139. Stolzoff, *Wake the Town*, 3.

140. Chang, *Can't Stop Won't Stop*.

141. Field notes, January 2009.

142. Silke Von Lewinski, *International Copyright Law and Policy* (Oxford: Oxford University Press, 2008), 33–34.

143. Okpaluba, "'Free-Riding,'" 384.

144. "Jamaican Artists Sing the Blues," *Jamaica Gleaner*, December 20, 2010, http://jamaica-gleaner.com/gleaner/20101220/lead/lead1.html.

145. Krista Henry, "Stop Order on 'Rampin Shop'—Ne-Yo's Publishing Company Writes Kartel," *Jamaica Star*, January 29, 2009, http://jamaica-star.com/thestar /20090129/ent/ent1.html.

146. Julie E. Cohen, "Pervasively Distributed Copyright Enforcement," *Georgetown Law Journal* 95 (2006): 1–44.

147. Government of Jamaica, "Copyright Documents—JIPO," Jamaica Intellectual Property Office, 2010, http://www.jipo.gov.jm/?q=node/69.

148. James, Vanus, *The Caribbean Music Industry Database: A Report Prepared for the United Nations Conference on Trade and Development (UNCTAD) and the World Intellectual Property Organization (WIPO)* (Geneva: UNCTAD, 2001).

Chapter 2

1. Emma Lewis, "Dancehall Directory? A New Yellow Pages Cover Stirs Controversy in Jamaica," *Global Voices* (blog), December 3, 2016, https://globalvoices.org /2016/12/03/dancehall-directory-a-new-yellow-pages-cover-stirs-controversy-in -jamaica/.

2. Jovan Johnson, "Phone Book Backlash—Church Lobby Forces Yellow Pages to Find Alternative Scene for Directory Cover," *Jamaica Gleaner*, December 1, 2016, http://jamaica-gleaner.com/article/lead-stories/20161201/phone-book-backlash -church-lobby-forces-yellow-pages-find-alternative.

3. Erin Macleod, "Lennox Coke on His Controversial Jamaican Yellow Pages Cover," LargeUp, December 19, 2016, http://www.largeup.com/2016/12/09/jamaica -yellow-pages-cover-dancehall/.

4. In fact, the backlash was less hostile and more publicly multisided than in the past, with many making Lennox's points, as well as criticizing a long history of public hostility to poor Jamaicans, and affirming the artwork's positive depictions of Black people's bodies. The phone book company's representative apologized only for giving offense and did not concede that the image itself was inappropriate, saying it was "a matter of interpretation." Johnson, "Phone Book Backlash."

5. Kevin O'Brien Chang and Wayne Chen describe sound systems as "the primary mode of musical dissemination" in *Reggae Routes: The Story of Jamaican Music* (Philadelphia, PA: Temple University Press, 1998), 175; while Norman Stolzoff asserts that "for the past fifty years, the soundsystems have been the driving force behind Jamaican popular music culture." *Wake the Town and Tell the People: Dancehall Culture in Jamaica* (New York: Routledge, Taylor & Francis, 2000), 4. Also see Robert Witmer, "'Local' and 'Foreign': The Popular Music Culture of Kingston, Jamaica, before Ska, Rock Steady, and Reggae," *Latin American Music Review* 8, no. 1 (1987): 15; David Katz, *Solid Foundation: An Oral History of Reggae* (New York: Bloomsbury, 2003), 1; or for a more philosophical argument, see Julian Henriques, *Sonic Bodies: Reggae Soundsystems, Performance Techniques, and Ways of Knowing* (New York: Continuum International, 2011).

6. Katz, *Solid Foundation*, 2.

7. "Boasy" is slang for "boastful" with a resistantly positive connotation: in the sense of being brash, well dressed, proud, and flamboyant. The term has class implications, especially as a street dance, because it implies one who has humble background but is not intimidated. See *West Indian Dictionary*, 2008, s.v. "Boasy," accessed April 8, 2013, http://wiwords.com/word/boasy.

8. The term "Passa Passa" is a Patwa idiom meaning "gossip-worthy drama." *West Indian Dictionary*, 2008, s.v. "Passa Passa," accessed April 8, 2013, http://www .wiwords.com/word/passapassa.

9. The term "Bembe" has several possible meanings, including the name of an Afro-Cuban drum rhythm (*bembé*) or a set of hand drums. "Dutty" is a Patwa version of "dirty" with similar connotations as English—including connotations of sex and of lower-classedness.

10. Obika Gray, *Demeaned but Empowered: The Social Power of the Urban Poor in Jamaica* (Kingston: University of West Indies Press, 2004), 9, 12, 324.

11. Louis Chude-Sokei, "The Sound of Culture: Dread Discourse and Jamaican Soundsystems," in *Language, Rhythm, and Sound: Black Popular Cultures into the Twenty-First Century*, ed. J. K Adjaye (Pittsburgh: University of Pittsburgh Press, 1997), 191.

12. James Holston, "Spaces of Insurgent Citizenship." In *The Urban Sociology Reader*, edited by Jan Lin, Christopher Mele, and Jan van Lin. (London: Taylor & Francis Group, 2012), 423.

13. Gray, *Demeaned but Empowered*, 91.

14. The Main Roads Act of Jamaica finds liable "any person who wilfully or negligently prevents, hinders or intercepts, the free passage of any other person or any carriage or beast, on any main road, or who draws up any carriage in such manner as to obstruct the free passage along the road." Ministry of Justice of Jamaica. Main Roads Act of Jamaica, § Town and Country Planning (1985), https://moj.gov.jm/laws /main-roads-act.

15. Sonjah Stanley-Niaah, *DanceHall: From Slave Ship to Ghetto* (Ottawa: University of Ottawa Press, 2010), 4.

16. Field notes, 2009.

17. Vice News, *Young and Gay: Jamaica's Gully Queens*, 2014, https://www.vice .com/en/article/kwpn4n/young-and-gay-jamaicas-gully-queens-288..

18. Vice News, *Young and Gay*, 2014.

19. Priscilla Frank, "These Are the Fearless LGBTQ Youth Who Live in Jamaica's Sewers," *Huffington Post*, August 29, 2016, https://www.huffpost.com/entry/christo -geoghegan-gully-queen-photos_n_57c09c34e4b085c1ff29586f.

20. Julia Felsenthal, "Meet the Gully Queens, the Transgender Women Defying Jamaica's Culture of Homophobia," *Vogue*, November 10, 2016, https://www.vogue .com/article/ray-blk-chill-out-video-premiere-gully-queens.

21. Shay Prietz, "10 Secrets about the Gully Queens, the Mole People Living underneath Jamaica's Streets," TheTravel, April 18, 2020, https://www.thetravel.com /gully-queens-mole-people-jamaica-secrets/.

22. VICE News, *Young and Gay*.

23. There appears to be no published work on this as yet, but a promising start is Michael Stephens, "Run to the Gully: Structural Escape of Jamaican Queer Communities under the Neoliberal Turn," in *Latin American, Caribbean, and U.S. Latino Studies Symposium*, March 4, 2017, https://scholarsarchive.library.albany.edu /lacsconference/2017/schedule/7.

24. Responses in conversation ranged from amusement to distaste. Two people I spoke with implied that foreigners like to go see parts of Jamaica that "decent" Jamaicans avoid. I was warned during election season that it would not be wise to cross town even in a taxi to get there, due to the risk of being caught in crossfire— not necessarily at Passa Passa but when driving through other garrison neighborhoods on the way. Personal conversations, February 2009.

25. Colin Clarke, *Decolonizing the Colonial City: Urbanization and Stratification in Kingston, Jamaica* (Oxford: Oxford University Press, 2006), 219.

26. Donna P. Hope, "Passa Passa: Interrogating Cultural Hybridities in Jamaican Dancehall," *Small Axe: A Caribbean Journal of Criticism* 10, no. 3 (2006): 125–39; Aldrie Henry-Lee, "The Nature of Poverty in the Garrison Constituencies in Jamaica," *Environment and Urbanization* 17, no. 2 (2005): 83–99.

27. As has been discussed elsewhere and as Gray emphasizes, local dons also supported their local communities through government connections and through

their increasing wealth from the drug trade and other sources—allocating resources among their supporters that they did not get from the state—sometimes including access to water and education.

28. As of 2019, Passa Passa has become legend, its ups and downs reflecting the uneasy power of dancehall spaces. In 2009, some organizers sought for it to be formally licensed and recognized; in 2010, newspapers publicly associated it with the wanted gangster and local "community leader" Christopher Coke and then had to publicly retract that assertion. The event faced repeated closures following a curfew enstated in Tivoli during the military incursion to extradite Coke to the United States. The event was officially shut down following a last event in 2012.

29. Noise Abatement Act of Jamaica, 1997.

30. Ulysse also describes these posted dress codes in "malls, hospitals and even police stations." Gina A. Ulysse, *Downtown Ladies: Informal Commercial Importers, a Haitian Anthropologist and Self-Making in Jamaica* (Chicago: University of Chicago Press, 2007), 222.

31. Mel Cooke, "Living by Law . . . Fletcher's Land Missing 'Dutty Fridaze,'" *Jamaica Gleaner*, October 31, 2010, http://jamaica-gleaner.com/gleaner/20101031/news/news1.html.

32. Lisa Douglass, *The Power of Sentiment: Love, Hierarchy, and the Jamaican Family Elite* (Boulder, CO: Westview, 1992), 38.

33. Although the poorest parts of town might be simply unpaved, road quality did not uniformly correlate with class position—uptown neighborhoods often had potholes or unpaved stretches, and wealthy people's luxury sport utility vehicles did serve a function in easing the way across uneven pavement (although it's unclear if that is worth the 100 percent import tax rate). This inconsistent public infrastructure hints at the lack of uniformity in the Jamaican state projects that contradicts easy assumptions about the rule of law and its ability to solve social problems.

34. Diane J. Austin-Broos and D. J. Austin, *Urban Life in Kingston, Jamaica: The Culture and Class Ideology of Two Neighborhoods*, vol. 3, Urban Studies (Montreux, Switzerland: Gordon and Breach Science, 1984), 35, 42.

35. Sound system crews include "five to fifteen men, with two to five selectors (DJs) and three to ten . . . roadies and technicians." Stolzoff, *Wake the Town*, 119.

36. Field notes, 2009.

37. Field notes, 2009.

38. Julian Henriques, "Sonic Dominance and the Reggae Soundsystem Session," *Auditory Culture Reader*, ed. Michael Bull and Les Back, (New York: Bloomsbury Academic, 2003), 451–80.

39. Mattathias Schwartz, "A Massacre in Jamaica," *New Yorker*, December 12, 2011, 42, http://www.newyorker.com/reporting/2011/12/12/111212fa_fact_schwartz.

40. Hope, "Passa Passa," 130.

41. "Apology to Organisers of Passa Passa," *Jamaica Gleaner*, August 2, 2010, http://jamaica-gleaner.com/gleaner/20100802/lead/lead8.html.

42. Cooke, "Living by Law."

43. Gray, *Demeaned but Empowered*, 197, 218–20, 285. Also see L. Alan Eyre, "Political Violence and Urban Geography in Kingston, Jamaica," *Geographical Review* 74, no. 1 (January 1, 1984): 24–37, https://doi.org/10.2307/214758.

44. Jamaicans for Justice, *Jamaica: A Long Road to Justice? Human Rights Violations under the State of Emergency* (London: Jamaicans for Justice / Amnesty International, May 31, 2011), http://jamaicansforjustice.org/nmcms.php?snippets=docmanager&p=docresults; Schwartz, "Massacre in Jamaica."

45. "Passa Passa's crowd might also include visitors from the U.S., Canada, Australia, Israel, Ireland, Sweden, Austria, Germany, England and Japan." Sadeke Brooks, "Italian Takes Passa Passa Photos to the World," *Jamaica Gleaner*, August 28, 2011, http://jamaica-gleaner.com/gleaner/20110828/ent/ent5.html; Passa Passa is also popular across the Caribbean. See Camille Hernandez-Ramdwar, "Shottas and Cubatoneros: Badmanism, Bling and Youth Crime in Trinidad and Tobago and Cuba," *Caribbean Journal of Criminology and Public Safety* 14, no. 1 (2009): 308.

46. Thompson provides a fascinating history of this in *Shine: The Visual Economy of Light in African Diasporic Aesthetic Practice* (Durham, NC: Duke University Press, 2015), https://doi.org/10.1215/9780822375982-003.

47. Cooke, "Living by Law."

48. Erin Macleod and Joshua Chamberlain, "Soundsystem Culture in Jamaica: Still the Voice of the People?" (Pop Conference, Seattle, WA, April 14, 2016).

49. "Passa Passa, the Authentic Tourism Experience," *Jamaica Gleaner*, March 4, 2007, http://jamaica-gleaner.com/gleaner/20070304/news/news5.html.

50. Ministry of Education, Youth, and Culture. "Towards Jamaica the Cultural Superstate: The National Cultural Policy of Jamaica." Kingston, Jamaica: Division of Culture, 2003.

51. Meaghan Frauts, "Resilience and the Creative Economy in Kingston, Jamaica," *Cultural Studies* 33, no. 3 (March 1, 2019): 405, https://doi.org/10.1080/09502386.2019.1584905.

52. "It became clear that there was no plan for how the removal of these dances from community spaces might affect the incomes of families if the zoning project came to fruition." Frauts, "Resilience," 406.

53. David Graeber, *Toward an Anthropological Theory of Value: The False Coin of Our Own Dreams* (Basingstoke, UK: Palgrave Macmillan, 2001), 225.

54. Graeber, *Toward an Anthropological Theory of Value*, 225.

55. Field notes, 2009.

56. Larisa Kingston Mann, "White Faces in Intimate Spaces: Jamaican Popular Music in Global Circulation," *Communication, Culture and Critique* 9, no. 2 (June 2016): 266–83.

57. Thompson, *Shine*.

58. "Women Fight for Video Light: Three to Be Sentenced after Brawl at Dance," *Jamaica Star*, August 12, 2008, http://jamaica-star.com/thestar/20080812/news/news1.html.

59. "Newspaper reports legitimized the dancers and made proving that they were bona fide entertainers much easier." Cooke, "Living by Law."

60. The Jamaica Copyright Act has a performance right, although ownership rests in the person who "by whom the arrangements necessary for the making of the recording . . . are undertaken," which means ownership could be a negotiation between soundman/promoter, videographer, and possibly the dancer. Jamaica Copyright Act, part 1, section 2(iii)(e).

61. Krista Henry, "Dancers to Copyright Moves," *Jamaica Star*, September 19, 2008, http://jamaica-star.com/thestar/20080919/ent/ent1.html; Curtis Campbell, "Dancers Want to Copyright Their Moves," *Jamaica Gleaner*, May 12, 2013, http://jamaica-gleaner.com/gleaner/20130512/ent/ent4.html.

62. Carmen Kate Yuen, "Scuffling for a Slice of the Ringtone Pie: Evaluating Legal and Business Approaches to Copyright Clearance Issues," *Vanderbilt Journal of Entertainment and Technology Law* 8 (2006): 541–50; Electronic Frontier Foundation, "ASCAP Makes Outlandish Copyright Claims on Cell Phone Ringtones: EFF Argues Phones Ringing in Public Do Not Violate Copyright Law," July 2, 2009, http://www.eff.org/press/archives/2009/07/02.

63. Krista Henry, "Stop Order on 'Rampin Shop'—Ne-Yo's Publishing Company Writes Kartel," *Jamaica Star*, January 29, 2009, http://jamaica-star.com/thestar/20090129/ent/ent1.html.

64. Digital Millennium Copyright Act, 112 Stat. 2860 (codified as amended at 17 U.S.C., 28 U.S.C., and 35 U.S.C.). The act protects hosting platforms like YouTube from infringement liability if they comply with copyright owner's requests to remove items identified as infringing. However, the original uploader is entitled to dispute the removal on various grounds.

65. Lee B. Burgunder, *Legal Aspects of Managing Technology* (Mason, OH: South-Western, Cengage Learning, 2011), 311.

66. Deirdre K. Mulligan and Aaron Perzanowski, "The Magnificence of the Disaster: Reconstructing the Sony BMG Rootkit Incident," *Berkeley Technology Law Journal* 22 (2007): 1157–232. In 2005, Sony installed software compromising the security of up to two million people's computers, attempting to enforce copyright protection on Sony CDs. Pamela Samuelson and Jason Schultz, "Should Copyright Owners Have to Give Notice of Their Use of Technical Protection Measures," *Journal on Telecommunications and High Technology Law* 6 (2007): 41–76.

67. Yochai Benkler, *The Wealth of Networks: How Social Production Transforms Markets and Freedom* (New Haven, CT: Yale University Press, 2007), 383.

68. Lori A. Morea, "The Future of Music in a Digital Age: The Ongoing Conflict between Copyright Law and Peer-to-Peer Technology," *Campbell Law Review* 28 (2005): 218; Lawrence Lessig, "Re-crafting a Public Domain," *Yale Journal of Law and the Humanities* 18 (2006): 60.

69. Burri gives an account of ways that networked digital technologies may alter cultural practices, in "Enquiry into the Notion of Cultural Protectionism in the Media and Its Dimensions in Cyberspace," in *Bits without Borders: Law, Communications and Transnational Culture in a Digital Age* (Cheltenham, UK: Elgar, 2012). It is important to note that the diasporic nature of Jamaican phonographic orality means that sonic homoegeity is unlikely to result from protectionism of the method of making Jamaican popular music. See, for example, Louis Chude-Sokei, "'Dr. Satan's Echo Chamber':

Reggae, Technology, and the Diaspora Process," *Emergences: Journal for the Study of Media and Composite Cultures* 9, no. 1 (May 1999): 47–59.

70. Shereika Grizzle, "Dancers Stand Alone," *Jamaica Gleaner*, February 1, 2016, http://jamaica-gleaner.com/article/entertainment/20160201/dancers-stand-alone.

71. Because Jamaican tunes tend to share instrumentals (riddims), it is common to hear the same riddim multiple times with different singers recorded over it.

72. Field notes, 2009.

73. There is a range between totally free street dances and elite nightclub events or "all-inclusive" parties in tightly secured locations. Bembe, while not free, relied on many of the practices of street dances in the way more elite clubs did not. It was in a partly enclosed space and appeared to admit famous dancers and singers from the street dance in free, their reputation in those places translating into social currency. Thus, it still reflected some orientation toward the authority of the street dance, while also catering to a slightly more well-off crowd—albeit one that wished, in Jamaica's still highly class-conscious environment, to spend time in a street-dance-like space.

74. Henriques, *Sonic Bodies*.

75. Interview, May 2009.

76. "Bottle-Throwing Bouts Smash 'Extravaganza,'" *Jamaica Gleaner*, December 24, 2004, http://jamaica-gleaner.com/gleaner/20011224/ent/ent1.html.

77. Carolyn Cooper, *Noises in the Blood: Orality, Gender, and the "Vulgar" Body of Jamaican Popular Culture* (Durham, NC: Duke University Press, 1995).

78. Lorder, *Royals* (Universal, 2012).

79. Busy Signal, *Well Prepared* (Turf Music, 2013).

80. Joseph P. Liu, "Copyright and Breathing Space," *Columbia Journal of Law and the Arts* 30, no. 3–4 (2007): 123. Also see Julie Cohen's discussion of "degrees of freedom" in "Creativity and Culture in Copyright Theory," *UC Davis Law Review* 40 (2007): 1190–91.

81. Denise Noble, *Decolonizing and Feminizing Freedom: A Caribbean Genealogy* (London: Springer, 2017), 277.

82. Cooper, *Noises in the Blood*; Janell Hobson, "The 'Batty' Politic: Toward an Aesthetic of the Black Female Body," *Hypatia* 18, no. 4 (Fall 2003): 87–105; Bibi Bakare-Yusuf, "'I Love Myself When I Am Dancing and Carrying On': Refiguring the Agency of Black Women's Creative Expression in Jamaican Dancehall Culture," *International Journal of Media and Cultural Politics* 1, no. 3 (December 2005): 263–76, https://doi.org/10.1386/macp.1.3.263/1; Tracey Skelton, "Ghetto Girls / Urban Music: Jamaican Ragga Music and Female Performance," in *New Frontiers of Space, Bodies and Gender*, ed. Rosa Ainley (London: Psychology Press, 1998), 142–54; M. Jacqui Alexander, "Erotic Autonomy as a Politics of Decolonization: An Anatomy of Feminist and State Practice in the Bahamas Tourist Economy," in *Feminist Genealogies, Colonial Legacies, Democratic Futures*, ed. Chandra Mohanty and M. Jacqui Alexander (New York: Routledge, 1997), 63–100.

83. Ulysse, *Downtown Ladies*, 222.

84. De Torres links traditions in men's dancehall fashion to the actor-boy character in Jamaican carnival tradition of Jonkonnu, arguing that these "characters are not Westernized hybrids of feminized masculinity analogous to the fop, dandy or maca-

roni. Actor Boy grows straight from the working classes and emerges as a construction of Jamaican counter-hegemonic gender identity." Lena Delgado de Torres, "Swagga: Fashion, Kinaesthetics and Gender in Dancehall and Hip-Hop," *Journal of Black Masculinity: The Philosophical Underpinnings of Gender Identity* 1, no. 2 (2011): 6.

85. Nadia Ellis, "Out and Bad: Toward a Queer Performance Hermeneutic in Jamaican Dancehall," *Small Axe* 15, no. 2 (July 1, 2011): 7–23, https://doi.org/10.1215/07990537-1334212.

86. Carolyn Cooper, "Erotic Maroonage: Embodying Emancipation in Jamaican Dancehall Culture," in *Proceedings of the Ninth Annual Gilder Lehrman Center International Conference at Yale University, Co-sponsored by the Yale Center for British Art* (Legacies of Slavery and Emancipation: Jamaica in the Atlantic World, New Haven, CT, 2007), 1, http://glc.yale.edu/sites/default/files/files/Cooper.pdf.

87. Gray, *Demeaned but Empowered*, 94.

88. Mann, "White Faces."

89. Mr. Vegas & Lexxus, *Video Light* (Greensleeves Records 2002).

90. Aside from Best's more wide-ranging cultural analysis in "Caribbean Cyberculture: Towards an Understanding of Gender, Sexuality and Identity within the Digital Culture Matrix," in *Constructing Vernacular Culture in the Trans-Caribbean*, ed. Holger Henke and Karl-Heinz Magister (Lanham, MD: Lexington Books, 2008), 377–98, most research on the penetration of technology in Jamaica has been done about cellular phones. See Heather A. Horst, "The Blessings and Burdens of Communication: Cell Phones in Jamaican Transnational Social Fields," *Global Networks* 6, no. 2 (2006): 143–59. Although internet access is officially low (10 percent of households in 2008), see Information and Telecommunications Department Office of the Prime Minister, "Information and Communications Technology (ICT) Policy" (Kingston: Government of Jamaica, Jamaica Information Service, March 2011), http://www.jis.gov.jm/pdf/GOJ_ICTPOLICY_March2011.pdf; in 2009, the internet was increasingly accessible (if not wholly or continuously reliable) for middle-class Jamaicans and not out of reach for some of the poor although not usually in their homes.

91. Skelton, "Ghetto Girls / Urban Music," Cooper, *Noises in the Blood*; Bakare-Yusuf, "'I Love Myself.'"

92. Thompson, *Shine*, 123.

93. Mann, "White Faces"; and see especially the discussion in Thompson, 112–68.

94. For a detailed discussion of the history of videography and visibility in the street dance, see Thompson.

95. Bennett and Peterson describe how "A translocal scene . . . serve[s] to produce affective communities that transcend the need for face-to-face interaction as a requirement for scene membership." Andy Bennett and Richard A. Peterson, *Music Scenes: Local, Translocal and Virtual* (Nashville: Vanderbilt University Press, 2004), 9. See also David Laing, "Rock Anxieties and New Music Networks," in *Back to Reality? Social Experience and Cultural Studies*, ed. Angela McRobbie (Manchester: Manchester University Press, 1997), 116–132.

96. "Boasy Tuesday 17 (DVD) Dancehall Reggae CD, Reggae DVD, Reggae Music and Dance Hall," n.d., http://cdselectaz.com/boasy-tuesday-p-4026.html; "DANCE

n STAGESHOW DVDs DOWNLOADS," Outtaroad—the Dancehall Mix CDs/DVDs Store, n.d., http://www.outtaroad.net/shop/index.php?_a=viewCat&catId=8.

97. Stanley-Niaah has also documented DVDs' global reach. Stanley-Niaah, *DanceHall*.

98. Some experts on Jamaican music have recently argued that this should change, although focusing more on roots reggae than dancehall. See, Niaah and Stanley-Niaah, "Bob Marley, Rastafari and the Jamaican Tourism Product," in *New Perspectives in Caribbean Tourism*, ed. Marcella Daye and Donna Chambers (London: Psychology Press, 2008). Promoters of the most established street dance have argued for its recognition as a tourist site. "Passa Passa, the Authentic Tourism Experience."

99. Riina Asamoa, "A Letter from a Dancehall Tourist—Police Keep Locking Off the Dance," Dancehall.mobi, April 1, 2011, http://www.dancehall.mobi/2011/01/04/a-letter-from-a-dancehall-tourist-police-keep-locking-off-the-dance/.

100. Bennett and Peterson, *Music Scenes*, 9.

101. This connection can, of course, be played with. I attended an event in Kingston's most expensive nightclub for a white U.S. artist debuting his album that relied heavily on Jamaican music, Jamaican vocals (both sampled and hired to perform), and images of Black Jamaican bodily performance. The event was reasonably well attended but not wildly so, the audience (consisting of those who could afford entrance or deemed famous enough to get in) did not appear particularly enthused, and it is unlikely that many of the Jamaican dancehall public were aware of the event—certainly it was not discussed or referred to; nor was his music played anywhere near a street dance at that time. But internationally the artist could—and did—say that he premiered his album in Kingston, Jamaica, and thereby gain some credibility.

102. Robert H. Mnookin and Lewis Kornhauser, "Bargaining in the Shadow of the Law: The Case of Divorce," *Yale Law Journal* 88 (1979 1978): 950–97.

103. Joanna Teresa Demers, *Steal This Music: How Intellectual Property Law Affects Musical Creativity* (Athens: University of Georgia Press, 2006), 10.

104. Demers, *Steal This Music*, 135.

105. Curtis Campbell, "Dancers Want to Copyright Their Moves," *Jamaica Gleaner*, May 12, 2013, http://jamaica-gleaner.com/gleaner/20130512/ent/ent4.html; Government of Jamaica, "Copyright Documents—JIPO."

106. Kristin Bumiller, "Victims in the Shadow of the Law: A Critique of the Model of Legal Protection," *Signs* 12, (1987): 438.

107. Cohen, "Creativity and Culture," 41.

108. Brian McPherson, *Get It in Writing: The Musician's Guide to the Music Business* (Winona, MN: Hal Leonard, 1999); "TheMU—Get It in Writing," accessed September 16, 2017, https://www.musiciansunion.org.uk/Home/Advice/Education/Contracts/Get-it-in-Writing.

109. Patricia Ewick and Susan Silbey, "Common Knowledge and Ideological Critique: The Significance of Knowing that the Haves Come out Ahead," *Law and Society Review* 33 (1999): 1025–41.

110. Starr Nelson, "Rock and Roll Royalties Copyrights and Contracts of Adhesion: Why Musicians May Be Chasing Waterfalls," *John Marshall Review of Intellectual Property Law* 1 (2001): i.

111. John Tehranian, *Infringement Nation: Copyright 2.0 and You* (Oxford: Oxford University Press, 2011), 187; Christoph Geiger, "Promoting Creativity through Copyright Limitations: Reflections on the Concept of Exclusivity in Copyright Law," *Vanderbilt Journal of Entertainment and Technology Law* 12 (2010): 515–947.

112. Cohen, in "Creativity and Culture," 1190, suggests that "serendipitous access to cultural resources and facilitation of unexpected juxtaposition of those resources" is crucial to creativity. See also Ernest A. Edmonds, Linda Candy, Terence Kavanagh, and Tom Hewett, *Creativity and Cognition: Proceedings of the Fourth Conference on Creativity and Cognition* (Loughborough, UK: Association for Computing Machinery, 2002), 173; Bjorn Alterhaug, "Improvisation on a Triple Theme: Creativity, Jazz Improvisation and Communication," *Studia Musicologica Norvegica* 30 (2004): 98, 111, 114.

113. Liu, "Copyright and Breathing Space."

114. Julie E. Cohen, "The Place of the User in Copyright Law," *Fordham Law Review* 74 (2006 2005): 349.

115. Rosemary J. Coombe, *The Cultural Life of Intellectual Properties: Authorship, Appropriation, and the Law* (Durham, NC: Duke University Press, 1998), 8.

116. "Challenges that postcolonial struggles pose . . . may not be appropriately met by habitual reliance on categories of thought inherited from the colonial era." Coombe, *Cultural Life*, 215.

117. Chude-Sokei, "'Dr. Satan's Echo Chamber,'" 191.

Chapter 3

1. "Busy Christmas Schedule for Chris Martin," *Jamaica Gleaner*, December 24 2011. The article quotes the Jamaican vocalist Cecile expressing her happiness at touring with the singer Chris Martin and "getting the chance to perform my counteraction to [his song] Cheater's Prayer."

2. The practice of combining aspects of oral cultural practices with recorded media. See Jason Toynbee, "Copyright, the Work and Phonographic Orality in Music," *Social and Legal Studies* 15, no. 1 (2006): 77.

3. Lloyd Bradley, *Bass Culture: When Reggae Was King* (London: Penguin Books, 2001); Carolyn Cooper, *Noises in the Blood: Orality, Gender, and the "Vulgar" Body of Jamaican Popular Culture* (Durham, NC: Duke University Press, 1995); Simon Jones, *Black Culture, White Youth: The Reggae Tradition from JA to UK* (Oxford: Macmillan Education, 1988); Norman Stolzoff, *Wake the Town and Tell the People: Dancehall Culture in Jamaica* (New York: Routledge, Taylor & Francis, 2000).

4. Jeff Chang, *Can't Stop Won't Stop: A History of the Hip-Hop Generation* (New York: Picador, 2005).

5. Julian Henriques, "Situating Sound: The Space and Time of the Dancehall Session," in *Sonic Interventions* (The Hague: Brill, 2007), 300; Dick Hebdige, *Cut 'n' Mix: Culture, Identity and Caribbean Music* (New York: Routledge, 2004); Christoph

Cox and Daniel Warner, *Audio Culture: Readings in Modern Music* (New York: Blooms-bury, 2004).

6. Katherine McKittrick, "Rebellion/Invention/Groove," *Small Axe* 20, no. 1 (2016): 81.

7. Ingrid T. Monson, *Saying Something: Jazz Improvisation and Interaction* (Chicago: University of Chicago Press, 1996).

8. Copyright law was long unavailable to Black jazz musicians for reasons paral-leling Jamaica: the U.S. rights management agency, ASCAP, refused membership to Black composers; there were many oral and collaborative traditions; and owner-ship was defined at the moment of audio recording, where white people were more likely to be in control. For more on this, see Larisa Mann, "If It Ain't Broke . . . Copy-right's Fixation Requirement and Cultural Citizenship," *Columbia Journal of Law & the Arts* 34 (2011): 201.

9. Peter Manuel and Wayne Marshall, "The Riddim Method: Aesthetics, Practice, and Ownership in Jamaican Dancehall," *Popular Music* 25, no. 3 (2006): 447–70.

10. Silvia Wynter, quoted in McKittrick, "Rebellion/Invention/Groove," 88.

11. McKittrick, 88.

12. Annie Paul, "The Turn of the Native: Vernacular Creativity in the Caribbean," in *Cultural Expression, Creativity and Innovation*, ed. Helmut Anheier and Yud-hishthir Raj Isar (New York: Sage, 2009), 126.

13. In one of many similar articles, the national newspaper discusses an artist famous for answer tunes / counteractions. "New Dancehall Acts," *Jamaica Gleaner,* July 30, 1999, http://jamaica-gleaner.com/gleaner/19990730/news/n7.html. Gringo, the "champ of counteractions," achieved some amount of success in 1995 with a popular reply to Beenie Man's "Big Up and Trust" and is now gaining notoriety in the dance halls with two new counteractions. One is to Bounty Killer's "Bulls of Chi-cago" and the other, a scathing but popular reply to Baby Cham's "Anywhere De Money De Mi A Go Fah."

14. In Jamaica, the schoolyard was not always separate from the recording stu-dio. One Jamaican musician I interviewed described being "discovered" as a singer by a studio owner who visited his school and heard him singing. Interview, February 2009.

15. "Ring the Alarm," produced by Winston Riley (Techniques Records, 1985).

16. "False Alarm," produced by Lloyd "King Jammy" James (Jammy's Records, 1986).

17. The response tune was on a different label, with a different producer, and thus technically violated the copyright held by the original producer.

18. Chinese Jamaicans have been involved in the music industry from its begin-nings. Stolzoff, *Wake the Town,* 43; Sonjah Stanley-Niaah, *DanceHall: From Slave Ship to Ghetto* (Ottawa: University of Ottawa Press, 2010), 68.

19. "Black Head Chinaman," produced by Dice (Prince Buster, 1963).

20. David Katz, *Solid Foundation: An Oral History of Reggae* (New York: Blooms-bury, 2003), 43; Heather Augustyn, *Ska: An Oral History* (Jefferson, NC: McFarland, 2010), 27.

21. Barry Wade, "Environmental Justice and the Poor in Jamaica" (United Nations Development Programme, December 16, 2011), 8. Some whole communities survive by living on land they have not rented, owned by people who cannot afford to develop it. Victor Cummings, "The Problem of Squatting in Jamaica," *Jamaica Gleaner*, May 24, 2009, http://jamaica-gleaner.com/gleaner/20090524/news/news1 .html.

22. Derrick Morgan, "Blazing Fire," produced by Leslie Kong (Beverly's Records, 1963).

23. Augustyn, *Ska*, 27.

24. Quoted in Katz, *Solid Foundation*, 43.

25. "DJs Mavado, Vybz Kartel Pledge to End Lyrical Feud," *Jamaica Gleaner*, December 9, 2009, http://jamaica-gleaner.com/gleaner/20091209/ent/ent5.html.

26. Tenor Saw, "Ring the Alarm," produced by Winston Riley (Techniques Records, 1985).

27. Nitty Gritty, "False Alarm," produced by King Jammy (Jammy's Records, 1986).

28. Echo Minott, "What the Hell" (Jammy's Records, 1986).

29. Mel Cooke, "Echo Minott Asks 'What the Hell the Police Can Do?,'" *Jamaica Gleaner*, November 15, 2009, http://www.jamaica-gleaner.com/gleaner/20091115 /ent/ent4.html.

30. Garth White, "The Development of Jamaican Popular Music, Part 2: Urbanization of the Folk; The Merger of Traditional and Popular in Jamaican Music," *African-Caribbean Institute of Jamaica Research Review* 1 (1984): 52; Bradley, *Bass Culture*, 305.

31. The word "screw" here probably denotes a Jamaican term, "screw-face," which describes a facial expression conveying extreme displeasure or disgust.

32. Lady Junie, "Tell the Police fe True" (Live and Learn Records, 1987).

33. Lovindeer, "Babylon Boops" (TSOJ Records, 1988).

34. In some contexts, copyright law distinguishes between the ability to own different elements. In the 1940s, U.S. law prohibited reusing melodies but not chord changes. Johnathan Z. King, "The Anatomy of a Jazz Recording: Copyrighting America's Classical Music," *Copyright Law Symposium (ASCAP)* 40 (1997): 277–330; U.S. law has on occasion denied ownership claims to rhythmic patterns. It is not a stretch to see particular cultural assumptions at work in what is deemed "worthy" of protection. Mark Rose, *Authors and Owners: The Invention of Copyright* (Cambridge, MA: Harvard University Press, 1993).

35. As described in chapter 2, few Jamaicans owned personal record players, especially in the first twenty or so years of the Jamaican recording industry.

36. Jones, *Black Culture, White Youth*, 26.

37. Walter Ong, "Psychodynamics of Orality," in *Perspectives on Literacy*, ed. Eugene R. Kintgen, Barry M. Kroll, and Mike Rose (Carbondale, IL: SIU Press, 1988), 34.

38. Toynbee, "Copyright, the Work Music."

39. Deanna C. Robinson, Elizabeth B. Buck, and Marlene Cuthbert, *Music at the Margins: Popular Music and Global Cultural Diversity* (New York: Sage, 1991), 89.

40. Riddimbase, "Riddimbase.Org," accessed February 5, 2011, http://www.riddimbase.org/riddimbase.php.

41. "The sociability of these [repetitive] musical relationships has been widely observed as condensing social and cultural relationships both in time and over time through invention and musical allusion." Ingrid T. Monson, "Riffs, Repetition, and Theories of Globalization," *Ethnomusicology* 43, no. 1 (Winter 1999): 36.

42. Although most now know the song via the Jamaican singer Dawn Penn's 1967 recording, the earliest known performance of the lyrics is by the American guitarist Willy Cobb in 1961, "You Don't Love Me" (Vee Jay Records, 1961), while others cite Bo Diddley and other references as well.

43. Remittances from overseas currently and for some time have made up a substantial part of GDP—larger than agriculture, mining, manufacturing, or construction. World Bank, "Personal Remittances, Received (% of GDP)—Data," Research and Statistics, September 2017, https://data.worldbank.org/indicator/BX.TRF.PWKR.DT.GD.ZS.

44. Ian Boyne, "Betrayal of 'Emancipendence,'" *Jamaica Gleaner*, August 3, 2009, http://jamaica-gleaner.com/gleaner/20080803/focus/focus1.html; also see Bradley, *Bass Culture*, 56, 351; Kevin O'Brien Chang and Wayne Chen, *Reggae Routes: The Story of Jamaican Music* (Philadelphia: Temple University Press, 1998), 3.

45. Paul Gilroy, *The Black Atlantic: Modernity and Double Consciousness* (London: Verso, 1993), 102.

46. Russell A. Potter, "Black Modernisms / Black Postmodernisms," *Postmodern Culture* 5, no. 1 (1994), http://search.proquest.com/docview/1426057173/abstract/242037973BA0488CPQ/1.

47. "Original Soca Songs From Jamaica—Page 2," Islandmix.com, July 23, 2005, http://www.islandmix.com/backchat/f16/original-soca-songs-jamaica-79576/index2.html.

48. Facebook discussion, accessed May 11, 2010, http://hr-hr.facebook.com/topic.php?uid=34854672920&topic=5075 (screenshot on file with author).

49. Gilroy, *Black Atlantic*, 95.

50. Raquel Z. Rivera, Wayne Marshall, and Deborah Pacini Hernandez, *Reggaeton* (Durham, NC: Duke University Press, 2009), 93.

51. As well, this practice is at the beginning of hip-hop and also has deeply influenced electronic dance music.

52. Busy Signal, "Well Prepared" (Turf Music, 2014).

53. Martha Woodmansee and Peter Jaszi, *The Construction of Authorship: Textual Appropriation in Law and Literature* (Durham, NC: Duke University Press, 1994).

54. "The anteriority of African civilisation is asserted not in order to escape this linear time but in order to claim it and thus subordinate its narrative of civilisation to a different set of political interests without even attempting to change the terms themselves." Gilroy, *Black Atlantic*, 191.

55. Wynter, quoted in McKittrick, "Rebellion/Invention/Groove," 85.

56. Neal Weinstock Netanel, "Copyright and a Democratic Civil Society," *Yale Law Journal* 106, no. 2 (1996): 356.

57. Joke Hermes, *Re-reading Popular Culture* (Hoboken, NJ: Wiley-Blackwell, 2005), 10; Jean Burgess, Marcus Foth, and Helen Klaebe, "Everyday Creativity as Civic Engagement: A Cultural Citizenship View of New Media," in *Proceedings 2006 Communications Policy and Research Forum*, September 24, 2006, https://eprints.qut.edu.au/5056/.

58. Shubha Ghosh, "Deprivatizing Copyright," *Case Western Reserve Law Review* 54 (Winter 2003): 395.

59. The musical background is often a separate composition from the vocals and can be owned by someone else. However, most Jamaican musicians do not own the tunes they sing or perform on unless they also own the studio where it was recorded.

60. Dave Simpson, "How We Made You Don't Love Me (No, No, No)," *The Guardian*, January 10, 2017, http://www.theguardian.com/music/2017/jan/10/how-we-made-you-dont-love-me-no-no-no-dawn-penn-clevie-browne-interview.

61. Christopher Brett Jaeger, "Does That Sound Familiar: Creators' Liability for Unconscious Copyright Infringement," *Vanderbilt Law Review* 61 (2008): 1903.

62. Julie E. Cohen, "Creativity and Culture in Copyright Theory," *UC Davis Law Review* 40 (2007): 1192.

63. Phanuel Antwi, "Dub Poetry as a Black Atlantic Body-Archive," *Small Axe* 19, no. 3 (November 1, 2015): 69.

64. Cohen, "Creativity and Culture," 1190.

Conclusion

1. Deborah A. Thomas, "Time and the Otherwise: Plantations, Garrisons and Being Human in the Caribbean," *Anthropological Theory*, March 2, 2016, 17, https://doi.org/10.1177/1463499616636269.

2. Thomas, "Time and the Otherwise," 17.

3. Victor Cummings, "The Problem of Squatting in Jamaica," *Jamaica Gleaner*, May 24, 2009, http://jamaica-gleaner.com/gleaner/20090524/news/news1.html; Jamaicans also make arguments defending the rights of the poor to take land and housing that is not being used based in English law; see Owen S. Crosbie, "Letter to the Editor: Squatters Have Rights," *Jamaica Gleaner*, November 16, 2010, http://jamaica-gleaner.com/gleaner/20101116/letters/letters4.html; and Craig Francis, "A Matter of Land: The 'Doctrine of Adverse Possession,'" *Jamaica Gleaner*, February 12, 2017, http://jamaica-gleaner.com/article/news/20170212/matter-land-doctrine-adverse-possession. And in international human rights law, see the comment on this article by Dully. "All I know every man and woman having a livable space is a HUMAN RIGHT under the international human rights charter. Almost a third of Jamaica's population are squatters more than 900000 is a disgrace and a violation of human rights." "Silly Approach to Squatting—Lecturer Blames Central Government for Expansion of Squatter Communities," *Jamaica Gleaner*, July 16, 2017, http://jamaica-gleaner.com/article/news/20170716/silly-approach-squatting-lecturer-blames-central-government-expansion-squatter.

4. Sally Engle Merry, *Human Rights and Gender Violence: Translating International Law into Local Justice* (Chicago: University of Chicago Press, 2005), 219.

5. Margaret Chon, "Intellectual Property and the Development Divide," *Cardozo Law Review* 27 (2005): 2821–912; Keith Aoki, "(Intellectual) Property and Sovereignty: Notes toward a Cultural Geography of Authorship," *Stanford Law Review* 48, no. 5 (1996): 1293–355; Keith Aoki, "Distributive and Syncretic Motives in Intellectual Property Law (with Special Reference to Coercion, Agency, and Development)," *UC Davis Law Review* 40 (2007): 717–801; Ruth L. Okediji, "The International Relations of Intellectual Property: Narratives of Developing Country Participation in the Global Intellectual Property System," *Singapore Journal of International and Comparative Law* 7 (2003): 315–85; Alan Story, "Burn Berne: Why the Leading International Copyright Convention Must Be Repealed," *Houston Law Review* 40 (2003): 763–802.

6. Nicole Foga and Masani Montague, *Electronic Commerce and Music Business Development in Jamaica: A Portal to the New Economy* (Geneva: UNCTAD, 2000); Michael Witter, *Music and the Jamaican Economy* (Geneva: UNCTAD/WIPO, 2004); Bruce Lehman, *Modernizing Jamaica's Intellectual Property System* (Geneva: International Intellectual Property Institute, 2000); Marlene Cuthbert and Gladstone Wilson, "Recording Artists in Jamaica: Payola, Piracy and Copyright," *Caribbean Popular Culture*, (Bowling Green: Bowling Green State University Press, 1990): 64–78; Zeljka Kozul-Wright and Lloyd Stanbury, *Becoming a Globally Competitive Player: The Case of the Music Industry in Jamaica* (Geneva: UN Commission on Trade and Development, 1998). Sympathetic observers from outside Jamaica have made similar arguments; see Krister Malm and Roger Wallis, *Big Sounds from Small Peoples: The Music Industry in Small Countries* (New York: Routledge, 1984); Dominic Power and Daniel Hallencreutz, "Profiting from Creativity? The Music Industry in Stockholm, Sweden and Kingston, Jamaica," *Environment and Planning A* 34, no. 10 (2002): 1833–54.

7. Annie Paul, "The Turn of the Native: Vernacular Creativity in the Caribbean," in *Cultural Expression, Creativity and Innovation*, ed. Helmut Anheier and Yudhishthir Raj Isar (New York: Sage, 2009), 125.

8. Erin Macleod and Joshua Chamberlain, "Soundsystem Culture in Jamaica: Still the Voice of the People?" (Pop Conference, Seattle, WA, April 14, 2016).

9. Foreigners may not always be threatened by the same local practices as are local elites. For example, foreign elites are far less reluctant to support Jamaican musical practices that involve performing sexual and stylistic flamboyance, even though these practices are still regarded as undesirable by locals. However, foreigners are not always as enthused about Jamaican practices of phonographic orality, which have been discussed as undisciplined and ignorant of intellectual property or artistic integrity.

10. James C. Scott, *Seeing Like a State: How Certain Schemes to Improve the Human Condition Have Failed* (New Haven, CT: Yale University Press, 1999); Marc Perlman, "The Paradox of Empowerment: Traditional Music between Stewardship and Ownership in International Intellectual Property Law," unpublished paper (Berkeley: University of California at Berkeley, April 18, 2008).

11. Obika Gray, "The Coloniality of Power and the Limits of Dissent in Jamaica," *Small Axe: A Caribbean Journal of Criticism* 21, no. 3 (November 1, 2017): 98–110, https://doi.org/10.1215/07990537-4272022.

12. Anupam Chander and Madhavi Sunder, "The Romance of the Public Domain," *California Law Review* 92 (2004): 1331–73.

13. Cheryl I. Harris, "Whiteness as Property," *Harvard Law Review* 106 (1993): 1707–91.

14. Hardin himself admits that his model of common ownership inevitably leading to self-destruction did not apply to most commonly held land in practice but only to specific "open-access" or "unmanaged" commons, which existed beyond the domain of a single community. See Garrett James Hardin, "The Tragedy of the Unmanaged Commons: Population and the Disguises of Providence," in *Commons without Tragedy: Protecting the Environment from Overpopulation—a New Approach*, ed. Robert V. Andelson (London: Shepheard-Walwyn, 1991), 162–85.

15. John Baden, *Managing the Commons* (Bloomington: Indiana University Press, 1998); Carol Rose, "The Comedy of the Commons: Custom, Commerce, and Inherently Public Property," *University of Chicago Law Review* 53, no. 3 (1986): 711–81.

16. Elinor Ostrom, *Governing the Commons: The Evolution of Institutions for Collective Action* (Cambridge: Cambridge University Press, 1990).

17. As presciently pointed out in James Boyle, "The Second Enclosure Movement and the Construction of the Public Domain," *Law and Contemporary Problems* 66 (2003): 33–74, unfortunately the historical materiality of commons management was largely not taken up in the defense of cultural commons that grew out of this work.

18. Bonnie J. McCay and James M. Acheson, *The Question of the Commons: The Culture and Ecology of Communal Resources* (Tucson: University of Arizona Press, 1990).

19. Edward P. Thompson, *Customs in Common: Studies in Traditional Popular Culture* (New York: New Press, 1991), 341.

20. James C. Scott, *The Art of Not Being Governed: An Anarchist History of Upland Southeast Asia* (New Haven, CT: Yale University Press, 2009).

21. Mark Goodale, "A Life in the Law: Laura Nader and the Future of Legal Anthropology," *Law and Society Review* 39, no. 4 (December 1, 2005): 7, 39, 49, https://doi.org/10.1111/j.1540-5893.2005.00251.x; Edward P. Thompson, *Whigs and Hunters: The Origin of the Black Act* (New York: Pantheon Books, 1975), 266.

22. Mark Fathi Massoud asked this question most poignantly in relation to the Sudan in *Law's Fragile State: Colonial, Authoritarian, and Humanitarian Legacies in Sudan* (Cambridge: Cambridge University Press, 2013).

23. Obika Gray, *Demeaned but Empowered: The Social Power of the Urban Poor in Jamaica* (Kingston: University of West Indies Press, 2004).

24. John Perry Barlow, "The Next Economy of Ideas," *Wired*, October 2000, http://www.wired.com/wired/archive/8.10/download.html; Nicholas Negroponte, *Being Digital* (New York: Random House Digital, 1996); David Lange, "At Play in the Fields of the Word: Copyright and the Construction of Authorship in the Post-Literate Millennium," *Law and Contemporary Problems* 55, no. 2 (April 1, 1992): 151, https://doi.org/10.2307/1191779; Bruce A. Lehman, *Intellectual Property and the National Information Infrastructure: The Report of the Working Group on Intellectual Property Rights* (Carby, PA: Diane Publishing, 1995), 130–31, warned that different national definitions of rights could render copyright essentially meaningless.

25. The case of Indigenous land rights illustrates how property rights are used to dispossess. "Johnson v. Macintosh stands for the principle that the extinguishment of the Indian title in North America was the sole prerogative of the appropriate Euro-American sovereign through either a purchase or conquest." Howard R. Berman, "The Concept of Aboriginal Rights in the Early Legal History of the United States," *Buffalo Law Review* 27 (1978 1977): 637. See also Harris, "Whiteness as Property." The student of peasant land rights in Europe also provides some support; see Karl Polanyi, *The Great Transformation: Economic and Political Origins of Our Time* (New York: Rinehart, 1944), 35; Edward P. Thompson, *The Making of the English Working Class* (New York: Vintage Books, 1963), 218.

26. Joseph E. Stiglitz, *Globalization and Its Discontents* (New York: W. W. Norton, 2003), 17; Benjamin F. Timms, "Development Theory and Domestic Agriculture in the Caribbean: Recurring Crises and Missed Opportunities," *Caribbean Geography* 15, no. 2 (2008): 101.

27. Jamaicans for Justice, *Jamaica: A Long Road to Justice? Human Rights Violations under the State of Emergency* (London: Jamaicans for Justice / Amnesty International, May 31, 2011), http://jamaicansforjustice.org/nmcms.php?snippets =docmanager&p=docresults.

28. Adidja Palmer, "Censorship vs. Free Expression—Critics Are Social Hypocrites," *Jamaica Gleaner*, February 9, 2009, http://jamaica-gleaner.com/gleaner /20090209/letters/letters8.html.

29. Jamaica Constitution of 1962, chapter 2, 22(2)(a)(ii).

30. "Rapporteurs Want New Laws for Freedom of Expression on Internet," *Jamaica Gleaner*, Summer 2011, http://jamaica-gleaner.com/gleaner/20110210/lead /lead51.html.

31. Carol Rose, "The Several Futures of Property: Of Cyberspace and Folk Tales, Emission Trades and Ecosystems," *Minnesota Law Review* 83 (1998): 129, 132.

32. Ruth L. Okediji and William L. Prosser, *The International Copyright System: Limitations, Exceptions and Public Interest Considerations for Developing Countries* (Geneva: UNCTAD/ International Centre for Trade and Sustainable Development, 2006), 243; Margaret Chon, "Intellectual Property from Below: Copyright and Capability for Education," *UC Davis Law Review* 40 (2006): 841.

33. Some important first steps are Olufunmilayo B. Arewa, "Piracy, Biopiracy and Borrowing: Culture, Cultural Heritage and the Globalization of Intellectual Property," *Bepress Legal Series*, no. 1114 (2006), http://law.bepress.com/expresso/eps /1114/; Chon, "Intellectual Property from Below."

34. Aoki, "Distributive and Syncretic Motives," 771; Chon, "Development Divide."

35. Kevin J. Greene, "Stealing the Blues: Does Intellectual Property Appropriation Belong in the Debate over African-American Reparations?," Thomas Jefferson School of Law Research Paper (n.d.), 343; Aoki, "Distributive and Syncretic Motives," 717; Okediji, "International Relations," 333; Graeme B. Dinwoodie and Rochelle C. Dreyfuss, "TRIPS and the Dynamics of Intellectual Property Lawmaking," *Case Western Reserve Journal of International Law* 36 (2004): 120.

36. The "capabilities approach" is associated with the philosophers Amartya Sen and Martha Nussbaum, focusing on the outcomes of policy in terms of human

being's actual capacity to flourish—it encompasses material security, political and expressive freedom, and equality as affirmative values toward which policies should be directed. Sen, *Development as Freedom*; Nussbaum, "Capabilities and Human Rights," 300. Also see Chon, "Development Divide," 2874–75.

37. Anjali Vats and Deidre A. Keller, "Critical Race IP," *Cardozo Arts and Entertainment Law Journal*, no. 3 (2018): 735–96.

38. Thomas, "Time and the Otherwise."

39. Jafari Sinclaire Allen, "For 'the Children' Dancing the Beloved Community," *Souls* 11, no. 3 (2009): 318.

40. Black women being at the intersection of multiple axes of structural oppression means that actions supporting their liberation will reach closer to the heart of coloniality. Kimberle Crenshaw, "Demarginalizing the Intersection of Race and Sex: A Black Feminist Critique of Antidiscrimination Doctrine, Feminist Theory and Antiracist Politics," *University of Chicago Legal Forum* 1, no.8 (1989): 139–67.

41. As described in chapter 1, the orphanage that gave rise to four generations of instrumentalists that formed the backbone of ska and reggae and continues, albeit in dire financial straits, to this day.

42. Boaventura de Sousa Santos, "The World Social Forum: Toward a Counter-Hegemonic Globalisation (Part I)," in Jai Sen, Anita Anand, Arturo Escobar and Peter Waterman (eds.) *World Social Forum: Challenging Empires*, (New Delhi: The Viveka Foundation 2004): 342–43; Boaventura De Sousa Santos, "The Future of the World Social Forum: The Work of Translation," *Development* 48, no. 2 (June 2005): 17.

43. Madhavi Sunder, "The Invention of Traditional Knowledge," *Law and Contemporary Problems* 70 (2007): 97–124.

44. Shane Greene, "Indigenous People Incorporated? Culture as Politics, Culture as Property in Pharmaceutical Bioprospecting," *Current Anthropology* 45, no. 2 (2004): 211–37.

45. Anjali Vats, *The Color of Creatorship: Intellectual Property, Race, and the Making of Americans* (Stanford, CA: Stanford University Press, 2020).

46. A growing field of writing, such as Susan Flynn and Antonia Mackay, eds., *Spaces of Surveillance: States and Selves* (New York: Springer, 2017); Helen Nissenbaum, *Privacy in Context: Technology, Policy, and the Integrity of Social Life* (Stanford, CA: Stanford University Press, 2009); Simone Browne, *Dark Matters: On the Surveillance of Blackness* (Durham, NC: Duke University Press, 2015); and activism, as discussed in Kate Conger, Richard Faussett, and Serge F. Kovalevsky, "San Francisco Bans Facial Recognition Technology," *New York Times*, March 14, 2019, https://www.nytimes.com/2019/05/14/us/facial-recognition-ban-san-francisco.html; and focusing on different communities, including Broderick Greer, "Gay Nightclubs and Black Churches Are Sanctuaries: Here's How to Make Them Safer," *Washington Post*, June 13, 2016, https://www.washingtonpost.com/news/soloish/wp/2016/06/13/gay-nightclubs-and-black-churches-are-sanctuaries-heres-how-to-make-them-safer/.

Index

173; on authorship, 13, 14, 46–47, 55, 57, 167–68; class politics and, 51–52, 58, 72–73, 82–84, 135–36; digital technology and, 17–18, 206n64; dub music and, 63; enforcement of, 174–76; ethnography and, 29; Jamaican independence and, 55–58; local authority vs., 132–36, 192n46; in musical reuse, 156–57; negotiating colonial, 179–82; vs. one-time fee negotiations, 71; in post-TRIPS era, 80–82; reggae and, 65–69; street dances and, 92, 115–19, 132. See also coloniality; intellectual property rights

Copyright Act (1911), 14, 40, 55–56, 191n41

Copyright Act (1977), 11–12, 65–66

Copyright Act (1993), 80, 191n41, 206n60

The Copyright Thing Doesn't Really Work Here (Boateng), 17

Coronation Market, 96, 103

counteractions. See answer tunes

counter-hegemonic globalization, 186

cover songs, 156–62, 184. See also reuse, musical

Cox, Christoph, 140

Creative Commons, 118

creative sovereignty, 165–70. See also cultural autonomy; sovereignty

Cuba, 70

cultural appropriation, 15

cultural authority, 104–8, 131. See also authority

cultural autonomy, 4–5, 86. See also agency; creative sovereignty; originality; poor population; resistance; street dances

cutting and mixing, 140–41

Daily Gleaner (publication), 74, 75

dancehall, 4; as commons, 177; formal scholarship on, 75; global circulation of, 70–71, 77; sexual expression in,

28; syncretism of, 69. See also Jamaican popular music; street dances

Dancehall Queen competition, 130

dancers, defined, 33

"Dancers Want to Copyright Moves" *(Jamaica Gleaner)*, 132

Darlington, Doris, 33, 37–38

decoloniality, 123–24, 162–65, 187–88. See also coloniality; power

Dekker, Desmond, 59

Demarco, 123

deregulation and privatization, 72, 74. See also power

diasporic musical expression, 33–41. See also Jamaican popular music

Diddley, Bo, 162

Digicel, 109

Digital Millennium Copyright Act (1998), 118, 206n64

digital technology, 17–18, 76, 77–78, 129, 206n64. See also music technology

DJ culture, as term, 179

DJ Kool Herc, 69

DJs: defined, 32; role of audience in street dances, 120–21

DMCA. See Digital Millenium Copyright Act (1998)

Dodd, Clement "Coxsone," 37–38, 44, 46, 167, 198n83

domestic violence, 150–53. See also safety considerations

DonGURALesko, 162

dons, 8, 60–61, 70, 91, 203n27. See also poor population

Douglass, Lisa, 100

drug trade, 70

drum machines, 76

drums, 34, 35

dub, 62–63, 169. See also Jamaican popular music

dubplates, 115–16, 129

dutty, as term, 202n9

Dutty Fridaze, 109, 115

economic migration, 69. *See also* remittances

economic policies and conditions, 69–70, 72–73, 186–87

economy of street dances, 108–19

education, 35, 211n14

electoral politics, 52, 60, 70, 97, 105, 203n24

Elephant Man, 94, 145

Ellis, Nadia, 28, 125

EMI record label, 18, 82

engineers, defined, 33

entrepreneurship, as term, 111

erotic marronage, 125–26

ethical rights *vs.* legal rights to authorship, 46–47, 57, 66–69. *See also* copyright

ethnographic methods, 19–23, 26–29

ethnomusicology, 19, 138, 189n5

exclusive riddim, 54

exilic spaces, 5, 7–8, 61, 90–92, 176, 178–79, 181–82, 190n13. *See also* accessibility, public *vs.* private; street dances

"False Alarm" (song), 145, 155

fandom, 46, 63, 115, 128–29, 148, 162. *See also* audience; participatory creative practices; shared knowledge

Fatal, DJ Rob, 131–32

Federal Records, 41

feminist research methodologies, 21–26

fife, 34

Fire Links sound system, 101

Fischlin, Daniel, 15

flexibility, 13, 59, 136, 155; authorship and, 81; creativity and, 165; of law, 11, 91

folk culture, 43–44, 46. *See also* Patwa

Folkes Brothers, 46

"Forward March" (song), 146

gangsters. *See* dons

garrisons and garrison communities, 60, 70, 97, 104

gender: coloniality and, 26–27; role in Jamaican music, 26, 27, 32–33; role in street dances, 114–17, 122–26; sexuality and, 95–96. *See also* masculinity

Gender Equality Report, 27

Gentleman, 77, 164

geographic respectability, 93–99. *See also* respectability

Germaican Records, 76–77

Germany, 76–77

Ghana, 17

Ghosh, Shubha, 166

Gilroy, Paul, 162, 163

Global Directories, 85

glossary of musical practitioners, 32–33

Graeber, David, 111–12

Gray, Obika, 6; on coloniality, 9; on exilic social space, 5, 7, 61, 90; on repair of cultural injuries, 126

gray markets, 58, 169. *See also* copyright

Gringo, 211n13

Guinness, 109

gully, 8, 89, 93–96, 99, 101. *See also* housing conditions; land ownership and populations; poor population

gully queens, 95–96

Hall, Stuart, 6

hand drums. *See* drums

Harriott, Derrick, 48, 79

Harris, Cheryl, 11

Hebdige, Dick, 140

Heble, Ajay, 15

Henriques, Julian, 104, 121, 140

higgling, 27

hip-hop: circular production of, 18, 77, 79, 123, 140; copyright and, 131; performance of, 69, 161

"Hold Yuh" (song), 119–20

homophobia, 27–28, 29, 95–96. *See also* queer communities; sexuality

Hope, Donna, 18, 28–29

housing conditions, 100–101. *See also* gully; land ownership and populations

Huffington Post, 95

ICE (choreographer), 94

income statistics of Jamaican music, 12. *See also* economic policies and conditions

independence of Jamaica, 55

"Independent Woman" (song), 81–82

India, 16

Indian Jamaicans, 3, 7, 34

Indigenous knowledge, 16–17, 21, 33, 187

individualism, 69, 70, 171

instrumentalists, defined, 32

intellectual property rights: citizenship and belonging in, 187; class politics and, 39–40, 178, 184; WTO on, 15–16. *See also* copyright

International Monetary Fund (IMF), 69–70

internet and creative works, 17–18, 76

intersectionality, 218n40

intersectional research methodologies, 19, 21–26

Irie FM, 72, 74

Island Records, 54–55

"Israelites" (song), 59

iTunes, 82

JACAP (Jamaica Association of Composers and Performers), 80–82, 107, 133

Jamaica Broadcast Corporation (JBC), 43, 151

Jamaica Coalition for a Healthy Society, 85

Jamaica Gleaner (publication), 104, 132, 148

Jamaica Labour Party (JLP), 52, 60

Jamaican economy. *See* economic policies and conditions

Jamaican popular music: anticolonial movements and, 59–60, 63–65, 197n38; capitalism and, 72–73;

central concepts and practices of, 4, 5–11; collaborative production process of, 33, 47–48; dub, 62–63, 169; mento, 34, 42, 49; Patwa and, 36–37, 50, 69, 157, 161; reggae, 12, 17, 18, 58–60, 74–75; ska, 46, 49–50; as sold and produced in England, 54–55; spaces and technologies of, 37–39; state intervention with, 31; in United States, 63–64, 76, 161. *See also* copyright; dancehall; phonographic orality; riddims

Jamaican rhythm and blues, 45. *See also* rhythm and blues

James, Lloyd "King Jammy," 150

Japan, 70, 71, 76

jazz, 18, 46, 59, 141, 166, 211n8. *See also* big-band jazz

JBC. *See* Jamaica Broadcast Corporation (JBC)

JFLAG, 95

jingles, 115–16

JIPO (Jamaica Intellectual Property Office), 82–83, 132, 173

JLP (Jamaica Labour Party), 52, 60

Jonkonnu, 207n84

Kamugisha, Aaron, 6, 9

Kartel, Vybz, 81–82, 117, 148, 162, 181

Keller, Diedre, 185

Kente cloth, 17

Khouri, Ken, 41–42

Kilimanjaro sound system, 48

King Tubby, 62

Kumina, 34, 46, 195n9

Lady Junie, 151–52, 153, 163

land ownership and populations, 3, 212n21, 214n3. *See also* gully; housing conditions

language. *See* Patwa

Latin population, 7

Lebanese Jamaicans, 3, 7, 33, 42

Lee, Bunny, 47–48, 53, 79

Leslie Kong, 146

Passa Passa: description of, 93, 96–97, 103–4, 119; police presence at, 105–6, 179; recognition and legacy of, 104–6, 110, 176, 204n28; as term, 202n8

Patwa: class and social location of, 36–37, 86, 98, 142; as official nation-language, 43–44; in song lyrics, 36–37, 50, 69, 157, 161; as term, 195n16

Paul, Annie, 142, 175

payola, 72

Penn, Dawn, 162, 166–67

pennywhistle, 34

People's National Party (PNP), 52, 60, 62

Performing Rights Society. See PRS (Performing Rights Society)

Perry, Lee "Scratch," 62

personhood, 7–8, 188. See also agency; cultural autonomy; resistance; sovereignty

phonographic orality, 5–7, 15, 20, 41–52, 71, 119–23. See also answer tunes; Jamaican popular music

piracy, musical, 58, 82. See also copyright

plantation economy, 171

plant knowledge. See Indigenous knowledge

"PLO" (song), 63

Pocomina, 34, 195n9

police brutality. See state violence

police discretion, 105–7

political resistance, 58–60, 105, 131. See also cultural autonomy; personhood

Poor and Boasy, 2

poor population, 4; call for government investment in, 185–86; cultural autonomy of, 31; dons and, 8, 60–61; education of, 35; exilic spaces of, 7–8; housing conditions of, 101; legal formalities and, 135–36; musical production and, 50–51; Patwa and, 36, 37; reggae's global success and, 64–65; ska and, 46, 49–50; as source of musical talent, 35–36; state violence against, 24; tourism industry and, 36. See also class politics; gully; Jamaican popular music; sovereignty

popular, as term, 3

popular music, as field of study, 3. See also Jamaican popular music

population, 3–4

Potter, Russell, 162

power, 8–11, 13. See also class politics; coloniality

private vs. public accessibility, 100–101

privatization, 72

propriety: challenges to, 46, 88, 93, 99, 108, 124–25, 139, 177, 181; colonial notions of, 30, 86, 127, 131. See also class politics; manners; morality

Prosperity Club, 49

PRS (Performing Rights Society), 40, 51, 65, 68, 72–73. See also copyright

public audience. See audience

public vs. private accessibility, 100–101, 129

quadrille, 34

queer communities, 95–96. See also homophobia

Quijano, Anibal, 6, 8–9

race, as concept, 8–9

racism, 4–5, 9, 127. See also anti-Blackness; class politics; colorism

radio technology, 37–39, 42–43, 72

Rae Town, 88, 104, 109

Ranglin, Ernest, 46–47, 57

Ranks, Cutty, 71

rapping, 91, 161. See also hip-hop

Rastafari, 34–35, 45–46, 62, 97

rebel music. See reggae

recording studios. See names of specific studios

record players and music technology, 37–39. See also sound system; vinyl recordings reggae: formal scholarship and studies on, 18, 74–75; as "intangible cultural heritage," 17; political resistance in, 58–60; worldwide income of, 12. *See also* Jamaican popular music

Reggae Studies Unit (UWI), 18, 74–75

Reid, Duke, 38, 66

Reid, Junior, 157, 160

religions, 34–35, 195n9

remittances, 213n43. *See also* economic migration

remixes, 156–62

reparations, 186, 188. *See also* class politics; power; slavery

reputational economy, 68, 80, 92, 110–15

resistance, 58–60, 105, 131. *See also* agency; cultural autonomy; personhood

respectability: Blackness and, 140, 177; bodily, 99–100, 124–25, 129–30; colonial notions of, 109–10; geographic, 93–99; sonic, 99, 104. *See also* rudeness, as concept

reuse, musical, 140–41, 153, 163–65. *See also* answer tunes

Revival religion, 34, 195n9

Revolutionaries (band), 63

rhythm and blues, 39, 49, 57, 59, 162. *See also* Jamaican rhythm and blues

Riddimguide.com, 67

"riddim method," 141

"The Riddim Method" (Manuel and Marshall), 18

riddims: defined, 7, 189n3; global circulation of, 70; originality of, 1–2, 155; production and use of, 53–54, 71, 76, 184; in sonic conversation, 154–56, 207n71. *See also* Jamaican popular music; samples

rights. *See* copyright; ethical rights *vs.* legal rights to authorship

Rihanna, 162

"Ring the Alarm" (song), 144, 145, 149, 155

RJR media group, 74

rocksteady, 52–53

"Royals" (song), 123, 164

royalties: class politics and, 58, 82–83, 199n87; enforcement of, 51, 56, 80–81; local translation of, 57, 66, 73, 115, 117, 135, 173–74; loss of, 65, 72–73; *vs.* one-time fees, 67–68, 116; promise of, 57, 109. *See also* copyright; PRS (Performing Rights Society)

rudeboy, as character, 10, 46. *See also* manners; respectability

rude citizenship, 130–37, 182–83. *See also* citizenship

rudeness, as concept, 10. *See also* manners; respectability

rumba box, 34, 35

safety considerations, 23, 24, 193n63, 203n24. *See also* domestic violence

samples: recording use of, 76, 77, 79, 156, 157, 162; royalties for, 65; sonic conversation of, 145, 156. *See also* riddims

Santos, Boaventura De Sousa, 186

screw-face, as expression, 212n31

Seaga, Edward, 52, 61, 97

Sean Paul, 86

Selassie, Haile, 35

Sen, Amartya, 185, 217n36

Sephardic Jewish population, 33, 42

sexuality, 95–96, 124. *See also* homophobia

sexual tourism, 23

Shabba Ranks, 74

Shaggy, 74, 75, 162

shared knowledge, 2, 50, 59, 76, 78, 141, 154–55, 165, 187. *See also* participatory creative practices

"Shepherd's Rod" (song), 34

ska, 46, 49–50. *See also* Jamaican popular music

Skatta, 1–2, 7, 13, 172

Skelton, Tracy, 127

skin bleaching, 127

slavery, 3, 5, 186. *See also* class politics; coloniality; power; reparations

Small Axe (publication), 18

Smalls, Minnie, 55

sonic conversation, 144, 145, 154–62, 207n71. *See also* answer tunes

sonic respectability, 99, 104. *See also* respectability

soul music, 45, 52, 57, 59, 64

soundmen, defined, 32–33

sound system, 32, 47–50, 184. *See also* record players and music technology; street dances

South America, 16

sovereignty, 10, 29, 165–70, 183, 197n38. *See also* creative sovereignty; Jamaican popular music; poor population

special, 54, 115–16

Spotify, 67, 176

squatting, 147, 172, 181, 214n3. *See also* gully; land ownership and populations

Stalag, 155, 160, 162

Stanley-Niaah, Sonjah, 18

state violence, 180–81; class politics and, 28; elections and, 60, 70; personal safety considerations and, 24, 203n24; against Rastafarians, 35; street dances and, 105–6. *See also* coloniality; parasitic state, as concept

Stony Hill Reformatory for Boys, 36

"The Stopper" (song), 71

street dances, 136–37; authority and, 104–8; class politics and, 86–88, 128–29; copyright and, 92, 115–19, 132; economy of, 108–15; as exilic spaces, 90–92, 181–82; in Kingston, 88–89; respectability and, 93–100; rude citizenship in, 130–37; visual artistic representation of, 85; visual media of, 126–28. *See also* cultural autonomy; dancehall; sound system

Studio One, 37, 49, 167. *See also* Dodd, Coxsone

syncretism, 6–7, 15, 33–37, 44–47

Taino population, 3, 33

telephone directories, 85

television, 42

"Tell You What the Police Can Do" (song), 151–52

Tenor Saw, 144, 149

textual conversation, 144, 145–54. *See also* answer tunes

"They Got to Go" (song), 145, 146, 147

"This is Why I'm Hot" (song), 157, 158

Thomas, Deborah, 10, 19

Thompson, E. P., 179

Thompson, Errol, 63

Thompson, Krista, 114, 127

Tivoli Gardens, 96–97, 104, 180

Tosh, Peter, 59–60

tourism industry, 23, 36

Towards Jamaica the Cultural Superstate (government), 111

Towse, Ruth, 192n56

Toynbee, Jason, 5, 18, 192n46

"traditional knowledge," as legal category, 16–17

transphobia, 95. *See also* antigay violence; homophobia; queer communities

The Travel (publication), 95

Trenchtown, 186

Trinidadian calypso, 34, 39

TRIPS (Agreement on Trade Related Aspects of Intellectual Property), 12, 16, 80

Trojan music label, 38

tu-tu-tweng, 160

Ulysse, Gina, 125

"Under Me Sleng Teng" (song), 72

UNESCO (United Nations Educational, Scientific and Cultural Organization), 16, 17

CPSIA information can be obtained
at www.ICGtesting.com
Printed in the USA
LVHW091314100322
713129LV00005B/134